Y0-BRY-328

The Computer & Literary Style

Kent Studies in English, Number 2

General Editor: HOWARD P. VINCENT

THE COMPUTER & LITERARY STYLE

Introductory Essays and Studies
Edited by Jacob Leed

KENT STATE UNIVERSITY PRESS
Kent, Ohio
1966

PN
98
E4
L4

9/30/68 Eastern 3,70

E + G Lit.

54067

CF

COPYRIGHT 1966 BY KENT STATE UNIVERSITY
LIBRARY OF CONGRESS CATALOG CARD NUMBER 66-22883

FOREWORD

THE ESSAYS in this volume are presented with the hope that they will be of use to scholars and students interested in new approaches to the old problem of analyzing style. A number of new studies rely heavily on computers to tally the objective features being examined and to manipulate the information that results. Some also rely on complex statistical formulations in conducting the analysis. A literary scholar who does not know much about computers or statistics finds it difficult to learn what is being done with the new techniques and difficult to see how they may be applied to literary problems he would like solved in his own field. Perhaps these essays will ease the difficulty. Most of them have been written for scholars-at-large, rather than for specialists, even though some very specialized material is presented.

I wish to thank the many scholars who answered my notes of inquiry at a time when very little bibliographical help was available in this area of work. A suggestion by Martin Nurmi began the project of assembling the material, and various particular encouragements along the way were given to me by Howard Vincent, Doris Franklin, Richard Goldthwaite, Thomas Knipp, Robert Hemenway, Arthur Sherbo, Robert Wachal, and Louis Milic, among others. Time made available to me by the English Department and by a Kent State University research grant during 1965 has been essential in preparing this collection. It has been very good to receive so much help and encouragement in arranging for these essays and studies to come before their readers.

J. L.

Kent State University
Kent, Ohio
May 1966

CONTENTS

A PREFACE TO COMPUTATIONAL STYLISTICS

Sally Yeates Sedelow
Walter A. Sedelow, Jr.

ABSTRACT: Stylistic analysis, the study of patterns formed in the process of the linguistic encoding of information, is of importance to any major research focused upon or dependent upon the production or analysis of language. Through the use of computers, it should be possible to achieve more accurate detection and delineation of such linguistic patterns than has hitherto been the case; a quantitatively rigorous and intense study of pattern or style in natural language we call "computational stylistics."

"Computational stylistics" has immediate, practical implications for work in areas ranging from machine translation and automatic abstracting to the social sciences and humanities. For adequate machine translations and automatic abstracts, algorithms of normative style for the textual genre being translated or abstracted must be available; the use of the computer for stylistic analysis will help make possible the recognition and specification of such algorithms. Stylistic analysis is also integral to the detection of idiosyncratic uses of language which distinguish one author from another. An author's style is his signature. Through analysis of individual style, researchers can find clues to unique characteristics in linguistic pattern; through the ability to recognize differing styles, researchers will have clues as to authorship, interpolations, etc. "Computational stylistics" should make possible detection of both more detailed and more encompassing linguistic patterns than have previously been apparent.

Stylistic analysis, which focuses upon certain distributional properties of linguistic units within and among natural-language strings, is the study of patterns formed in the process of the linguistic encoding of information. Such patterns serve to distinguish one language-user from another, one sub-culture from another, and — in subtle ways as well as obvious — one civilization from another. Such patterns also serve to confuse or clarify, bore or interest, persuade and entrance, or repel and disengage the people responding to them.

NOTE: Inasmuch as this article was written for readers who do not have special training in literature, it contains a very general treatment of both the history of literary criticism and of approaches to the analysis of style. We hope these sections of the article will be informative to the reader whose interests are not primarily in literature just as we hope other sections of the article will be informative and suggestive for the literary scholar, as well as for the general reader. This article originally appeared as System Development Corporation document SP-1534, February 17, 1964.

Stylistic analysis is integral, therefore, to the solution of problems germane to the analysis of the propagation and effect of information. Natural language invariably contains stylistic (structural) patterns. These patterns serve as clues to the methods used to encode and to transmit information; they may also be used to help detect information structured to elicit certain responses. An intense, quantitatively rigorous study of pattern, or style, in natural language we may call "computational stylistics;" such study should markedly contribute to the efficiency with which information can be transmitted, received, and analytically manipulated. Prior to the use of computers, the detection of such patterns in any sizable data base was exceedingly difficult and unreliable because the quantity of detail tended to defy human patience and accuracy. Although computers have made such analysis feasible, there nevertheless has been no research *directly* addressed to defining reliable operational measures of style — possibly because other, earlier problems preempted attention and because of a relative dearth of professional experience in stylistics among people who have been practically concerned with the automatic manipulation of language.

Not only the feasibility of stylistic analysis but also its importance has become increasingly evident with the advent of computers and the attempts they have engendered at automatic manipulation of language. As a first step applicable to machine translation and automatic abstractings, experts in linguistics have given their primary attention to the sentence as a comparatively isolated unit, focusing their study on its syntax. For meaningful analysis of language, however, extra-syntactic as well as syntactic interrelationships among groups of sentences, as well as within the isolated sentence, must be taken into account. Even isolated sentences depend upon more than correct syntax for their semantic impress, as Chomsky has demonstrated with the syntactically correct but essentially meaningless sentence: "Colorless green ideas sleep furiously."[1] The presumptive intraneural associations words have with object representations and with other words must be considered if a meaningful sentence is to be produced. Specialists in manual stylistic analysis[2] have pointed out that a wide range of stylistic variables determines the information in any given text—variables which are often dependent upon more context than that provided by the isolated sentence.

---

[1] Noam Chomsky, *Syntactic Structures,* p. 15.

[2] See especially the close textual analyses by Cleanth Brooks and Robert Penn Warren (1959, 1960), Clay Hunt (1954), William Empson (1953), Joseph Summers (1954), Arnold Stein (1953, 1957) and other scholars in the "new critical" tradition. (Works by these authors are listed alphabetically, by author's name, under References, a procedure followed throughout this paper).

The stylistic variables customarily considered of first importance are form and texture. There are two main approaches to form: (I) a description, primarily based upon operational definitions, of the way the text looks on the page, and (II) a description of the text in qualitative, non-operationally defined terms. Under the first category of form, the stylistic attributes usually discussed are (1) discriminators for differentiating prose and poetry; (2) prosody;[3] (3) rhyme scheme (which may, of course, be located in prose as well as in poetry); (4) number of lines (also sometimes relevant to analysis of prose); (5) syntax. Latent in these broad categories are many other divisions. For instance, a discussion of prosody would imply examination of paragraph length, sentence length, and word length and the interrelationships among these variables, as well as the study of syllabic stress. The second category of form would include classification of the text as to genre — whether it is an informatve or indicative abstract, for instance, or a political tract. Such classifications should and could be operationally defined because they depend heavily upon types of words appearing in the text (abstract nouns as opposed to concrete nouns, for instance) and upon the frequencies of specific words.

Texture, the second major stylistic variable, has many interpretations. Two interpretations which are important to the possible research areas suggested later in this paper are tone and patterns of word association. Tone refers to the generalized semantic impact of the words in the text: incorrect mood can undercut the foundations of information; and incorrect colloquialism, or unusual mixture of colloquial and formal language, might reveal a non-native user of a language or stylist of unusual complexity. Patterns of word association range from interrelated similes and metaphors to etymologically interrelated content words.

It is within a multi-sentence context — and, after all, the frequency of one-sentence texts is demonstrably low—that such stylistic variables as form and texture become increasingly important. If, for instance, a number of sequential sentences follow an identical form, each sentence having a similar rhythm, the ensuing monotony might well tend to reduce the alertness and comprehension of the reader. Thus the transmission of information could be obstructed by the form in which the information is encoded. In this larger textual context, the transmitter(s) of information must be particularly mindful of tone because uncontrolled variations weaken the infor-

---

[3] Perhaps the most monumental works in this area are Saintsbury's *A History of English Prose Rhythm,* and *A History of English Prosody from the Twelfth Century to the Present Day.*

mational structure of a text; verbal patterns become too diffuse or too dissonant to be clearly perceived and the reader sometimes may not know within which verbal subpattern(s) a particular tonal detail is to be fitted. Aspects of form and texture can provide clues as to authorship. For instance, when examining the Federalist papers, Mosteller and Wallace (1963) discovered that those written by Hamilton and Madison could be discriminated on the basis of the frequency of function words such as "by," "upon," and "to."[4] A good research model will provide for the delineation of overall patterns of the usage of function words, because such patterns may well distinguish not only between individual authors but also between types or genres of texts.

Patterns of word association, integral to texture, are valuable stylistic discriminators. In literature such patterns are sometimes called chains of images; in psychology they are sometimes designated as part of a personality syndrome;[5] in intelligence analysis they are sometimes singled out as clues to political trends. To date, most attempts to use automated equipment for singling out such patterns demand that human beings define the pattern in advance.[6] Impressive as some of the achievements have been, the disadvantage of such programs is that although what is sought may be found, important word associations may go unnoticed because they have not been described in advance. A desirable information retrieval program for some intelligence purposes, for instance, would be one that finds the unexpected, not what is already known. Pre-prepared association lists might well be unsatisfactory for this purpose; dependence upon the text for new, unspecified clues thus becomes a prime desideratum.

The range of activities conventionally subsumed under the term stylistic analysis precludes a thorough description of them here, but the importance of the detection of verbal patterns should be clear; since both the transmission and reception of language depend upon giving it pattern, research workers ranging in interests from machine translation and automatic abstracting to the detection of impending revolutions must be concerned with stylistic analysis.

[4]Their work is particularly impressive when compared with the attempts at manual analysis of the Federalist papers, even those by such a distinguished scholar as Douglass Adair (1944).

[5]For a recent example of such usage, see Nunnally and Flaugher's "Psychological Implications of Word Usage" (1963).

[6]A notable example—notable in part because of its wide acceptance—is "The General Inquirer," developed by Stone et al. (1961), at Harvard University's Laboratory of Social Relations. See also Mosteller and Wallace (1963), mentioned above.

Review of Relevant Work

Examination of texts in terms of style has been the major preoccupation of literary critics for the past twenty years. John Crowe Ransom (1941) emphasized the interest of the "new critics" in developing techniques which would permit statements about the style of literary texts and genres. The new critics' emphasis upon the text itself marked a departure from the predominant older orientation of American and English literary historians toward study of the work's environment.[7] Emphasis upon stylistic analysis is now the standard technique of literary critics in the English-speaking world, particularly in the United States, and their work has provided many useful analytical categories.[8]

Before the broad range of analytical tools for stylistic analysis can be used to govern a computerized version of them, more rigorous definitions are need. G. Udny Yule's (1944) pioneering study of noun frequencies, primarily in *De imitatione Christi* and in the religious works of Gerson, and James Whaler's (1956) attempt to work out the statistics of the rhythm in *Paradise Lost* are among the few non-computer efforts to make more rigorous statements about a small aspect of the style of individual works. Among recent efforts using a computer, Mosteller and Wallace's (1963) study of the Federalist papers and the Reverend Andrew Morton's work on the Pauline epistles are notable.[9] Like Mosteller and Wallace, Morton tabulated occurrences of certain commonly occurring words, apparently concentrating upon the word και which is roughly equivalent to the English word *and.* Morton's study, described in an article in the *New York Times* by Lawrence Fellows (1963), also took note of distances between occurrence of the words tabulated.

In the field of content analysis, another aspect of style as here defined, *The Language of Politics: Studies in Quantitative Semantics* by Lasswell, Leites, *et al.* (1949) is an important pre-computer milestone. Bernard Berelson (1952), in *Content Analysis in Communication Research,* laid some stress on the qualitative, as well as the quantitative, approach to the study of content. *Trends in Con-*

[7]For an outline of trends in manual literary criticism and for descriptions of certain aspects of contemporary criticism, see Wellek and Warren's *Theory of Literature* (1949), Stanley Hyman's *The Armed Vision* (1948), and W. K. Wimsatt's *The Verbal Icon* (1954).

[8]For further examples of stylistic analysis, see works by Bevis (1956), Cope (1956), Bradbrook (1951), and other listings under References.

[9]It may serve to indicate how little has been done to observe that in his remarks at a recent colloquium at the University of California at Los Angeles, Mosteller cited Yule's work of nineteen years before as a principal point of departure for his recent study.

tent Analysis, edited by Ithiel de sola Pool (1959), described the value of content analysis for the exploration of phenomena ranging from an individual's emotions to submerged policy indicators in enemy propaganda, but no attention was given to the use of the computer for such investigations. Computer specialists in information retrieval have been interested in locating clusters of word associations, but for the most part their work depends heavily upon manually prepared thesauri.[10] As a departure from dependence upon manual analysis, Lauren Doyle (1962) has proposed a technique for using a computer to construct maps of word associations, and William B. Eldridge and Sally F. Dennis (1962), in a project for the American Bar Foundation, propose to use a computer to construct a thesaurus geared specifically toward retrieval of information from legal literature.

Another effort in the direction of more extensive analysis of language is reported by RCA (Climenson, 1962), whose research scientists are working on text units larger than the sentence. But so far they are restricting themselves to analysis of syntax.

The importance of semantics, as well as syntactics, for machine translation has been stressed by Ross Quillian (1962) in "A Revised Design for an Understanding Machine." M. Kay (1962) proposes the construction of semantic indices to aid more meaningful analyses of texts. Although their reports to date indicate a concentration upon syntax, Householder and Lyons (1962) are engaged in research on *The Automation of General Semantics*; so they presumably intend to give some attention to semantics.

Clearly, there is an incipient recognition of the importance of a wider-ranging, extra-syntactic stylistic anaylsis for effective automatic investigation of language.

Areas of Possible Research

Initially, research on computational stylistics probably would be asyntactic, although without doubt there will come a time when these two complementary approaches will be of mutual value and will mesh for optimum manipulation of language.[11] Another caveat to bear in mind is that we currently do not know all the linguistic categories to explore, and we may well not know a majority, or even the most promising of them. One of the stringent constraints on stylistic analysis heretofore has been human inability to cope with data in both sufficient quantity and detail to discover empirically

---

[10]See reports by Gurk and Minker (1961), Needham (1962), Pietsch (1962), Swanson (1960), Tasman, *et al.* (1962), and Wall (1962).

warranted broad patterns within which finer delineations might be traced. Our goal at the moment is to test analytical techniques which look as though they may be powerful and, at the same time, to work toward providing the computer with self-adaptive abilities so that the advantages accruing from its capacity for accurate attention to multitudinous details can be most effectively utilized.

Initial research, designed to discover both lexical and distributional patterns of word associations, is underway. This first computer program focuses upon (1) the construction of a thesaurus which contains *only* words which appear in a given text or in the works of a given author, and (2) a distributional representation of the function and content words in the text. For a description of the program as it now operates and of the kinds of patterns it may be expected to discover, the reader is referred to Sedelow and Bobrow (1964), TM-1753.

In addition to the research already in progress, there are many other avenues which seem worthy of exploration. One would be the study of the juxtaposition, grouping and positioning of words. Do certain words or certain types of words tend to occur in one (relative) position in a sentence more than in other positions? If there is no such overall pattern, are there not isolated patches (possibly within clauses, certainly within phrases) of such occurrences? (For instance, varieties of parallel structure have distinguished writers ranging from the sixteenth-century Elizabethan John Lyly to the twentieth-century Elizabethan Winston Churchill.) Do certain words or certain types of words tend to occur in a particular type of sentence, such as an imperative sentence, or a question, or exclamation, or classes of declarative sentences, more than in others? What are the maximum and minimum distances between occurrences of words, or a group of words? Does the occurrence distribution between the maximum and minimum distance follow a normal curve, or is it skewed toward one or the other of the boundaries? If one were to abstractly represent word occurrences between commas, or prior to and subsequent to dashes, or clustered around any form of punctuation, would recurring patterns appear?

When studying words, a stylistic analyst would also be interested

---

[11]One circumstance, among others, in which a certain sort of syntactic concern almost immediately would become a phase of a computational-stylistic analysis is a comprehensive assault on one author's attributes of style. Here the stylistic analyst would be seeking not for a high-generality parsing program or any of the other goals of automatic syntactics, but for a use-profile of the author's stylistic repertory, so as to identify among the hallmarks of his style propensities toward particular grammatical and rhetorical stratagems, etc.

in the length of individual words, the derivation of words (i.e., is the vocabulary heavily Latinate, for instance, or Anglo-Saxon?), as well as the occurrences of words not native to the language under examination.

The study of groups of letters within and among words is highly informative stylistically, but, again, because of the demands upon human accuracy and patience, such information has been infrequently available. Literary critics, for instance, may be willing to discuss alliteration or internal rhyme as it occurs in a sonnet, but much less so for a long poem, and they are thoroughly discouraged by more than a paragraph of prose—and, with the exception of a few lines, the description of even the sonnet may be fairly general. In order to get a computer to do a first-class job of detecting rhyme, one might resort to phonetic spelling. But the computer could do some interesting work on the basis of letters, or groups of letters, alone, and with addition of some rules of equivalence, it might do a moderately adequate job.

The computer could also be used to detect and analyze the occurrences of modules such as *tion, pre,* etc. It could be interesting to know, for instance, whether the incidence of prefixes in a given text is higher than that of suffixes, or vice versa.

Punctuation patterns are also stylistic discriminators. The nature of the uses of dashes, or question marks, or semicolons, or any type of punctuation mark may well form a pattern providing clues as to the style of an author, or the characteristics of usage in a particular genre, or in a specific subculture.

Another approach to the problem of finding both normative and idiosyncratic usages of language would be to compare the overall lexical population of the text, texts, or subsections of text under examination with some other lexical population. For instance, one might ask what fraction of the words and classes of words in a standard dictionary, such as Webster's Collegiate, appears in a given text. Or, lexical distribution patterns in one text might be projected against the background formed by those patterns in another text, or group of texts. Overall consistencies would of course have implication for the format of automatic language production.

Using a dictionary based on historical principles, a time profile indicating the neologistic phase of the words used by a particular author or in a particular genre could be delineated. Such profiles might be very useful for distinguishing among specific styles. (Presumably Jack Kerouac's profile, for instance, would differ in significant ways from that of Stafford Beer). In addition, time profiles might provide more precise meaning for rather vague stylistic descriptors. The word *vivid,* for instance, which is a great favorite in bookreviews, technical writing guides, etc., tends to fade into meaninglessness under close scrutiny. It might turn out, though, that for specific genres or other classes of text there is a correlation between a style which is termed "vivid" and a particular time profile. Perhaps vividness depends in some specifiable contexts upon a high proportion of "twentieth-century words," for instance, and, in others, upon a generous sprinkling of terms from the "Middle Ages."

It is possible that one of the most distinctive characteristics of an individual style, as well as the most important concomitant of a readable style,[12] is rhythm. Although the perception of rhythm and variations in rhythm has long been of interest to students of the use of language, no careful, accurate measures have been made of just what is being perceived as rhythm and how whatever is perceived is recognized. Earlier in this paper, there was the suggestion that word, sentence, and paragraph length play a role in determining rhythm; using the computer, these particular rhythmic variables and their inter-correlations would be relatively easy to pick out and study. The currently operating stylistic analysis program[13] makes patterns of function words and content words apparent; these patterns may well have rhythmic significance and, in fact, one could talk about one type of rhythm in these terms. It would be interesting to see whether correlations exist between these or other patterns and the results of experiments registering readers' eye-movements when reading given texts. Conventionally, the assumption is that readers proceed word by word, phrase by phrase, or, in the case of a speed reader, paragraph by paragraph. However, it is probably the case that if these conventions do indeed hold, they are nonetheless influenced by length of word, recurrence of certain groups of letters, the familiarity of words or combinations of words encountered, etc. Insights into the relative importance of these rhythmic variables could have real importance for stylistic specifications for automatic language processing, as well as for the design of various types of display equipment.

Meter, the aspect of rhythm to which perhaps most attention has traditionally been paid, seems at the moment one of the most difficult rhythmic problems for our current computer capabilities. The study of meter tends to focus upon what is represented to be perception of stress, or accent, within individual words; and it has never been

---

[12]Admittedly, "readable" is a hazy stylistic criterion. Its implications are that the facts in a given article or the plot in a given book have been successfully communicated or made "memorable" for the reader. Thus, in this sense, readability is measurable.

[13]See the document by S. Y. Sedelow and D. G. Bobrow (1964).

clearly determined whether accent results from pitch, length of time required to pronounce a given syllable, some combination of the two, or, if it is a combination, just what the proportion of the stress ingredients may be. Ultimately, a precise computer pattern-recognition ability focused upon sound spectrographs should make possible the study of metrical patterns, although achieving consistency in the production of such spectrographs will continue to pose formidable problems. In the meantime, concentration upon intra-word and inter-word patterns may, in fact, produce the same results, stylistically, because the stress patterns are implicit in the words; thus the value and necessity of distinguishing metrical patterns may be obviated.

The proportion of words having operational content also varies from one author to another and from one type of document to another. An article on chemistry, for instance, is likely to have a much higher proportion of operationally defined words than a "humanistic" article. This distinction is frequently made in terms of words which are concrete and those which are abstract; such a distinction could be of real value, not only for purposes of discrimination but also for specifying relative proportions in order to produce articles or précis in language idiomatic to the potential reader's experience. The major obstacle to making such discriminations by computer is that they would seem largely to be problems of semantics. And, although attacks are being made on the problems of semantic analysis,[14] that battle is not yet won; it may have scarcely begun. Again, it is possible that recognition of other kinds of patterns may make it possible to bypass this semantic quagmire by rendering the importance of the abstract-concrete word proportion pattern less immediate so far as the automatic production of readable texts is concerned. Further, there is the additional possibility that other patterns may throw light on semantic patterns; for instance, certain meanings of words may correlate with particular rhythmic patterns. Factor-analytical manipulation may then eliminate the need to find certain of these other values.

The importance of discovering and making use of stylistic discriminators cannot be overstressed. In addition to their very real importance to certain kinds of "detective" projects, stylistic discriminators are necessary for satisfying the demands of contemporary computer technology. Without research in stylistic analysis, empirically-based denotations for commonly used stylistic descriptors will be lacking, and without stylistic descriptors, the prospects for automatic language production look dreary indeed. The forebodings of the

---

[14] See articles by Quillian (1962), Garvin (1963), and Katter (1963).

many who fear "the machine" may come to seem justified if the flood of natural language which will presently pour out of computers is of one consistency. Unrelieved by stylistic variation, this black tide could drown not only the serious reader—the casual reader will have earlier departed for an illiterate shore—but also the creativity born of variant structurings of language. To achieve linguistic variety, alternatives for the computer will require meaningful specification. Without such specification, an adjuration to write "vividly," for instance, or "commandingly" will go unheeded, as will, very possibly, the information the computer is trying to transmit.

References

Adair, Douglas. "The Authorship of the Disputed Federalist Papers, Part I," *The William and Mary Quarterly*, Vol. 1, No. 2, pp. 97–122 (April 1944).
————. "The Authorship of the Disputed Federalist Papers, Part II," *ibid.*, Vol. 1, No. 3, pp. 235–264 (July 1944).
Berelson, Bernard. *Content Analysis in Communication Research*. Glencoe, Illinois: Free Press, 1952.
Bevis, Dorothy. "*The Waves*: A Fusion of Symbol, Style and Thought in Virginia Woolf," *Twentieth Century Literature*, 2:5–20 (1956).
Bradbrook, Frank W. "Style and Judgment in Jane Austen's Novels," *Cambridge Journal*, 4:515–537 (1951).
Brooks, Cleanth, and Robert Penn Warren. *Understanding Fiction*. 2nd ed., New York: Appleton-Century-Crofts, 1959; 3rd ed., New York: Holt, 1960.
Chomsky, Noam. *Syntactic Structures*. 's-Gravenhage: Mouton and Co., 1957.
Climenson, W. D. Report from Data Systems Center, Radio Corporation America, *Current Research and Development in Scientific Documentation*, No. 11, National Science Foundation, November 1962, pp. 313–314.
Cope, Jackson, "Seventeenth-Century Quaker Style," *PMLA*, 71:725–754 (1956).
Crane, William G. *Wit and Rhetoric in the Renaissance: The Formal Basis of Elizabethan Prose Style*. New York: Columbia University Press, 1938.
Doyle, Lauren B. "Indexing and Abstracting by Association," SDC Document, SP-718/001/00, April 9, 1962.
Eldridge, William B., and Sally F. Dennis. Report on Research for American Bar Foundation, *Current Research and Development in Scientific Documentation*, No. 11, National Science Foundation, November 1962, pp. 62–63.
Empson, William. *Seven Types of Ambiguity*. 3rd ed., Norfolk, Connecticut: New Directions, 1953.
Fellows, Lawrence. "Cleric Says Computer Proves Paul Didn't Write 14 Epistles," *New York Times*, Western Edition, November 7, 1963.
Garvin, Paul L. "Inductive Methods in Semantic Analysis," Technical Note No. 6, AF49(638)–1128. Thompson-Ramo Wooldridge, Inc., Canago Park, California, January 15, 1963.
Gurk, H. M., and J. Minker. "The Design and Simulation of an Information Processing System," *Journal of the Association for Computing Machinery*, Vol. 8, No. 2, pp. 260–270 (April 1961).
Householder, F. W., Jr., and J. Lyons. *The Automation of General Seman-*

tics. Quarterly report No. 3, September 1–November 30, 1960, Indiana Univesity, Bloomington, Indiana.

————. *The Automation of General Semantics.* Quarterly report No. 4, December 1, 1960–February 28, 1961, Indiana University, Bloomington, Indiana.

Hunt, Clay. *Donne's Poetry.* New Haven: Yale University Press, 1954.

Hyman, Stanley Edgar. *The Armed Vision.* New York: A. A. Knopf, 1948.

Jacobs, Melville. *The Content and Style of an Oral Literature: Clackamus Chinook Myths and Tales.* Wenner-Gren Foundation, New York, 1959.

Katter, Robert V. "Language Structure and Interpersonal Commonality." SDC Document, SP–1185/00/01, June 17, 1963.

Kay, M. "Rules of Interpretation—An Approach to the Problem of Computation in the Semantics of Natural Language." Presented at International Federation of Information Processing Congress, Munich, Germany, August 1962.

Lane, Robert. *The Liberties of Wit: Humanism, Criticism and the Civic Mind.* New Haven: Yale University Press, 1961.

Lasswell, Harold D., Nathan Leites, and Associates. *The Language of Politics: Studies in Quantitative Semantics.* New York: G. W. Stewart, 1949.

Lasswell, Harold D., Ralph D. Casey, and Bruce Lane Smith. *Propaganda and Promotional Activities, An Annotated Bibliography.* Minneapolis: University of Minnesota Press, 1935.

Miles, Josephine. *Major Adjectives in English Poetry from Wyatt to Auden.* Berkeley: University of California Press, 1946.

————. *Pathetic Fallacy in the Nineteenth Century.* Berkeley: University of California Press, 1943.

————. *The Primary Lanuage of Poetry in the 1640's.* Berkeley: University of California Press, 1948.

————. *The Primary Language of Poetry in the 1740's and 1840's.* Berkeley: University of California Press, 1950.

————. *The Primary Language of Poetry in the 1940's.* Berkeley: University of California Press, 1951.

————. *Renaissance, Eighteenth-Century, and Modern Language in English Poetry: A Tabular View.* Berkeley: University of California Press, 1960.

————. *Wordsworth and the Vocabulary of Emotion.* Berkeley: University of California Press, 1942.

Miller, George A. *Language and Communication.* New York: McGraw Hill Book Company, 1951.

Mosteller, Frederick, and David L. Wallace. "Inference in an Authorship Problem: A Comparative Study of Discrimination Methods Applied to the Authorship of *The Federalist Papers,*" *Journal of the American Statistical Association,* 58: 275–309 (1963).

Needham, R. M. Report from Cambridge Language Research Unit, *Current Research and Development in Scientific Documentation,* No. 11, National Science Foundation, November 1962, pp. 74–75.

Nunnally, Jum C., and Ronald L. Flaugher. "Psychological Implications of Word Usage," *Science,* Vol. 140, No. 3568, pp.775–781 (May 17, 1963).

Pietsch, E. H. E. Report from Gmelin Institute Documentation Center, *Current Research and Development in Scientific Documentation,* No. 11, National Science Foundation, November 1962, p. 99.

Pool, Ithiel de sola, ed. *Trends in Content Analysis.* Urbana: University of Illinois Press, 1959.

Quillian, Ross. "A Revised Design for an Understanding Machine," *Mechanical Translation,* Vol. 7, No. 1, pp. 17–29 (July 1962).

Ransom, John Crowe. *The New Criticism*. Norfolk, Conn: New Directions, 1941.

Ribner, Irving. *Patterns in Shakespearian Tragedy*. London: Methuen, 1960.

Saintsbury, George Edward Bateman. *A History of English Prose Rythm*. London: Macmillan and Co., 1912.

————. *A History of English Prosody from the Twelfth Century to the Present Day*, Vol. 3. 2nd ed., London: Macmillan and Co., 1923.

Sedelow, Sally Yeates. *The Narrative Method of Paradise Lost*. Ann Arbor, Mich., Microfilm, 1960.

————, and Daniel G. Bobrow. "A LISP Program for Use in Stylistic Analysis." SDC Document, TM-1753, February 17, 1964.

Sedelow, Walter A., Jr. "Cummings' What if a much of a which of a wind," *The Amherst Review*, 2:15–19 (1960).

————. "Marvell's To his Coy Mistress," *Modern Language Notes*, 71:6–8 (1956).

Spurgeon, Caroline. *Shakespeare's Imagery*. Cambridge: University Press, 1935.

Stein, Arnold. *Answerable Style: Essays on Paradise Lost*. Minneapolis: University of Minnesota Press, 1953.

————. *Heroic Knowledge: An Interpretation of Paradise Regained and Samson Agonistes*. Minneapolis: University of Minnesota Press, 1957.

Stone, Philip, Robert F. Bales, J. Zvi Namenwirth, and Daniel M. Ogilvie. *"The General Inquirer": A Computer System for Content Analysis and Retrieval Based on the Sentence as a Unit of Information*. Laboratory of Social Relations, Harvard University, Cambridge, Mass., November 1961.

Summers, Joseph. *George Herbert, His Religion and Art*. London: Chatto, 1954.

Swanson, D. R. "Searching Natural Language Text by Computer," *Science*, Vol. 132, No. 3434, pp. 1099–1104 (October 1960).

Tasman, J. E., P. M. Nobbs, and Edward F. Thode. Report from Pulp and Paper Research Institute of Canada and The Institute of Paper Chemistry, *Current Research and Development in Scientific Documentation*, No. 11, National Science Foundation, November 1962, pp. 139–140.

Wall, Eugene. Engineers Joint Council, *Current Research and Development in Scientific Documentation*, No. 11, National Science Foundation, November, 1962, pp. 91–92.

Wellek, René, and Austin Warren. *Theory of Literature*. New York: Harcourt, Brace, 1949.

Whaler, James. *Counterpoint and Symbol: An Inquiry into The Rythm Milton's Epic Style*. Copenhagen: Rosenkilde, 1956.

Wimsatt, William K. *The Prose Style of Samuel Johnson*. New Haven: Yale University Press, 1941.

————. *The Verbal Icon*. Lexington: University of Kentucky Press, 1954.

Yule, G. Udny. *The Statistical Study of Literary Vocabulary*. Cambridge: University Press, 1944.

ON USING A COMPUTER

Robert S. Wachal

It may seem strange to begin an article such as this by debunking the computer, but unfortunately these machines come in two kinds. First of all there is the real computer, which is a gigantic and dynamic *tabula rasa,* a sort of high-speed, tireless idiot with a big memory and not a jot of common sense. Then there is the computer of journalistic myth, an nth-power Einstein capable of doing everything from turning out poetry to predicting election results accurately —a super *Literary Digest* served by slaves who keep its lights flashing, its dials quivering ecstatically, and its voracious maw filled with unfolded, unspindled, and unmutilated punched cards.

We may as well begin, then, by clearing up several possible misapprehensions. First of all no mathematical background is necessary either to prepare material for a computer or to operate it. Secondly, it is not necessary nor often even possible to directly operate the computer. Such work can be hired out if desired, and unless the computer is a relatively small one (say an IBM 650 or 1620), one may consider himself lucky if he sees more of the machine than a glimpse through an observation window will allow. One gets his closest contact with a large computer when he hands a deck of punched cards to a human clerk. And finally, computers do not, in most people's concept of the word, think. If a computer composes poetry, analyzes style, detects literary influence, and referees authorship disputes, it does so in a highly metaphoric sense. That is, some human agent with insight, imagination, ingenuity, and a great amount of time has first determined a completely specified procedure (called an *algorithm*) for doing part of a complex job. That procedure, broken down into steps of staggering simplicity, is coded into a special, but usually non-mathematical, language, and the resulting program is then communicated to a computer, which quickly, accurately, tirelessly, and insensibly executes thousands of times over the series of routine chores given it. It then communicates the results of its drudgery back to the human, who interprets these results with insight, imagination, ingenuity, and, if he has done his original job well, in a small amount of time.

The purpose of this article is to give the reader some idea of just what the above process entails so that he can better understand literary studies done with the help of computers, so that he can decide whether or not to try using a computer himself, and so that he can communicate with computer specialists.

The major difficulty in using a computer is not the communication process as such but the reduction of the problem to the level on which the computer operates. If one so chooses and has funds, a professional programmer can be hired who will do all of the communicating with the computer and some of the reducing of the problem. However, even before a programmer can be employed effectively, the problem must be completely specified without so much as the ghost of a concealed assumption. This is not so easy to do as one might think. Suppose, for example, that we want to compile a word-frequency list based on the known work of a given author for an attribution study. Suppose further that there is no uniform edition of the author's several works and that we have the best available editions punched onto cards as running text with as many words per card as space allows. Before computer processing of this data deck can be done, a set of instructions must de devised, coded into a computer language, and punched onto cards to form a program deck, which precedes the data deck into the machine and gives the computer precise directions for the processing task. But we cannot ask a programmer to write a program for determining the frequency of occurrence of each different word in our texts until we have defined "different" and "word."

The problem of "same" vs. "different" is really three separate problems: spelling variation (*go, goe*), inflectional variation (*go, goes, going, went, gone*), and homonymy (*art* as in *thou art* and as in *graphic art*). One can choose simply to ignore these problems and pay the consequences, although it is still important to be aware of the choice and to inform others of the decision. The alternative is rather more complex. It involves formulating rules wherever possible that will recognize and then normalize the different forms of what we may choose to regard as the same word. This can be done for inflections and for some spelling variants (e.g. *-oe* occurring at the end of a word would be changed to *-o*). Forms not covered by rules (e.g., *shoe*) can be put in a list or dictionary of variants with their normal or canonical forms, and this dictionary can be stored in the computer or in an accessory unit. Of course, homonyms cannot in isolation be distinguished by the computer. A choice must be made between post-editing—separating the homonymous frequencies after the text has been processed (a difficult task unless a concordance type of output is available)—and pre-editing—affixing discriminant symbols to potential homonyms before processing (*art* would become either *art 1* or *art 2*). Perhaps when more research has been done in linguistic semantics, homonyms can be discriminated by machine on the basis of context. This could be done now for simple cases such as *art 1* vs. *art 2*, but imagine the complexity of analysis and span of context required to distinguish "leadership" from "a heavy metal" in a clause like ". . . he took the lead . . . " or even more in ". . . he took the lead in the race to the linotype machine . . ." even if the necessary clues were somewhere available in the text.

Defining "word" requires another set of decisions. It is not true that everyone knows what a word is, and even if it were, "everyone" should not be construed as including a computer. A collection of wires, magnets, and transistors lacks even the most elementary *Sprachgefühl*. We might begin by provisionally defining "word" as "any string of symbols (excluding the space) occurring between spaces." Then, the knotty problem of editorial and authorial inconsistency must be faced: *matchbox* vs. *match-box* vs. *match box, cannot* vs. *can not*. There is also the inconsistency of the language itself: *nevertheless* vs. *in spite of, into* vs. *out of.* We can normalize the text, a big job, or simply look the other way. But even if we opt for ignoring the problem, we still must specify how the hyphen is to be interpreted. Often, we might want to treat the hyphen as a word delimiter, as in *well-known authority, hard-working student,* and *up-to-the-minute record.* Yet we would not want to split *co-operate, pre-existent, re-sort,* or *un-American.* An arbitrary decision which would probably result in a high percentage of desired choices is the specification that a hyphen be interpreted as a word delimiter only if it is preceded by a string of four or more letters.

We are not yet out of the wandring wood, however. If we proceeded on the basis of decisions made so far and turned our problem over to a programmer, we would get embarrassing results. Our computer-made frequency list would not only have entries like *go* followed by a frequency figure, but it would also have separate entries for *go., go,,* and *go).* Punctuation marks precede the space and must therefore be included in our list of word delimiters. Whatever else the use of a computer does for us, at the very least it forces our hidden assumptions into the open.

Computer Logic

Whether communicating with a computer directly or through a programmer, one should have some sort of conceptual model of the computer in mind, some framework within which problems can be thought about and described. Computer languages provide such a framework, of course, but an analogical model could be suggested which, while it might be less precise, would be considerably easier to apprehend.

We can construct our model out of four components. First of all we would need an electric typewriter or something like a tele-type-writer for moving information into or out of the computer. So that we can store information, we would next need thousands of pigeon-holes each capable of storing one good-sized number and each having a bracket in which to put a label by which the contents can always be addressed or found. We could have permanent addresses if we wanted, but it is more flexible and convenient if we supply our own labels which can have some mnemonic relation to the contents. The third component would be an ordinary desk calculator and the fourth some kind of controller, a simple-minded administrator capable of performing four kinds of tasks: routing information between typewriter and storage pigeonholes, routing information between storage and desk calculator, rearranging information within storage, and operating the desk calculator. He will tirelessly follow simple instructions to the letter, whether they are sensible or obviously ridiculous. Our model, then, consists of a typewriter, a storage area, a calculator, and a controller.

Suppose now that a text already occupies a block of pigeonholes in the storage area. The first pigeonhole in the block contains the first word of the text, the second pigeonhole contains the second word of the text, and so on. We could have labelled each pigeonhole with a mnemonic address, e.g. WORD 1, WORD 2, etc., but to make things simpler, we have labelled only the first pigeonhole in the block, and its address will be "WORD." All other pigeonholes will be counted from it, so that the pigeonhole containing the second word of the text will have the relative address "WORD + 1." The third word of the text can be found by addressing "WORD + 2," and so on.

The pigeonholes contain words only in a metaphoric sense. Actually each pigeonhole is capable of storing one number. However, we can assume that our typewriter or our controller codes each word into a number for us, and that is all ye know on earth, and all ye need to know. But in order to make things clearer, let's set up an analogical coding system. Assuming, for ease of illustration, that each pigeonhole can contain a twelve-digit number and that no word in our text exceeds six letters, we can set up a simple code in which A is represented by 01, B by 02, and so on down to Z by 26. So that we can use this scheme later for alphabetizing, we will ensure that all words are of full length by simply filling out the unused space to the right with zeros. Consequently THEIRS will be representd by 200805091819, while THE will be represented by 200805000000, and of course no matter where the word THE, or any other word, appears, it will always be represented by the same number.

If we have chosen the following bit of deathful prose, "Nor snow nor rain nor dark of night shall stay these men from their just rounds," it will be stored like this:

Text	Pigeonhole Address		Pigeonhole Contents
NOR	WORD		141518000000
SNOW	WORD +	1	191415230000
NOR	WORD +	2	141518000000
RAIN	WORD +	3	180109140000
NOR	WORD +	4	141518000000
DARK	WORD +	5	040118110000
OF	WORD +	6	150600000000
NIGHT	WORD +	7	140907082000
SHALL	WORD +	8	190801121200
STAY	WORD +	9	192001250000
THESE	WORD +	10	200805190500
MEN	WORD +	11	130514000000
FROM	WORD +	12	061815130000
THEIR	WORD +	13	200805091800
JUST	WORD +	14	102119200000
ROUNDS	WORD +	15	181521140419

The numerical representation of alphabetic material not only simplifies the making of machines (most of which are based on binary numbers rather than decimal, but that needn't concern us), but it also makes it easier to specify certain operations. For example, specifying the necessary steps for alphabetization, including assumptions about priority, is fairly complex. But given a machine with a built-in number system and a built-in letter-to-number conversion code, we simply ask the machine to rearrange the numbers representing words into numerical order. When these are reconverted, the words will be in alphabetical order. Also if we wanted to compare two words to see whether they were alike, how would we do it, how would we define "compare" and "alike"? If we have a machine that can subtract and that can recognize whether the result is positive, negative, or zero, we can compare two numbers just by subtracting one from the other and examining the result. If the result is zero, then the numbers are alike, otherwise they are not. If we convert our two words to numbers, we can compare them in the same way. We will use this capability in the following problem to be worked out with our stored text.

Suppose we want to find out the number of times the word *nor* occurs in our stored text. We simply give the administrator or controller the following list of instructions, which it will execute in successive order unless told otherwise:

1. Find an empty pigeonhole anywhere in the storage area. Label it NOR and put the numerical equivalent of *nor* into it.

2. Find another empty pigeonhole. Label it N-NOR (i.e., the number of times *nor* appears in the text) and put a zero into it. Now in addition to the stored text there are two more pigeonholes containing information:

Information	Pigeonhole Address	Pigeonhole Contents
The word *nor*	NOR	141518000000
A *nor* counter	N-NOR	000000000000

3. Find the pigeonhole labelled WORD. Subtract its contents (i.e., the number representing the first word of the text) from the contents of NOR (i.e., 141518000000). If the result is zero (i.e., if WORD=NOR, if the first word of the text is *nor*), go to step 4, otherwise go to step 5.

4. Increase N-NOR by one (i.e., N-NOR will now contain 000000000001).

5. Find WORD + 1. Subtract its contents from the contents of NOR. If the result is zero go to step 6; otherwise go to step 7. (With the present text, step 6 will in fact be skipped and control will pass to step 7).

6. Increase N-NOR by one.

7. Find WORD + 2. Subtract it from NOR. If the result is zero go to step 8, otherwise go to step 9.

8. Increase N-NOR by one. (With the present text, step 8 will be executed, since the third word is in fact *nor* and the pigeonhole labelled N-NOR will then contain 000000000002).

9. Find WORD + 3 . . . .
(and so on until all of the text has been examined down through WORD + 15)
At the end of this process, the pigeonhole labelled N-NOR will contain the number of occurrences of *nor,* which, with the present text, will be 000000000003.

However, the program or set of instructions could be considerably shortened by use of iteration. Instead of referring to WORD, WORD + 1, WORD + 2, etc. we could refer each time to WORD + I and let the letter I assume successive values from zero to one less than the total number of words. Thus we would have an abstract address which could become particular addresses under the following conditions:

Abstract address: WORD + I
Particular addresses:

Value of I	Associated Address
0	WORD + 0*
1	WORD + 1
2	WORD + 2
. . .	. . .
. . .	. . .
. . .	. . .
15	WORD + 15

*i.e.., WORD

Thus the program might now read:

1. Label an empty pigeonhole NOR and insert *nor*.
2. Label an empty pigeonhole N-NOR and insert zero.
3. Label an empty pigeonhole I and insert zero.
4. Find WORD + I. Subtract it from NOR. If the result is zero, go to step 5, otherwise go to step 6.
5. Increase N-NOR by one.
6. Increase I by one.
7. Go to step 4.

Whereas the first program will require about twice as many statements as the number of words in the text to be processed, the second program can handle a text of any length (up to the limit of the storage area) with a small fixed number of statements.

A more ambitious task, namely a frequency list of all the words in a text, can be performed by again using the result of a subtraction to provide a branching in the program as in step 4 above. Starting with the text stored in the pigeonholes as in the previous problem, we could re-sort the text (that is, the set of numbers corresponding to the text) into numerical sequence. This could be done by searching the text block for the smallest number in it (found by subtraction with a negative result vs. a positive or zero result) and removing this number from the text block and putting it into a new location, for which we'll need a new address, say, LOGOS. The search would be repeated in the remainder of the text block and the result would be pulled out and put in LOGOS + 1. This process would continue until locations WORD through WORD + 15 were empty. Then LOGOS through LOGOS + 15 would contain the entire text in numerical (and, hence, alphabetical) order. (LOGOS + 16 is added for a purpose that will become clear later.)

List	Pigeonhole Address	Pigeonhole Contents
DARK	LOGOS	040118110000
FROM	LOGOS + 1	061815130000
JUST	LOGOS + 2	102119200000
MEN	LOGOS + 3	130514000000
NIGHT	LOGOS + 4	140907082000
NOR	LOGOS + 5	141518000000
NOR	LOGOS + 6	141518000000
NOR	LOGOS + 7	141518000000
OF	LOGOS + 8	150600000000
RAIN	LOGOS + 9	180109140000
ROUNDS	LOGOS + 10	181521140419
SHALL	LOGOS + 11	190801121200
SNOW	LOGOS + 12	191415230000
STAY	LOGOS + 13	192001250000
THEIR	LOGOS + 14	200805091800
THESE	LOGOS + 15	200805190500
(Blank to signal end of text)	LOGOS + 16	000000000000

Note that once the words are in alphabetical order, all like words are grouped together — in this case, the three *nor*'s.

The computer next examines the re-ordered set of words (the LOGOS block), following these instructions, which use the typewriter for output and have a provision for stopping the machine when the task has been completed:

1. Set up an indexing pigeonhole. Label it with the letter I and set it equal to zero.

2. Set up a counting pigeonhole. Label it NUMBER with a value of one (every word examined will have occurred at least once).

3. If LOGOS+I=zero (this condition will be satisfied in our present text only when I = 16, i.e. when the end of the list has been reached), stop the machine. Otherwise, go to step 4.

4. Subtract the contents of LOGOS+I from the contents of LOGOS+I+1 (i.e., determine whether the currently examined word is like the next word in the list). If the result is zero, go to step 5; otherwise, go to step 8.

5. Increase NUMBER by one.

6. Increase I by one.

7. Go to step 3.

8. Skip the typewriter to the next line and type out the word in LOGOS+I and the number in NUMBER, following the spacing instructions in step 9.

9. Skip 3 spaces. Type the alphabetic character in LOGOS+I,

allowing 6 spaces. Skip 5 spaces. Type the integer in NUMBER, allowing 4 spaces.

    10. Increase I by one.

    11. Go to step 2.

When all of the text has been processed, the paper in the typewriter will contain a complete word-frequency listing of the text.

    Such a routine is easily expressed in a programming language called FORTRAN. In FORTRAN a list would be referred to by the notation LOGOS(I) rather than LOGOS+I and the lowest value of I would be one rather than zero, but the principle is the same. The branching statement takes the form IF (   ) 2, 6, 9, which means "if the expression in parentheses is negative, go to statement 2, if zero to statement 6, if positive to statement 9." Furthermore the symbol "=" should be read "is reset equal to." The section of a FORTRAN program that would perform the task above would read as follows (the numbers to the left in parentheses refer to the above set of instructions and are not part of the FORTRAN program):

```
(1)         I = 1
(2)         1 NUMBER = 1
(3)         2 IF (LOGOS (I)) 4,3,4
            3 STOP
(4)         4 IF (LOGOS (I + 1) — LOGOS (I)) 6, 5, 6
(5)         5 NUMBER = NUMBER + 1
(6)          I = I + 1
(7)          GO TO 2
(8)         6 PRINT 7, LOGOS (I), NUMBER
(9)         7 FORMAT (3X, A6, 5X, I4)
(10)         I = I + 1
(11)         GO TO 1
```

Programming logic similar to that of the preceding problem can be used to construct a text concordance. First, each word in the stored text would be tagged with a location number which would remain with it throughout its existence in the machine. This location number might either be the number of the line in which the word occurs or be the distance from the beginning of the text expressed in number of words. The text with its location numbers would then be duplicated and one copy would be sorted into alphabetical order as in the previous problem. The location numbers accompanying the alphabetized list would be used to control the printing of the concordance line by line. If line numbers were used and the first location number in the sorted list were 517, then line number 517 would be printed from the stored copy of the original text. If 517 were a word number, the 517th word would be located in the original text. A line would be formed by counting off in each direction a set number of characters from the beginning of word 517, and this line would then be printed.

The solutions to the above problems may seem obvious enough, once stated. In fact, if they were not in some sense obvious, they would not be translatable into computer language. Yet the thinking habits required to produce such solutions are not the kind to which one may be accustomed; they must be cultivated.

However, when one can produce solutions of the kind illustrated, the problem of translating them into a programming language is trivial. One can hire a programmer or learn one of the simpler programming languages himself. These languages are easy enough to learn. It is the conceptualizing which must accompany them that causes the difficulty.

Programming Languages

Computer programming languages vary between two extremes: languages that are easy for the computer to digest but hard for the programmer to write (e.g., strings of binary numbers) and languages which require a good bit of processing before the computer can use them but which are fairly easy to compose in (e.g., FORTRAN, COMIT, and others). Fortunately for us humans, it is the computer itself which does the processing of these higher level languages by following ingenious programs already designed.

It is convenient to distinguish three levels of computer languages:

1. *Machine languages* are composed of strings of numbers, usually binary, which need no processing by the machine.

2. *Symbolic languages* are composed of decimal numbers and short mnemonic alphabetic codes for standard instructions. They are a good deal easier to use than machine languages and are just as flexible; all of the capabilities of the computer can be fully utilized and added shortcuts are available. Yet these languages are still fairly difficult to learn and use. The computer translates a source program written in a symbolic language into an object program in machine language by means of an assembly program. These symbolic languages, one for each kind of computer, often have acronymic titles, e.g., MAP, FAP, SAP.

3. *Problem-oriented* languages allow programs that resemble an ordinary statement of the problem. Some flexibility and power is lost, but such programming languages are easily learned, are much simpler and quicker to write in than are the machine-oriented symbolic languages and are, as a consequence, likely to be more free of errors to begin with and easier to correct when errors do occur. There are a number of these languages, each designed for particular applications, e.g., FORTRAN for scientific work, COBOL for com-

merce, COMIT for machine translation and linguistic analysis, and many others. Unfortunately, the purpose for which a programming language was designed must often be relegated to minor consideration; often far more important are considerations of availability, universality, and efficiency. The closest thing to a programming *lingua franca* in this country is FORTRAN; any academic computing center is likely to have it available, fellow scholars can readily trade programs, and it has a high-speed translator. The fact that FORTRAN was designed to accommodate algebraic formulas is not the disadvantage that one might suppose. It is a highly flexible instrument that can be adapted to many problems in literary data processing.

The difference between a symbolic language and a problem-oriented language can be illustrated with programs for executing a task described earlier: counting the number of occurrences of a given word. Suppose that we have a 2500-word text with no word containing more than twenty-four letters and that we wish to know the frequency of *nor*. We'll begin with a symbolic language program for the IBM 7040.[1] Because a 7040 machine location will hold only a six-letter string, four such locations must be set aside for each word, with unused spaces filled by zeros. The required 10,000 locations can be labelled 0 through 9999. This means that the first word begins in location #0, the second in location #4, the third in location #8 and so forth. In addition to the text, the following program constants will be stored: 10,000 in a location labelled L10000, zero in L0, and *nor* (i.e., NOR followed by three zeros) in LNOR. In the program that follows, the numbers on the left are for our reference only and are not part of the program. Explanatory notes follow the program.

(1) There is a special kind of pigeonhole used for control and counting; it's called an *index register* and there are three of them. Index register #1 will be used to control the address of the word called for so that not all 2500 words need be addressed specifically or directly (which would require a program 2500 times as large as the one above). This instruction sets index register #1 at 10,000; that is, the contents of L10000 are transferred into it.

(2) Index register #2 will be used for counting the number of *nor*'s. This instruction sets it at zero.

---

[1] This program is taken with slight modifications from the very helpful article by Sidney M. Lamb, "The Digital Computer as an Aid in Linguistics," *Language*, XXXVII (1961), 382-412, now available in the Bobbs-Merrill Reprint Series in Language and Linguistics. An article dealing with a smaller machine (the IBM 650) is Thomas A. Sebeok's "Notes on the Digital Calculator as a Tool for Analyzing Literary Information," *Poetics*, ed. Donald Davie *et al.* (The Hague, 1961), pp. 571 - 590.

Memory Location	Operation	Address
(1)	LXA	L10000,1
(2)	LXA	L0,2
(3)	CLA	LNOR
(4) A	CAS	10000,1
(5)	TRA	B
(6)	TRA	C
(7) B	TIX	A,1,4
(8)	TRA	PRINT
(9) C	TXI	B,2,1

(3) The part of the "desk-calculator" component used for addition and subtraction is called the *accumulator*. This instruction clears it (sets it at zero) and adds into it the numerical equivalent of *nor,* which is stored in location LNOR.

(4) This statement, which has a specified memory location so that a loop, a repeated series of statements, can be set up transferring control back to it, is a three-way branching instruction. It means Compare Accumulator with Storage; that is, the content of the accumulator (the numerical equivalent of *nor*) is compared for size with the content of a given storage location containing the first six letters of a word of text. If the number in storage is less than the one in the accumulator, control is transferred to the next instruction (#5); if the numbers are equal (i.e., if the given word of text is a *nor*) control goes to the second following instruction (#6); and if the storage number is greater than the accumulator number, control goes to the third following instruction (#7). The storage location chosen for the comparison is determined by the address portion of this instruction. The address "10000,1" means "10,000 minus the contents of index register #1." As we will see later, this instruction begins a loop. The first time through the loop, index register #1 will contain 10,000 and hence the address will be 10,000 minus 10,000, which is zero, the location of the first six letters of the first word of text. Each time the loop is executed, index register #1 will be reduced by 4 so that successive word beginnings will be called for as follows:

Execution Number	Address Base	— Index Register	= Effective Address
1	10,000	— 10,000	= 0
2	10,000	- 9,996	= 4
3	10,000	- 9,992	= 8
. . .	. . .	. . .	. . .
. . .	. . .	. . .	. . .
. . .	. . .	. . .	. . .
2500	10,000	- 4	= 9,996

(5) This instruction merely transfers control to instruction B (#7).

(6) This instruction transfers control to instruction C (#9). Note that if the storage word is *nor,* control goes to C, if it is not *nor,* control goes to B. Thus the original three-way branch is now, in effect, a two-way branch.

(7) This instruction subtracts four from index register #1 and transfers control back to A, thus establishing a loop from A to B to A that is traversed whenever the storage word is not *nor.* This loop in a sense does nothing except move us on to the next word. It does have one additional feature, however. When index register #1 has less than four in it (i.e., when four can no longer be subtracted from it without getting a negative result), control is not transferred to A, but to the very next statement (#8).

(8) This statement, which can only be reached when all of the specified amount of text has been examined for *nor,* transfers control to a section of the program beginning at a memory location named PRINT, which presumably will guide the computer in printing the results of our *nor* count.

(9) This instruction adds one to index register #2, our *nor* counter. It must not transfer control directly to A, for then the same word, *nor,* would be re-examined, and we would appear to have a 2500-word text containing *nor* an infinite number of times. Control must first be transferred to B, which will reset the location counting index register and will automatically return control to A. Thus our second loop, traversed whenever the storage word is *nor,* goes from A to C to B to A. It tallies a *nor* and then moves us on to the next word. The first time through, the instructions are handled in the following order: 1-2-3-4. From this point on, one of three loops are followed, 4-5-7-4, 4-6-9-7-4, or 4-7-4. Note that in each loop the last two numbers are 7-4. When the final word is being compared, the last two numbers will be 7-8.

In the equivalent *problem-oriented language program,* the text will be stored in locations labelled LWORD(1), LWORD(2), . . . LWORD(10000), allowing four LWORDs per word of text to permit twenty-four letters per word, if needed. In addition to the text, two constants will be stored: NNOR = 0, and the word *nor* in location LNOR. In the following program, the numbers to the left are for our reference only and are not part of the FORTRAN program.

```
(1)     DO 6 I = 1, 100000, 4
(2)     IF (LNOR – LWORD(I) ) 6,5,6
(3)   5 NNOR = NNOR + 1
(4)   6 CONTINUE
(5)
```

(1) The word DO indicates the beginning of a loop. It means: Do the things specified by the following statements down through statement 6 (#4) over and over again. The first time around, interpret I as 1, and each successive time increase I by 4. When I exceeds 10,000, do not re-execute the loop, but proceed instead to the statement following 6 (i.e., to #5).

(2) This is a three-way branch statement similar to the CAS of the previous program except that the branches are specifically numbered and can therefore be anywhere in the program. It means: If LNOR — LWORD(I) results in a minus quantity, transfer control to statement 6, if zero to statement 5, and if plus to statement 6.

(3) This statement, which can be reached only if LWORD(I) is a *nor,* increases the NNOR counter by one. It means: Replace the contents of NNOR by a number which is one larger than the present contents of NNOR. After the tally is made, control passes to the next statement.

(4) This is a dummy statement to take care of an inflexibility of the programming language. Only by going here, to the specified last statement of the DO-loop (DO 6), can the program increase I by one. Consequently it wouldn't work to replace the sixes in #2 by a statement number referring to #1, for control would then transfer back to the DO statement but the index I would remain unchanged and the machine would therefore try to execute this loop an infinite number of times. CONTINUE means: "Carry on."

(5) This point in the program would be reached after the entire text had been examined and all the *nor*'s had been tallied. We would probably want a printing instruction here.

Another problem-oriented programming language is COMIT, designed specifically for machine translation and having some useful features for dealing with alphabetic data. Under the COMIT program, all available computer space is divided, like Gaul, into three parts. The part that concerns us here, called the *workspace,* must contain whatever data is to be manipulated. We will assume that our 2500-word text is in normal (i.e., original) order in the workspace and that we have inserted at the head of the text the word *TALLY/.0. As far as the computer is concerned, this word is on a par with any other word in the workspace. Any constituent (i.e., word, or any other unit for analysis) can have subscripts, separated from it by a slash. These subscripts can contain information about the constituent: e.g., "noun, singular" or "verb, past perfect, active" or "metaphor" or "anacoluthon" or "Q1, Q3, Q4, F2," or a number preceded by a period if the constituent and its subscript are to be used as a counter as they are here. To prevent having our counting word confused with a word in the text, we begin it with a star. We could just as well have used anything whose absence in the text is a certainty: e.g., CNT or QNT.

Counting in COMIT somewhat resembles the game of leapfrog. We should imagine a line (text) of boys (words), some of whom are wearing green caps (they represent *nor*'s). At the beginning of the line there is a kangaroo (*TALLY/.0). If our model were to be perfect, the kangaroo would need have 32,767 fingers on his right hand, but we shall plead allegorical license. The kangaroo sights down the line of boys until he sees one with a green cap. He then leaps to the position in front of the sighted boy and holds up one finger (*TALLY/.1). He continues to do this until there are no more boys with green caps ahead of him, at which time the number of upraised fingers (*TALLY/.3) equals the number of green-capped lads (*nor*'s) in the line (text).

The COMIT program for counting *nor*'s is as follows (the numbers at left in parentheses are not part of the program):

	Rule Name	Instruction	Traffic
(1)	FIND	*TALLY + $ + NOR = 2 + 3 + 1	COUNT
(2)	*		PRINT
(3)	COUNT	*TALLY = 1/.I1	FIND

(1) This rule locates three parts of the workspace; one of them, *TALLY, is named explicitly. NOR refers to the first occurrence of NOR after *TALLY. $ is anything in between *TALLY and NOR, which may be nothing. These parts are found by the left half of the instruction, i.e., that part of the instruction left of the equal sign. The right half of the instruction re-orders these parts from 1-2-3 to 2-3-1 (i.e., $ + NOR + *TALLY). The traffic section of this rule specifies that the next rule to be executed is the rule named COUNT. However, the traffic section is ignored if the parts named in the left half cannot be found. See (3) below.

(3) The rule named COUNT merely increases the subscript of our counter, *TALLY, by one and transfers control back to the first rule, which is named FIND. Thus we have a two-rule loop which transfers *TALLY to just after the first occurrence of NOR, changes *TALLY/.0 to *TALLY/.1, transfers *TALLY to just after the second occurrence of NOR, changes *TALLY/.1 to *TALLY /.2, and so on until there are no more occurrences of NOR appearing after the location of *TALLY. At this point the condition specified in the left half of the first rule cannot be met. This is known as left-half failure and results in automatic transfer to the very next rule (#2).

(2) This rule merely transfers control to a rule named PRINT, which will be used to print out the word *TALLY with its subscript,

which, at this point, is equal to the number of *nor*'s in the text. The PRINT rule could just as well be placed in this position instead of the asterisk rule, thereby making the program one rule shorter.

In the preceding three programs, economy was several times sacrificed to clarity (although it may seem to the reader that the reverse was true). Consequently no rigorous comparison of the three languages would be possible even if we ignored the obvious limitation of drawing general conclusions from a very small sample. Nevertheless the general impression given is accurate: a FORTRAN program is likely to be considerably shorter than a symbolic-language program. If we restrict ourselves to the manipulation of language data rather than numerical data, a COMIT program will be shorter than an equivalent FORTRAN program. It is also apparent that one could accommodate his thinking to FORTRAN or COMIT statements a good deal more easily than to symbolic statements. FORTRAN in particular reads a good deal more like English in its instructions; e.g., READ, WRITE, DO, IF, CONTINUE, STOP, END, RETURN, and even that standby of the Elizabethan stage —GO TO.

The problem-oriented languages are also easier to learn. MAP, the symbolic language for the IBM 7040 computer, has a repertoire of roughly 200 instructions. Not all of these are needed for literary-linguistic work; Sidney Lamb[2] lists fifty-six key operations (not counting input-output statements). But contrast this with FORTRAN, which has a total repertoire of about thirty statements (and one can get along nicely with about twenty of these). COMIT can, in turn, be more quickly learned than FORTRAN. Furthermore, problem-oriented languages tend to be relatively uniform even when implemented on machines of different manufacturers, while symbolic machine languages must of necessity differ for each kind of machine even though from the same manufacturer.

However, chosing a problem-oriented language over a machine-oriented language is not without its complications. For literary data-processing FORTRAN does have a few disadvantages. First of all, if a text is stored as a list of words, then it is nearly impossible to get at parts of words. One way around this is to store text as a series of letters. There are also extra-legal ways around this but these vary from machine to machine. In COMIT, on the other hand, text is initially stored as a series of letters, but from then on groups of letters can be contracted into words and expanded back into groups of letters at will by using a single rule. In a symbolic program, words may be stored as words initially and still be

[2]"The Digital Computer as an Aid in Linguistics."

broken apart. The other major disadvantage of FORTRAN is its algebraic orientation; terms that are entirely numeric are treated as constants, i.e., as pigeonhole contents, and terms that are entirely or partially alphabetic are treated as variables, i.e., as labels for pigeonhole contents. One way around this is to store the desired alphabetic constants in pigeonholes whose labels are equivalent to their contents; e.g., *A,B,C,D,* can be stored in pigeonholes named "A", "B", "C", "D", or the constant *THE* can be stored in a pigeonhole named "THE."[3] Both COMIT and the symbolic family of languages are a good deal more flexible in this respect. Also, it would be unfair not to mention that the two dodges suggested for getting around FORTRAN limitations may cause some programming inconveniences, but they are genuine solutions nonetheless.

COMIT has some disadvantages too. Although it is the easiest language to learn of those mentioned and has the most convenient notation for literary problems, it is, at least in its present form, relatively slow and therefore rather expensive in computer time. Furthermore, it is not nearly so widely available as FORTRAN. The designers of COMIT have been working on a new version, COMIT II, which promises to be much faster and to have some additional programming features. It is perhaps partly up to us, the potential users of a literary-linguistic data processing language, to help overcome its lack of general availability. In the meantime, many who want a fast-running program and one that can be widely disseminated will probably continue to write in FORTRAN. Dissemination can be very important if one has developed a procedure which he wants tested as extensively as possible.

Input and Output

Physical means of communicating with a computer are several. The most intimate link is the typewriter connected to the computer console. This dual input-output device is used by the operator to run the computer and handle unforeseen problems. In the normal run of things, it is not the channel of communication which a computer user is likely to encounter. Instead he will communicate with the computer through the media of punched cards, punched paper tape, magnetic tape, magnetic disk, or, for output only, printed sheets. Initially, one's input will probably be on cards, which may, for speed and convenience, be converted to a magnetic medium. The output may initially be magnetic but finally may be converted to printed pages or punched cards or both. If the output is likely

---

[3]This circumvention is not possible in some older versions of the language such as IBM's FORTRAN II and Control Data's FORTRAN 60.

to be the input for some future program, it should be saved on cards or, if there is a lot of it, on magnetic tape.

The format of the output is controlled by the program, subject only to the limitations of the output device and medium. One cannot exceed the card length of eighty columns or the length of the printed line (119 characters is common, although there are others). Another limitation is the availability of characters. It is possible but very expensive to have printing wheels or chains made to order. Similarly upper and lower case is available, but few installations have it as yet and the required equipment is somewhat costly. Consequently one is limited to numbers, upper-case letters, and a set of special characters—a business set or a scientific set. Most academic computer centers will probably have the scientific set, consisting of plus and minus signs, the equal sign, parentheses, period, comma, slash, dollar sign, asterisk, hyphen (apostrophe on some machines) and blank.

Input format is also flexible and specified by the program: the eighty characters represented by eighty card columns can be interpreted as eighty separate items, called "fields," or as ten eight-character fields or as a ten-character field followed by an eight-character field, followed by an eleven-character field, etc. Any desired configuration can be specified. One is again limited by the card length of eighty columns and by the available characters listed above. The problem, then, is how to accommodate one's text to these limitations.

First of all, it should be emphasized that, considering the cost of keypunching, nothing less than full text should ever be put on a card. One never knows what aspect of the text will be needed for some future analysis either by oneself or someone else.[4] Often it is desirable or even necessary to put information on cards in addition to the raw text—e.g., phonological, grammatical, rhetorical, or typographical data. For the same economic reason, nothing short of the best available text should ever be used.

---

[4]Attempts are being made to set up a central agency for maintaining an index of all texts that are available on cards or tape. Computer users derive much mutual advantage from sharing programs and data. In *Natural Language in Computer Form,* Memorandum RM-4390-PR (Santa Monica, California: The Rand Corporation, February 1965), Martin Kay and Theodore Ziehe propose a standard format for storing text on magnetic tape in a form that allows for all printing conventions, including different alphabets and fonts. Their proposal combines the virtues of uniformity with flexibility by allowing the text to be punched onto cards in any form convenient for keypuncher and user. A standard program then converts the text on cards into a magnetic tape text in standard form. Anyone planning on punching a text deck of any size ought certainly to avail himself of the details of their proposal.

In converting a text into punched cards, we are faced with decisions about two matters: coding, the way in which unavailable characters (e.g., semicolon, capital letters, italics) are to be represented, and format, the way in which data is to be arranged on a card. If the services of a professional programmer are being used, he should be consulted about both kinds of decision, for they may affect programming efficiency and ease. If it turns out that coding decisions are arbitrary with respect to the programmer, then the keypuncher ought to be considered. Such mnemonic devices as using two periods for a colon, a period followed by a comma for a semicolon, and a dollar sign for capitalization[5] may speed up keypunching if it is done directly from the text. On the other hand, if no immediate use of punctuation, capitalization, and typographical data is contemplated, then such information may best be represented by numbers, rather than letters or special characters. Thus a typographical word (anything between spaces) can be converted to a textual word simply by stripping it of any characters with a value less than ten, for all alphabetic and special characters are represented inside the machine by numerical values greater than nine. If the original text contains numerals, these can be preserved by prefixing them with a special character, say an asterisk, and specifying that only those typographical words which do not begin with an asterisk are to be stripped of their numeric affixes. If the specific numeral is of no moment, such a specification could be omitted and the asterisk would still remain as a symbol of a numerically expressed number. Another alternative would be to convert all numerals in the original text to their alphabetic counterparts, but this assumes that one knows exactly how a given author would have pronounced combinations of numerals. Would 24 become *twenty-four or four-and twenty*? Would *1984* be *nineteen-eighty-four, nineteen-hundred eighty-four* or *one-thousand nine-hundred and eighty-four*? This is the same problem that must be faced if we wish to add prosodic information to the text: how to determine the correct reading.

Settling on a card format also should be done with programming convenience in mind. Economy is a factor too: the more information per card, the smaller the data deck, resulting in savings of keypunching time, card costs, and storage space. The most compact method is to punch running text onto cards and let the program break the eighty columns up into typographical words and each typographical word into punctuation code, textual word, and additional information code. A simpler method from the standpoint of pro-

---

[5]This ingenious pun was unveiled at IBM's Literary Data Processing Conference (Yorktown Heights, N. Y., September 9 - 11, 1964) by the Reverend Joseph G. Devine, S.J.

gramming is to use a fixed field format. For example, a convenient format for the detailed examination of a short but heavily augmented text might be as follows:[6]

Columns	Contents of Field
2—30	Textual word
32—33	Initial punctuation (e.g., open parenthesis, open quote, dash)
35	Capitalization
37	Type font (e.g., italic, bold face)
39—41	Final punctuation
43—47	Name of speaker (if dialogue)
49	End of line (if poetry)
51—52	Part of speech
54	Number of syllables
56—59	The syllable numbers of poetically stressed syllables
61—68	Syntactic information
70—74	Deck identification name
75—80	Serial numbering of deck

Unmentioned columns are left blank to facilitate proofreading.

The computer can read a card punched in a fixed field format, ignore any specified columns and automatically store other fields in pigeonholes with any desired label. This is all a part of the normal read-in procedure in FORTRAN, for example. It requires only two statements and no analysis of data. The varying-field format requires the same two statements to read in all eighty columns and then additional analysis to determine word boundaries. However, no space is lost in a varying field, but think of the space wasted in a fixed word-field if the word is *a* or *the*.

Regardless of which method is adopted, space should be left on the card for serial numbering and identification. If decks are dropped, no matter how badly they become scrambled, they can be restored on a high-speed mechanical sorter. A deck identification name is easy enough to put on all the cards because the keypunch duplicates any desired field automatically.

Statistics and Canned Programs

Important extensions of the computer are the prepared programs available to computer users. These are especially valuable to the

---

[6]Another format, especially useful for textual studies, was proposed by Professor Thomas Clayton of U.C.L.A. at the LDP conference (see preceding note).

humanist engaged in any kind of numerical analysis of texts, for many past studies have been vitiated by their statistical naivete. The canned statistical program not only frees the investigator from tedious computation, it frees him from knowing how such computations are performed as well. Thus with an elementary knowledge of statistics, with a statistician to check over one's plans and with a canned program to do the work, the literary scholar can do a respectably sophisticated job of numerical analysis.

Some knowledge of statistics is not so very hard to come by if one knows where to start. Probably, it would be best to start by asking the advice of someone who knows more about statistics than the author of this article does. However, without claiming to have looked at more than a dozen or two of the hundreds of statistics books in print, I shall mention five which have been very useful to me.

Paul G. Hoël's *Elementary Statistics* (New York, 1960) is an extremely lucid and very elementary beginner's book and one (I've been assured) of high repute among mathematicians. Anglophiles and those who prefer their statistics delivered with some stylistic adornment and a bit of wit may also enjoy M. J. Moroney's *Facts from Figures* (3rd edition, Baltimore, 1956). An intermediate text which begins at the beginning but makes no concession in speed or to those whose "deficiency in mathematics is . . . accompanied by an emotional reaction to symbols" is *Psychological Statistics* by Quinn McNemar (3rd edition, New York, 1962). This book is also highly lucid and goes a good deal beyond the information given in the two elementary texts. Bernard Ostle's *Statistics in Research: Basic Concepts and Techniques for Research Workers* (2nd edition, Ames, Iowa, 1963) is somewhat more advanced, although its organization and terseness make it easier to use as a reference than as a self-teaching text. It is very useful. A fifth book, which exclusively treats ways of dealing with many variables at once (and with their interactions) and which gives FORTRAN programs for each statistical technique described, is *Multivariate Procedures for the Behavioral Sciences* by William W. Cooley and Paul R. Lohnes (New York, 1962). This book is a good deal more advanced than the two intermediate texts just cited, and at times its prose style approaches impenetrability, at least for the uninitiated reader.

Project Planning

The first decision to be made in planning a project is whether to use a computer at all. If the text to be analyzed is short, if the analysis is highly complex and if the procedure to be developed is unlikely to be useful in analyzing other texts, and if the amount of time available is little, then one should probably not compute.

The development of a complex computer program requires many man-hours to write and a fair amount of human time to get into working order, although computer time itself may be brief. The first draft of a program seldom works. It must be submitted to the computer and revised after its return any number of times before the desired result is obtained. During this process, known as *debugging*, one is more or less at the mercy of the speed at which his computing center processes and returns programs. In any case, saving time with a computer has this in common with making money by investment: a large initial outlay is necessary.

The second decision is whether to hire a programmer or to do one's own programming. Both choices are common practice and depend largely on personal preference. Having tried both methods, I can say that I vastly prefer the second, both because it leaves one more independent and because programming is a highly interesting task. In any case, it is convenient to know something about FORTRAN to facilitate communicating with a programmer. Computer manufacturers generally publish descriptions of the FORTRAN dialect acceptable to each of their machines. Many schools offer regular and short courses in FORTRAN. Some useful texts are *A Guide to FORTRAN Programming* by Daniel D. McCracken (New York, 1961) and *A FORTRAN Primer* by Elliott I. Organick (Reading, Mass., 1963). The major shortcoming of these texts from the standpoint of the literary scholar is that the problems, which must be worked to gain a real grasp of the language, are largely mathematical. Vinton Dearing has been working on a text designed to teach symbolic language programming to literary scholars. COMIT can be easily learned from *An Introduction to COMIT Programming* (revised edition, Cambridge, Mass. 1962). More general works, which do not attempt to teach programming but which contain a great variety of information for computer users as well as descriptions of some unusual applications, are *Digital Computers in Research: An Introduction for Behavioral and Social Scientists* by Bert F. Green, Jr. (New York, 1963), *Computer Applications in the Behavioral Sciences,* edited by Harold Borko (Englewood Cliffs, N. J., 1962) and *Natural Language and the Computer,* edited by Paul L. Garvin (New York, 1963). Mr. Green's book is an especially clear and detailed general introduction to the subject.

Program and data decks are produced on a keypunch machine, which somewhat resembles a typewriter but which has some excellent automatic tab-spacing and duplicating features. It not only punches the proper holes, but it also prints the corresponding characters across the top of the card. The prepared deck is then processed (preferably by someone other than the person who punched it) on a verifier, a machine which works very like a keypunch except that instead of punching the holes corresponding to a given keyboard character, it senses whether such a hole (or holes) has been punched, and if not it warns the operator by flashing a red light. Although this almost doubles the deck preparation time, it is a standard and necessary step if any kind of accuracy is to be achieved. But even a deck that has been punched and verified by two expert keypunchers will have some errors. Consequently the deck should be run through one of several kinds of machines that print out a listing of a deck of cards, one card per line, for checking by a third person, preferably someone acquainted with the text. Even so, some words may have been entirely omitted without having been caught, so that one may wish to write a simple program which reads in the cards, reconstitutes the text, and prints it out in somethng like the original format for additional checking. All of this precaution may sound old-grand-motherly to someone who has never tried to get a text onto cards with complete accuracy, but experience will show him otherwise.

Two other basic machines which aid in deck preparation are the reproducing machine, which automatically produces a duplicate deck, and the collator, which is useful for checking to see whether the cards are in numerically sequential order. Both machines can be made to do a number of other things too.

The remaining information needed to plan a project fully—cost of computer time, cost of basic machines, local wages for programmers and keypunchers—must be obtained from the computing center which one hopes to use. Of course, to get usable advice from someone at a center, one should have clearly in mind precisely what it is he wants to do and how much material he wants processed. It is to the end that he may communicate effectively with such an advisor that this article has been written. Of further assistance is a user's manual (computers can be habit forming), which lists the conventions and requirements of a given center as well as the canned programs available through it.

Conclusion

If this article has shown that the computer is a tool with which the humanist can come to grips, it will have done its job. There can be no doubt that the solution of many literary problems can be automated in part; many studies have demonstrated that. The computer can take over the drudgery and some of the jobs too vast for a human to perform in several lifetimes, leaving for the humanist the creative part of the scholarly enterprise. It is probably not too much to hope that the scholar of the near future will begin work on an author with an assemblage of texts in any form from letterpress to microfilm, that these texts will be automatically scanned by optical equipment, that a variorum edition and a concordance will be automatically produced along with possible emendations and textual trees suggested by the machine for the consideration of its human master. Furthermore, automatic syntactic analysis will allow frequency counts of linguistic features as well as vocabulary counts, and the two together will offer the rudiments from which the scholar, free from dependence on a sometimes fallible memory, will be able to build *his* analysis and determination of authorship, literary influence, style, and theme with an ease and sophistication not now feasible except with short texts.

Since the above article was written, IBM has announced a new language, PL/I, to be implemented on its new line of 360 computers. If a full dialect of this langauge becomes widely available, it will be a boon to all who wish to process natural-language data, for it combines the simplicity and many of the features of FORTRAN with the flexibility of machine symbolic languages. Furthermore, it uses a much expanded set of character and provides convenient means of handling character strings as well as the facility for storing data in tree structures, useful to the generative grammarian and the textual historian alike.

AN EXPOSITION

OF A STATISTICAL APPROACH

TO THE FEDERALIST DISPUTE

Ivor S. Francis

Two DAYS before his fatal duel with Aaron Burr on July 11, 1804, Alexander Hamilton visited Egbert Benson and ostentatiously concealed in his friend's bookcase a slip of paper. All the *Federalist* papers had been published over the name "Publius," whose identity was a secret. On the slip of paper Hamilton listed by number the authors of the various essays. The three authors were James Madison, John Jay, and himself.

Neither Madison nor Jay chose to challenge the Benson list when it was found. It was not until 1817 that a friend of Madison's challenged the Benson list and claimed for Madison some of the papers that Hamilton had claimed to have written. Then in 1818 Madison formally announced his claim in Jacob Gideon's edition of *The Federalist*. Few of Madison's contemporaries doubted this carefully considered claim and there the matter rested until the Civil War. From 1861 the Virginian's fame as a constitutional statesman declined while Hamilton's reputation grew with the rise of Federalism, so that by 1886, with the publication by Henry Cabot Lodge of a new edition of *The Federalist,* the Benson list was being reconsidered.

Three quarters of a century later the authorship of these disputed papers remained an historical controversy and it was into this arena that two innocent statisticians stumbled. This article describes the attempts made by Frederick Mosteller and David L. Wallace to

NOTE. The writer acknowledges with thanks the many helpful comments and suggestions of Professor Frederick Mosteller. For work on the manuscripts thanks are due to Miss Marguerite O'Leary, Miss Jacqueline Wollan, and also to Mrs. Marianne Blackwell and Miss Frances Suda.

The quotations from the book *Inference and Disputed Authorship: The Federalist,* by Frederick Mosteller and David L. Wallace, are reprinted by permission of the copyright owners, Addison-Wesley Publishing Company, Inc., Reading, Massachusetts.

This work was facilitated by a grant from the National Science Foundation (GS-341).

resolve the controversy, not by the usual methods of historical literary analysis, but by methods of mathematical statistics.

1. Background

The statistical or mathematical approach to the study of language is not new. Whatmough (1957) points out that a Sanskrit grammarian of the Sutra period (500 - 200 B.C.) gave the number of hymns, verses, words, and even syllables contained in the Rig-Veda. More recently, in 1854, George Boole records in Laws of Thought how the principle of determinate frequency was applied to the deciphering of Ogam and cuneiform. In 1887 Mendenhall investigated the difference between the literary styles of Dickens and Thackeray insofar as the length of words was concerned. He studied the frequency distribution of the length of words—the proportion of one-letter, two-letter, three-letter words, etc. In a later article (1901) he used word-length frequency distributions in a study of the authorship of Shakespeare's play (see Section 4). Figure I shows the distributions for Bacon (based on a count of 200,000 words from his Henry VII, The Advancement of Learning, and many essays) and for Shakespeare (based on a count of 400,000 words including nearly all of his most famous plays).

The frequency distribution of the number of words in a sentence was proposed by Yule (1938) as another element of style that seems to be characteristic of an author. He investigated the style of De imitatione Christi and compared it, in respect to the distribution of sentence length, to works of Thomas à Kempis and Jean Charlier de Gerson. His results were consonant with the view that à Kempis was, and Gerson was not, the author of the work.

In 1944 Yule published a further attempt to decide the authorship of De imitatione Christi. This time he studied a feature of vocabulary, namely the distribution of the number of nouns used once, twice, etc.

In 1941 Frederick Williams introduced Frederick Mosteller to the problem which we shall consider in detail in this paper, namely the problem of the authorship of the disputed Federalist papers. Williams and Mosteller, influenced by the work of Yule and of C. B. Williams (1939), studied the undisputed Federalist works of Hamilton and Madison but found that sentence length did not discriminate between the two authors. They then computed for each known paper the percentages of nouns, of adjectives, of one- and two-letter words, and of the's. On the basis of these data they constructed a statistic that was intended to separate Hamilton's writings from Madison's. This statistic, however, was not sensitive

FIGURE I.   Word-Length Frequency Distribution for
Bacon and Shakespeare
Redrawn from Mendenhall (1901)

Bacon ————
Shakespeare Poetry - - - - - - -
Shakespeare Prose ——— – ———

Number of
Occurrences
Per 1000 words

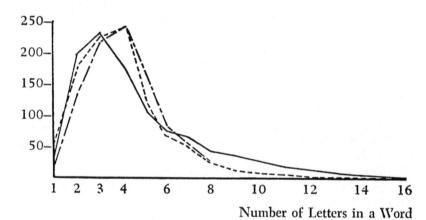

Number of Letters in a Word

enough to assign the disputed papers with any degree of confidence,
although it pointed to Madison for most of them.

William and Mosteller did not resume their joint work and it
was only a few years ago that Mosteller's interest was revived. In
1959 Douglass Adair informed Mosteller that he had found a pair
of words (later called marker words) that distinguished Hamilton
from Madison quite well when the words occurred. Hamilton uses
while and Madison, in a corresponding situation, uses *whilst.* It
was around such words that Mosteller and Wallace built their
case described in their book *Inference and Disputed Authorship:
The Federalist* and summarized in a paper entitled "Inference in
an Authorship Problem" (*J. A. S. A.,* 1963). As mathematical statisticians the authors' major concern was the comparison of a number
of statistical methods of discrimination all based on much the same
data. But they were also interested in solving the authorship question of the *Federalist* papers and in proposing routine methods for

solving other authorship problems. This paper attempts to give readers unfamiliar with mathematical statistics a summary of the problem and the results, besides reporting briefly the authors' advice to those who would undertake similar projects. The writer of this article assisted in several parts of the *Federalist* project and will quote frequently from the book and paper. The tables are taken from the *J. A. S. A.* paper

For a more detailed account the reader is referred to the book which, though statistically oriented, separates much of the mathematics from the exposition so that a non-mathematical reader should have little difficulty in following the main arguments. A reader who is interested in this study because of its contribution to the literary controversy may feel, after viewing the complexity and power of the main Bayesian study, that nuclear weapons have been used to defoliate a forest when weedkiller would have done the job. He should be reminded that Mosteller and Wallace realized that, though the methods of their earlier work may have been adequate for the immediate purpose of deciding authorship, the problem presented an opportunity for a systematic comparison of two general methods of attack. Thus the study became more involved than a simple resolution of the controversy would have required.

The authors admit in retrospect that the methodological analysis could have been restricted to sets of papers whose authorship is known, but the responsibility of making judgments about authorship in disputed cases added a little hard realism and promoted additional care that might otherwise have been omitted. The book describes four different studies—four different approaches to the dispute. The first, the main study, exhibits the so-called Bayesian approach, and the second, the weight-rate study, follows the so-called classical tradition of statistical inference. These two large-scale studies, parts of which were carried out on a high-speed computer, contrast the two methods of attack. The main study, especially, required considerable use of the computer. Mosteller and Wallace believed that lighter artillery would have done the trick so they carried out two small-scale studies, one Bayesian in character and the other essentially classical. These two studies were less sensitive than the two large-scale studies but required only desk-calculators or slide rules for the calculations. They are described in Chapters 6 and 7 of the book and will not be treated in this paper.

2. The Federalist

The *Federalist* papers were published anonymously over the pseudonym "Publius" in 1787 - 1788 by Alexander Hamilton, John Jay, and James Madison, to persuade the citizens of the State of New

York to ratify the Constitution. Of the 77 essays, 900 to 3500 words in length, that appeared in newspapers, it is generally agreed that Jay wrote five: Nos. 2, 3, 4, 5, and 64. Hamilton and Madison, as well as historians, agree upon the authorship of an additional 57 papers, 43 by Hamilton and 14 by Madison. On the other hand, they dispute the authorship of another 12 papers referred to as the "disputed papers." Finally there are three papers which will be referred to as "joint" papers—Hamilton said they were joint papers, and Madison claimed to have written them using Hamilton's notes. The issue concerning these three papers is the extent of each man's contribution.

Over the past 150 years numerous lists have been published, some claiming the disputed papers for Hamilton and some for Madison. Adair (1944a) has noted that the preference shown for each man's claim has, over the years, swung with the popularity of the man's views. The available historical evidence today is modest enough that a reasonable skeptic can maintain that it is not convincing one way or the other.

This brief summary of the case Hamilton versus Madison certainly does not do justice to the controversy. The reader is referred to Adair (1944a, 1944b) and Cooke (1961) for more complete historical accounts.

3. Statistics and Style

In Section 1.1 of their book Mosteller and Wallace write: "From the point of view of statistical methods, authorship problems fall into a general area called discrimination or classification problems. In these problems the task is to assign a category to an object or individual whose true category is uncertain. In our authorship problem the objects are essays written by either Hamilton or Madison. We reduce our uncertainty about the authorship of an 'unknown' essay by comparing its properities with information obtained from essays whose authorship is known. Classifying plants in biology, skulls in anthropology, candidates for parole in criminology, and subjects according to personality in psychology are related operations that sometimes employ similar methods, even though the properties that aid the classification vary drastically from one area to another. The methods used to study one problem in discrimination can sometimes be extended to other areas of research." But where does the statistical method stand from the point of view of historical and linguistic methods? How much can we hope to accomplish toward resolving this controversy?

At best we can make statements like "It is very likely that Madison wrote paper No. 57." When we make such a statement about one of the disputed papers, clearly we have no direct evidence that Madison wrote paper 57. We are merely stating that, with respect to certain stylistic attributes, paper 57 is much more like Madison's known writings than Hamilton's. But surely this is nothing new. The difference between the statistical method and the standard methods of historical research is that the stylistic attributes used in the statistical method are formal ones that are treated quantitatively. Mosteller and Wallace treated these attributes merely as fingerprints: fingerprints say nothing about the character of their owner but they do help to identify him. Referring to the selection of vocabulary items for such classification problems, Yule (1944) said: "All these are mere details; details certainly quite useful in relation to the controversy, providing valid evidence . . . *but they give no faintest notion as to what his vocabulary is really like as a whole.* To tell me that there is a small mole on Miranda's check may help me to identify the lady, and may in conceivable circumstances be quite useful information to the police, but it hardly amounts to a description of her alluring features." For the purpose of studying authorship Mosteller and Wallace were not interested in the writers' overall style or in the use of their total vocabulary. They just searched for and found tell-tale fingerprints.

We can take this analogy further. Suppose there are two suspects for a certain burglary. Police are familiar with the techniques of both suspects and are certain that one of the two committed the crime. There were some hairs left at the scene of the crime but, unfortunately for the police, not only do both suspects have the same color hair but the texture is almost identical. Analogously the average sentence length for Hamilton is practically the same as for Madison, and also the variability of sentence length (as measured by the standard deviation) is practically identical for the two authors. So these measures prove to be of no use in detecting authorship for *The Federalist.*

The detectives felt that there were subtle differences between the techniques of the two suspects but had difficulty in putting their fingers on specific things. One thing—there may have been other more subtle clues—that did differentiate the crimes of one suspect from those of the other was the fingerprints. Thus Mosteller and Wallace, as we shall see below, settled on the frequency of occurrence of certain selected words as their clue, these particular words because they had proven successful in differentiating between the known writings of Hamilton and Madison. Note that in this analogy the fingerprints correspond to the particular selected words, *not* to words in general. Words *not* selected correspond to clues such as the hair which did not distinguish between the two suspects, and the admission of inconsequential evidence into a trial will only succeed in clouding the issue and obscuring the important evidence contained in the fingerprints.

The analogy can take us one step further. If only one partly smudged fingerprint could be found, it is doubtful that a jury would be convinced on that evidence alone. Likewise if Mosteller and Wallace based their final classification on only one marker word or pair of marker words, such as "while-whilst" mentioned above, it is doubtful that many people would be convinced. But as another print is found, then another and another, the case tightens, so that with several prints found, smudged though they might be, the evidence points more and more to one of the suspects. Likewise with the *Federalist* problem, each distinctive word by itself is not convincing enough, but the combined evidence of all the selected words presents a case which should convince a very skeptical juror.

4. Sentences, Words and Letters

In most authorship studies the problem of deciding what variables to use as discriminators will be easier than it was in the *Federalist* study. Both Hamilton and Madison had developed a style of writing much admired in their period, rather in imitation of the *Spectator* papers. Douglass Adair (1944a) writes that "like Hamilton and Jay, Madison was a master of that Addisonian prose style which had all but standardized the tone of eighteenth century essays." Also one author might have tried to imitate the other, since they were writing over the same *nom de plume.* So not only were clues that distinguished Hamilton from Madison hard to find, but stylistic attributes which could be easily imitated were not to be trusted.

Sentence length is one attribute that could be easily imitated, and in this respect the two authors are pratically identical. In fact any single attribute that can be recognized can be imitated, especially if a writer is given plenty of time. So it would be unwise to attribute authorship to a paper on evidence from one attribute alone.

In this *Federalist* study the researchers went to great lengths in trying to choose variables which were not subject to the whims of the writer. It is unlikely that a writer would be aware of small but consistent changes in the use of high frequency words: for example a change in the use of *an* from 6 times per thousand words to 4½, or a change in the use of *of* from 64½ times per thousand to 58, etc.

Moreover, the attribution of authorship to the disputed *Federalist* papers was based not on a single attribute or variable, but on many variables. Mosteller and Wallace believe that their authorship attributions are not vulnerable to the possibility that one author wrote but the other edited the disputed papers: only a virtual rewriting would provide all the necessary differences (see Section 16, part A). We know that *The Federalist* was written at great speed so the authors were forced to work independently of each other. Adair (1944b) believes that "the very speed with which *The Federalist* had to be written guaranteed that the writing of both men would reveal sharp differences which they had no time to level off into perfect editorial unity."

Another danger with sentence length as a discriminating variable is that the proportion of long and short sentences may differ from one essay to another depending, for example, on context. An essay on law or philosophy may have more long sentences than an essay on farming. In more technical language we would say that the *frequency distribution* or the *probability distribution* of sentence length might depend on context.

The notion of a distribution is important so we shall digress briefly to discuss it. Figure I displays three examples of *frequency distributions*. If we divide the numbers on the vertical axis by 1000, we have three *probability distributions*. For instance, Shakespeare's poetry graph would then give the probabilities attached to each word length for a word drawn at random from Shakespeare's poetry: there is a probability of about .05 (or equivalently, 50 chances in 1000) that this randomly selected word is one letter in length; a probability of .175 that it is two letters long; a probability of .225 that it is three letters long; etc. Since this distribution was obtained from counting the length of several hundred thousand words, it should come very close to his true distribution, his long-run distribution, for poetry. If we took a sample of 500 words from his poetry we would expect the proportions of words of the various lengths to be something like the true or long-run probabilities, but not necessarily very close.

Notice that Shakespeare's poetry distribution is different from his prose distribution. There seems to be a slight but systematic change in his vocabulary when he changes from poetry to prose. It is this kind of change that we were concerned about above when we suggested that the probability distribution of sentence length might depend on context. If it changes significantly when the author changes subject we might be led to believe that it is a different author writing. For this reason Mosteller and Wallace used only those words which were not contextual and which seemed to have consistent rates over a variety of subjects.

The frequency distribution of the length of words might be similarly subject to change in context and therefore suspect as a discriminator. And an author might change his word-length distribution when he imitates another author. Mendenhall (1887, 1901) named the graph of the word-length distribution the *characteristic curve of composition*. In his 1887 paper he pointed out, however, that Mr. Edward Atkinson, in two addresses on the same subject, made greater use of long words in his speech to the alumni of the Andover Theological Seminary than in his speech to a group of working men of Providence. (Some of these items were brought to my attention in an unpublished paper by Patricia Phillips, 1964.)

Again in his 1901 paper Mendenhall studied the characteristic curve, this time for Shakespeare and some of his contemporaries. Shakespeare's curves, differing only slightly between his prose and poetry, were different from the curves of Bacon, Ben Jonson, Beaumont and Fletcher, and others, but were remarkably similar to Marlowe's. But Mendenhall ended by throwing cold water on his conclusions in reporting a count made of a brochure written by Professor Shaler of Harvard University, entitled "Armada Days." Professor Shaler had endeavored to "compose in the spirit and style of the Elizabethan Age. Although too small to produce anything like a 'normal' curve it was counted and plotted, and the diagram indicated that Professor Shaler had not only caught the spirit of the literature of the time, but that he had also unconsciously adopted the mechanism which seems to characterize it. In the excess of the four-letter word and in other respects, the curve was rather decidedly Shakespearean, although it was written before its author knew anything of such an analysis as this" (Mendenhall, 1901, p. 105).

So while there is evidence that an author is consistent in his word lengths in his normal writings — Brinegar (1963) exhibits statistics to indicate that Mark Twain was similarly consistent — there is also evidence that a particular frequency curve can be simulated. One might then question Brinegar's conclusion — that the Quintus Curtius Snodgrass (QCS) letters were not the work of Mark Twain — since it was based on the fact that the frequency curves of Twain and QCS were dissimilar. Twain would seem to have had good reasons for not being identified as QCS; so might he not have affected a different style?

The *Federalist* problem is easier than Brinegar's problem and probably most authorship problems, in that Hamilton and Madison were the only two contenders. Everyone agrees that either Hamilton or Madison wrote the disputed papers; so if we become satisfied that a disputed paper is much more like Hamilton's writing than Madison's, we have resolved the controversy for that paper. But Brinegar had no list of authors which he was certain contained the name of the true author of the QCS letters. So even if he had found Mark Twain's frequency curve (or use of certain words) to be like QCS's, he could not have said that Twain was QCS with the same confidence that we could say that Hamilton wrote the paper in question.

Mosteller and Wallace in their book report briefly on their attempt to use the Mendenhall statistics to discriminate between the known papers. Unfortunately, the variation from paper to paper *within* an author's writings was greater than the difference *between* the two authors.

The reader can probably think of candidates other than sentence length and word length which might be useful discriminators. Section 15 suggests several.

5. Words as Discriminators

Joshua Whatmough (1957) has said that "languages obey laws as stable as any that have been found in human behavior, if not as those of astrophysics (which are not entirely stable)." Kepler's laws provide a mathematical model of the motion of a body, for example a planet, in the solar system. They describe approximately, in mathematical terms, the path that a planet actually traces in space — approximately because no mathematical model can ever describe a physiscal process exactly. For instance Kepler's model assumes that a planet is subject only to the attractive force of the sun and neglects the effect of the other planets. So the planet's true path is not quite the ellipse that Kepler's model describes, but for many purposes an ellipse is an adequate description of the path.

A mathematical model enables us to assemble information from different sources to strengthen our inference. "It can be manipulated in the absence of the structure it represents . . . [and] consequences can sometimes be derived from the mathematics that are not obvious from inspection of apparatus or data" (Mosteller and Wallace, 1964, p. 22). The next few paragraphs describe two possible models, one called the Poisson model and the other the negative binomial model, which attempt to describe the process by which an author produces words. We shall see that the negative binomial model, the more complicated of the two, appears to be significantly better than the other in describing the process: that is to say, when the mathematics of the two models is manipulated, the distributions of word occurrences predicted by the negative binomial model are very close to the actual observed distributions.

A simplified model of the use of words by an author could be the following: an author uses each word in his vocabulary at a constant average rate. In addition, the occurrence of a particular word is independent of the previous occurrence of that same word. This is called a Poisson model after S. D. Poisson, a nineteenth century French mathematician.

For example, an author might use the word *on* at the average rate of 5 times per thousand words. This is not to say that *on* will appear 5 times in every block of 1000 words, but he tends to average 5 times per thousand in a very large text.

The independence assumption in the model implies that the occurrence (or non-occurrence) of a particular word gives absolutely no information about its next occurrence — it might come in the same sentence again, or it might not come for another thousand words. The only thing that governs the occurrence of this word is its overall rate.

Notice that this model contrasts with a second, more realistic model in which one occurrence of a certain word would bring two counter-pressures to bear on the next occurrence of that word. A writer's attempt to avoid repetition of a word isolates it and spaces its occurrences, thus making the rate constant. On the other hand, he may repeat a word several times in a brief passage for emphasis, parallelism, or clarity. This tendency to cluster can be built into the more complicated negative binomial model.

If the Poisson model is a reasonable approximation of reality we would expect that the frequency distribution of word occurrences — the proportion of times in passages of fixed length that a word occurs once, twice, etc. — could be closely approximated by a Poisson distribution. Consider, for example, the word *any* as used by Hamilton. Mosteller and Wallace broke up a collection of *Federalist* papers into 247 blocks of approximately 200 words, and tabulated the frequency distribution of counts for each of many different words. The distributions for a few words are given for Hamilton in Table 1.

Notice that out of the 247 blocks, 125 had no occurrence of *any*, 88 had exactly 1 occurrence, 26 had exactly 2 occurrences, 7 had 3, no block had 4, 1 block had 5, and no block had more than 5. This gave a total of 166 occurrences in a total of 247 blocks for an average (or mean) number of occurrences in a 200-word block of 166/247, or .672 words per block.

In the specification of the Poisson model above we required two things: independence of one occurrence from the next, and a constant rate. For a particular rate this model gives rise to a particular Poisson distribution, and that distribution is completely specified by that rate. Thus we call the collection of all the Poisson distributions a "one-parameter" family since one number, or parameter (in this case the average rate), specifies which member of the family we are talking about. The Poisson distribution has a mathematical formula, in which this number (parameter) appears, giving the proportions of zero occurrences, one, two, etc., expected under the Poisson model. These proportions will of course depend on the parameter—the average rate. So now we can verify whether Hamilton used "any" as if he followed a Poisson model by comparing the observed frequencies with the frequencies expected from the Poisson distribution which has the same average rate. This process of calculating the observed rate (in our example, .672), then calculating the expected frequencies given by the Poisson distribution having that same rate, is termed "fitting" a Poisson distribution to the data. Recall that the Poisson is a *one*-parameter family: just *one* number

TABLE 1. Observed and fitted Poisson and negative binomial distributions for selected words—Hamilton

	Occurrences:							
	0	1	2	3	5	4	6	7 or more
an								
obs.	77	89	46	21	9	4	1	
Poisson	71.6	88.6	54.9	22.7	7.0	1.7	.4	.1
N.B.	81.0	82.7	49.2	22.0	8.2	2.7	1.0	.2
any								
obs.	125	88	26	7	0	1		
Poisson	126.3	84.6	28.5	6.4	1.1	.2		
N.B.	same as Poisson							
may								
obs.	128	67	32	14	4	1	1	
Poisson	109.9	88.9	36.0	9.7	2.0	.3	.1	
N.B.	128.2	69.4	30.1	12.1	4.6	1.7	.6	.3
upon								
obs.	129	83	20	9	5	1		
Poisson	121.6	86.1	30.6	7.3	1.3	.2		
N.B.	131.1	77.1	27.9	8.2	2.1	.5	.1	
his								
obs.	192	18	17	7	3	2	4	3
Poisson	131.7	82.7	26.2	5.5	.9	.1		
N.B.	192.2	23.8	11.0	6.4	4.0	2.7	1.9	5.0

specifies a particular Poisson distribution, so that the "fitting" involves the equating of only *one* number (parameter), in this case the mean rate. (Shortly we shall discuss a *two*-parameter family of distributions. The fitting of one of these distributions to some data involves the equating of *two* parameters.)

Returning to the Poisson and our example, we calculate the expected frequencies given by the Poisson distribution having a mean rate .672. The results are in Table 1 under the observed counts for *any*. Out of a total of 247 blocks we would expect 126.3 blocks to have zero occurrences, 84.6 to have one occurrence, etc. It can be seen that the Poisson distribution fits the data very well. (Even if our observed data had come from an artificial process which is truly Poisson, it is quite likely that the observed and expected frequencies would differ by more than they do in this example.) So we can say that in the writings of Hamilton that were studied the word *any* occurs as if it obeyed the Poisson model.

This is gratifying, but a glance at Table 1 will show that not all words are as Poissonian as *any*. The observed frequences for *may* and *his* differ drastically from those expected from Poisson processes having the same mean rates of occurrence. What we need is another family of distributions which are like the Poisson—because, after all, the Poisson fits *any* very well—but which allows a little more flexibility, or gives us a wider choice of distributions. We say we need a "richer" family. Notice that the tails of the observed distributions (we call the "tail" that part furthest from the mean) are fatter than the tails of the fitted Poisson distributions. This might arise from the word's being repeated for emphasis, and this repetition means that the occurrences of the word are not independent as required by the conditions of the Poisson model.

One way, therefore, in which we would like this new family to be flexible is that it allow for fatter tails. A family which does this is the negative binomial family. The negative binomial model allows the author to vary slightly, from one block of writing to another, his rate of usage of a word. More formally, we suppose that before writing a block the writer chooses a rate for that block and then behaves according to the Poisson theory for that rate and that block. For the next block he chooses another rate and so on. If he chooses his rates randomly in a certain reasonable way, he ends up with a negative binomial model.

But this is no exception to the rule that you never get something for nothing. The negative binomial is a two-parameter family, so we pay for the increased flexibility by having to fit a distribution with two parameters and more generally by having to work with a much more complicated mathematical formula. The first parameter is again the average rate. The second measures how fat the tail of the negative binomial distribution is, compared with the tail of the corresponding Poisson distribution. This parameter is termed the *non-Poissonness parameter*.

Table 1 shows clearly how the negative binomial distributions come very close to the observed data even in the tails.

6. Pools of Words

Initially every word in an author's vocabulary is a candidate for selection as a discriminator. Fortunately many can be rejected immediately. Mosteller and Wallace wanted variables that depended as nearly as possible only on the author and not, for example, on the subject under discussion. For instance the word *war* would likely occur frequently in an essay on the armed forces but seldom in an essay on voting. Such contextual words are probably bad discriminators, and therefore unlikely survivors of a screening test, and they are potentially dangerous if they survive the screening test. That they proved to be bad discriminators and dangerous will be demonstrated later. One source of words, found in an independent study to be largely non-contextual, was a list of "function" words made up by Miller, Newman, and Friedman (1958). Their list gives frequency counts, for 363 words, based on 35,000 words of text taken from the King James Bible, William James, and *The Atlantic* (1957). "Function" words are "filler" words as opposed to "content" words. They would include Russell's "logical" words which are associated with the structure of a sentence so that they may not be changed without changing the structure. It is likely that these words will discriminate, but certain other function words, such as personal pronouns and auxiliary verbs, might be dangerous. The 70 most frequent words of the Miller-Newman-Friedman list became one pool of words along with a random set of 20 from their low-frequency words. The 70 high-frequency function words are listed in Table 2, and the random sample of 20 appear in Table 3.

A second source of words—chronologically the first—was a screening study. Some known papers of both authors were studied in waves, and words were scored by the number of papers in which they appeared. There were 18 Hamilton and 14 Madison papers. Words like *enough,* which appeared in 14 Hamilton papers and no Madison papers, *commonly* (9, 1), *whilst* (0, 13), and *language* (2, 10), were retained. About 3000 different words started but only 28 survived. The survivors, which by the nature of their selection were low-frequency words, appear in Table 3 with an asterisk beside them.

A number of papers for both authors had been typed on to punched cards, then stored on magnetic tape of a high-speed computer. These papers, 18 by Hamilton and 19 by Madison totalling 70,000 words, provided a concordance of 6700 different words. Those uncontextual words which displayed an uneven split between the two authors were retained. The 48 survivors, which are not listed here, brought the total number of words in the pool to 165.

7. The Main Study: Bayes' Theorem

Statistical inference is the process of drawing conclusions about unknown quantities from propositions which are supposed to be true. For example, knowledge of the characteristics of a sample allows inferences to be made about the population from which the sample was drawn. Or, information about the features of typical Hamilton and Madison essays, together with the corresponding information

TABLE 2. Function words and their code numbers

1 a	11 been	21 had	31 its	41 one	51 that	61 was
2 all	12 but	22 has	32 may	42 only	52 the	62 were
3 also	13 by	23 have	33 more	43 or	53 their	63 what
4 an	14 can	24 her	34 must	44 our	54 then	64 when
5 and	15 do	25 his	35 my	45 shall	55 there	65 which
6 any	16 down	26 if	36 no	46 should	56 thing	66 who
7 are	17 even	27 in	37 not	47 so	57 this	67 will
8 as	18 every	28 into	38 now	48 some	58 to	68 with
9 at	19 for	29 is	39 of	49 such	59 up	69 would
10 be	20 from	30 it	40 on	50 than	60 upon	70 your

TABLE 3. Additional words and their code numbers

*71 affect	*83 contribute	*94 innovation	106 still
*72 again	*84 defensive	*95 join	107 those
*73 although	*85 destruction	*96 language	*108 throughout
74 among	86 did	97 most	109 under
75 another	*87 direction	98 nor	*110 vigor
76 because	*88 disgracing	*99 offensive	*111 violate
77 between	89 either	100 often	*112 violence
78 both	*90 enough	*101 pass	*113 voice
*79 city	(and in	102 perhaps	114 where
	sample of 20)		
*80 commonly	*91 fortune	*103 rapid	115 whether
*81 consequently	*92 function	104 same	*116 while
*82 considerable	93 himself	105 second	*117 whilst

about a particular disputed essay, allows conclusions to be drawn about the authorship of the disputed essay.

What is the mechanism by which statistical inferences are made? How is evidence combined to change a prior belief into a conclusion or posterior belief? In the main study these questions are answered by Bayes' Theorem. Degrees of belief in propositions such as "Hamilton wrote paper No. 52" are expressed by numerical probabilities, and Bayes' Theorem adjusts the probabilities for the evidence in hand.

Consider the problem of assessing the evidence regarding the authorship of a single disputed paper. With the help of a simple form of Bayes' Theorem we first assess the evidence of a single word, then use the theorem again to combine the evidence from several words.

Suppose that for the word *also* Hamilton's true average rate is known to be .25 words per thousand and Madison's .50, and that both authors follow the Poisson model. Then for a 2000-word paper the probabilities that each author used *also* 0 times through 6 times are given in Table 4. If Hamilton wrote the paper there is a probability of .607 that *also* did not occur at all, a probability of .303 that *also* appeared once, and so on. But if Madison wrote a 2000-word paper there is a probability of only .368 that *also* will not occur at all, and an equal probability that it will occur once, and so on.

Suppose now that *also* appears four times in our disputed paper. Table 4 shows that the probability of *also's* occurring four times in a Hamilton paper is .00158, but in a Madison paper it is .0153, or about ten times as much. A betting man would interpret these numbers as betting odds: if he had only a very vague opinion on the dispute prior to his looking at the evidence from *also,* he now

TABLE 4. Poisson probabilities for a word from a 2000-word paper: Hamilton's rate being .25 and Madison's .5

Frequency	Hamilton	Madison
0	.607	.368
1	.303	.368
2	.0758	.184
3	.0126	.0613
4	.00158	.0153
5	.000158	.00307
6	.0000132	.000511

would bet .0153 to .00158, or approximately 10 to 1, that Madison wrote the paper. Thus the data provide evidence in the form of *odds,* or, as the ratio .00158/.0153 is called, in the form of a *likelihood ratio.*

If, however, our betting friend had previously read of this dispute and had formed an opinion on the matter, how should he change his belief in the light of this new, independent information provided by the data? Suppose he could express this prior opinion in the form of odds, say 1 to 3 that Hamilton wrote it. These are his *initial* or *prior* odds. What we want are his *posterior odds* which combine his prior information with that obtained from the data. Appealing to Bayes' Theorem we find that his posterior odds are simply his prior odds multiplied by the likelihood ratio: 1/3 multiplied by 1/10 giving 1/30; that is, his odds now are 1 to 30 that Hamilton wrote the paper.

Notice that a different friend who had prior odds of 2 to 1 in favor of Hamilton now has odds of 1 to 5 in favor of Hamilton, or 5 to 1 in favor of Madison. So the data strengthened the opinion of our first friend, whereas it altered the opinion of our second friend.

8. Combining the Evidence of Several Words

Our first friend now has odds of 1 to 30 that Hamilton wrote the paper in question. Suppose that both authors' use of the word *an* is likewise well represented by independent Poissons, and that for *an* Hamilton is known to have an average rate of 6.00 words per thousand and Madison 4.50. Suppose further that *an* appeared 7 times in the disputed paper in question. From tables of the Poisson distribution we find that the likelihood ratio for this outcome ·is .0437/.117 or approximately 3/8. Before looking at this new information our friend's *new prior odds* are 1 to 30 (see Figure II). Bayes' Theorem once again tells us how to combine this new evidence and we see that his latest posterior odds are 1/30 times 3/8 or 1/80. So his new odds are 1 to 80 that Hamilton wrote the paper. By repeating this procedure we can combine the evidence of all the words.

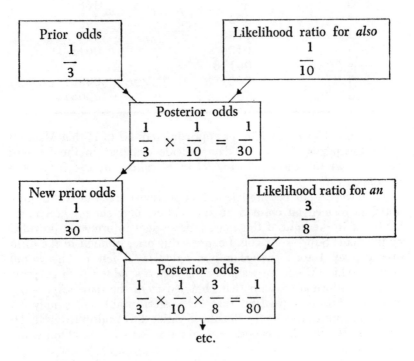

FIGURE II. Block Diagram Showing Progression from Prior Odds to Posterior Odds

Notice that his latest odds, 1/80, factor into the product of the initial odds 1/3 and the combined likelihood ratio of the two words, 3/80. In other words, the assessment of the initial odds can be separated from the statistical analysis needed to determine the likelihood ratio. Because different people have different prior odds, the statistical analysis in this study concentrates on the likelihood ratio term.

9. Criterion for Selecting Final Words

We now have a guide for selecting final words from the three pools described earlier: we select only those whose discriminating power is high, that is, whose likelihood ratio is very different from unity. We saw that the likelihood ratio for 4 occurrences of *also* was approximately 1/10, and for 7 occurrences of *an* it was 3/8. The product of these was 3/80. The addition of a few more good words will build up this combined likelihood ratio to such an extent that it will swamp any reasonable initial odds. In contrast, consider the word *because*. It can never hope to contribute much to the combined likelihood ratio since its individual likelihood ratios for 0, 1, 2, and 3 occurrences are respectively 1.11, 1.00, .90, and .81, so that no matter how many times *because* appears in a disputed paper it will be of very little help in classifying the paper one way or the other. Such words may be discarded since they add significantly to the complexity and cost of the enterprise, yet provide little discriminating power.

What has been described in the last few sections is a simplification of a real-life analysis. Many of the assumptions made are too strong and a real analysis must make allowances for the deviations. For instance, the rates for *also* and *an* were assumed known. If we know the true rates for all words, picking out the best discriminating words does not introduce any bias. But when the rates have to be estimated, the selection and regression effect arises because some of the selected variables are not as good at discriminating as they appear to be. (The regression effect will be discussed in Section 11.)

Allowances can be made for each of the troubles and the combined allowance will provide an adjustment to the final odds. If the final adjusted odds still favor one author strongly, the conclusions remain strong.

10. Unkown Parameters: A Second Use of Bayes' Theorem

The preceding sections have described the logical process which takes the information relating to authorship from the sample and unites it with the prior odds of authorship to produce the posterior odds. This is the skeleton of a Bayesian analysis. One of the assumptions made in this simplified analysis, namely that the parameters (the average rates in this case) were known, was rather bold. In the actual problem, of course, the true rates were unknown and had to be estimated from some rather vague prior information and a moderate amount of sample data. The prior information comes from a few existing studies of word rates, and the sample data comes from 94,000 words of Hamilton's text and 114,000 words of Madison's. This is a large amount of text, but for the purpose of estimating rates it is surprisingly little. This section describes how the rates are estimated.

Since the exact values of the rates are unknown, we would like to express the knowledge that we do have, not by point estimates (e.g., .25 and .50), but in the form of probability distributions. These would enable us to make probability statements about the unknown parameters: for example, instead of stating that Hamilton's rate for a particular word is .25, we could state that there is probability of 1/20 that his rate is less than .15; a probability of 1/10 that it is between .15 and .20; 1/3 that it is between .20 and .25; and so on. (These are hypothetical figures.)

Here, for a second time, Bayes' Theorem gets into the act. The prior information about word rates is summarized into a probability distribution—the *prior* distribution of the rates. The information contained in the known works of the two authors concerning the rates of various words is summarized into likelihood ratio terms. Then Bayes' Theorem combines the prior distribution and the likelihood ratio terms into the *posterior* distributions of the rates. Unfortunately these posterior distributions turn out to be very complex and unmanageable even with the help of high-speed computers; so we have to be satisfied with new, improved point estimates derived from the posterior distributions. For example, the rates with which Hamilton and Madison used *also,* as estimated from the known works, are respectively .28 and .71 occurrences per thousand words of text. But the new, improved estimates, which take the prior information into account, are .31 and .67.

We shall now discuss this procedure in somewhat more detail. Firstly, where do the prior distributions come from? This question is perhaps the one most frequently asked of Bayesians. (The term "Bayesian" is applied to someone who would carry out such an analysis as this, using Bayes' Theorem to combine prior distributions with sample information to form posterior distributions. The weight-rate study, to be discussed briefly in Section 14, is an example of a non-Bayesian analysis.) Some Bayesians would choose prior distributions with first consideration being their mathematical form. They would choose forms that make the mathematics easy in the application of Bayes' Theorem. Unfortunately it will often happen that the distribution with the most convenient mathematical form does not describe the prior information as well as some other distribution could. Mosteller and Wallace believe that, where possible, prior distributions should be empirically oriented: they should be founded on data. This attitude leads them into mathematical and computational difficulties, but these seem to be facts of life in all but the simplest Bayesian analysis.

In the Poisson model there are two parameters for each word: the average rate for each author. In the negative binomial model, which we believe more accurately describes the word-producing process, there are four parameters for each word: the average rate and the non-Poissonness parameter for each author. We shall look briefly at the problem of assigning prior distributions to the Poisson parameters to illustrate the essential ideas. The priors (i.e., prior distributions) for the negative binomial parameters will not be treated in this paper.

Let μ_H denote Hamilton's true average rate for a particular word, and let μ_M denote Madison's true average rate for the same word. The exact values of these two parameters are unknown. The problem is to try to summarize all prior information about the parameters into a probability distribution. Mosteller and Wallace found it easier to think in terms of two related quantities which they called σ and τ:

$$\sigma = \mu_H + \mu_M$$

$$\tau = \frac{\mu_H}{\mu_H + \mu_M}$$

σ measures the combined rate for the word because $\frac{1}{2}\sigma$ is the average of the two authors' rates. τ measures the disparity between the two rates, so it is a measure of the discriminating ability of this word. For example, if $\mu_H = 1$ and $\mu_M = 2$, then $\sigma = 3$ and $\tau = 1/3$, and this word is a potential good discriminator. But if $\mu_M = 101$, and $\mu_M = 102$, then $\sigma = 203$ and $\tau = 101/203$. With rates of 101 and 102 the word will not be a useful discriminator. The further τ is from $\frac{1}{2}$ the better the word is for discrimination.

Notice that if we know μ_H and μ_M we can calcuate σ and τ and vice versa. And theoretically, if we know the distributions of μ_H and μ_M we can derive the distributions of σ and τ, and vice versa. So the task of obtaining priors on μ_H and μ_M is equivalent to that of obtaining priors on σ and τ. Mosteller and Wallace found it easier to work with σ and τ. (In technical language we say that σ and τ are transformed variables, or that the problem has been reparameterized.)

Prior information on σ, arising from a few existing word-frequency studies on many authors, writing in many styles, over several centuries, was almost negligible compared with the information contained in the *Federalist* material. So the mathematical form of the prior distribution on σ was not critical so long as it expressed only vague or diffuse information.

What is a reasonable prior for τ? For the two authors, writing together on the same topic at the same period, Mosteller and Wallace supposed that, for most words, their two rates would not differ by much, and that, for a word picked at random, the higher of the two rates would just as likely be Hamilton's as Madison's. These requirements mean that the prior on τ should be symmetric around $\tau = \frac{1}{2}$ and concentrate most of the probability in the vicinity of $\tau = \frac{1}{2}$ (see Figure III). It is possible that for high-frequency words τ will not vary as much from $\frac{1}{2}$ as it might for low-frequency words. This means that the prior on τ should depend on the average rate or, in other words, on σ.

The distribution chosen to fulfill these requirements was a symmetric beta distrubtion whose parameter γ depended on σ:

$$\gamma = \beta_1 + \beta_2\sigma$$

where β_1 and β_2 are called underlying constants. Two members of the family appear in Figure III. The one with parameter $\gamma = 10$ is the prior distribution of τ for the set of underlying constants $\beta_1 = 10$, $\beta_2 = 0$.

Because of the imprecise nature of the prior information about τ, Mosteller and Wallace preferred not to choose one and only one distribution to represent this information. Instead they chose several so that they could be sure that one of the chosen distributions represented the prior knowledge accurately. Then they carried out the complete analysis for each prior. If it turned out that all analyses gave the same allocation of the unknown papers, they would be very confident about their conclusions. Each prior distribution is determined by its underlying constants β_1 and β_2, and looks similar to the distributions in Figure III.

The prior distributions for σ and τ now had to be combined by Bayes' Theorem with the likelihood terms to give the posterior distributions of σ and τ. The likelihood terms contained the information from the known papers regarding σ and τ. Unfortunately the mathematical forms of the prior distributions and of the likelihood terms were such that it was quite impracticable, if not impossible, with existing mathematical and computational methods, to obtain the entire posterior distributions for σ and τ. It was possible, however, to obtain a certain amount of information about these posterior distributions, namely posterior point estimates of σ and τ. Since

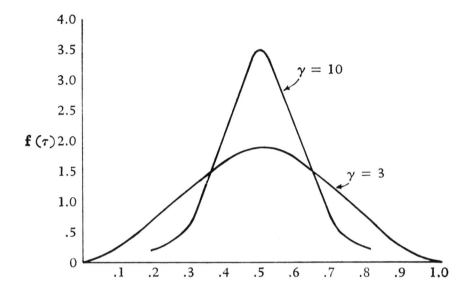

FIGURE III. Two Symmetric Beta Distributions.

these point estimates were derived from the posterior distributions they contained the combined information of the prior estimates (obtainable from the prior distributions) and the samples estimates (obtainable from the likelihood term).

An example might clarify things a little. For the word *also* the prior estimate for τ was .5 (see Table 5).The estimate based on the observed rate, or equivalently on the likelihood term, was .282. The estimate obtained from the posterior distribution (based on one of the priors for τ) was .316. So the posterior estimate .316 is a weighted combination of the prior .500 and the sample .282,

TABLE 5.   Estimates of the Poisson Parameters
For *also* ($\beta_1 = 10$, $\beta_2 = 0$)

Parameter	Prior Estimate	Sample Estimate	Posterior Estimate
τ	.500	.282	.316
σ	very vague	.99	.99
μ_H		.28	.31
μ_M		.71	.67
$\mu_M - \mu_H$		.43	.36

the weights being determined by the relative precision of the two estimates. The prior has the effect of watering down the sample estimate, thus making allowance for the regression effect (to be discussed in the next section.) On the other hand the posterior estimate of σ, .99, was the same as the sample estimate because the prior distribution on σ contained only the vaguest information, giving the prior estimate almost zero weight compared with the sample estimate.

Earlier in this section we noted that knowledge of μ_H and μ_M was equivalent to knowledge of σ and τ, and vice versa. So the posterior estimates of σ and τ provide posterior estimates of μ_H and μ_M (see Table 5).

With the new posterior estimates of the rates in hand we can now proceed to use *also* for the classification of a disputed paper just as in section 7. There we supposed that .25 and .50 were the known true average rates for *also*. We can never know what the true average rates are, but we do have estimates, .31 and .67, which we hope are as close to the true rates as possible. Pretending that these estimates are the known rates introduces certain errors. Consequently the final odds have to be adjusted accordingly. This adjustment is not discussed here.

Figure II can now be amended as in Figure IV. The analysis of *an* and of all the other words is similar. This example has assumed

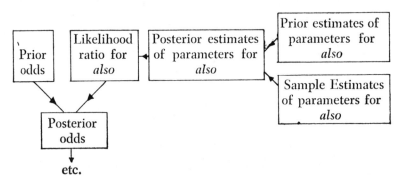

FIGURE IV. Extension of Figure II when parameters have to be estimated.

a particular prior distribution of σ and τ. For each different prior the example could be repeated and different priors would produce slightly different posterior estimates of μ_H and μ_M.

We have discussed only the Poisson case. Mosteller and Wallace carried out the entire study for both the Poisson model and the negative binomial model. Recall that the negative binomial family of distributions is a two-parameter family whereas the Poisson has only one parameter, so assigning priors to the negative binomial is at least twice the problem it is for the Poisson. For both the negative binomial and the Poisson models several priors were used and the whole study carried through with each of them. Each of the priors is characterized by a set of five numbers called underlying constants, and altogether twenty-one different sets were used in some phase of the study. It turns out that the final conclusions regarding the authorship of the disputed papers are the same for all prior distributions studied. And the confidence, or degree of belief, associated with these conclusions is affected only slightly by a change of the prior. This is gratifying. However, changing the data distribution from the Poisson to the negative binomial has a marked effect, not on the allocation of authorship which remains the same, but on the confidence associated with the allocation. This confidence or degree of belief is measured by the posterior odds of authorship, and the negative binomial analysis concludes that the final odds should be much weaker (though still very strong) than the odds given by the Poisson model. This suggests that some of the assumptions in the Poisson model were not justified. More on this in a later section.

11. The Regression Effect

What is the regression effect? Suppose that I want to find a biased coin with which I hope to win money gambling. I collect all the coins I have in my desk, pockets and piggy bank, and I toss each coin 10 times. One of them turns up 1 head and 9 tails. All the others turn up less extreme results. I select this coin as the one I shall gamble with because it appears to be the most biased of all my coins. Since it turned up 1 head out of 10 trials I might estimate the probability of a head's turning up for that coin as 1/10. But if I play my game, believing that the probability is 1/10, I am likely to be sorely disappointed with the amount of money I win. The number of heads turning up in the next 10 trials will probably be more than 1, so the proportion of heads—this proportion was 1/10 in the first experiment—will *regress* towards ½. This is the selection and regression effect, or sometimes called simply the regression effect.

In practice, of course, I would not believe that the probability was really 1/10 because my prior knowledge of coins tells me that the probability of a head's turning up is almost certainly much closer to ½. If I approach my game with a more conservative estimate I am not likely to be so disappointed.

Occasionally the selected variable will not regress. If one of of my coins had been actually quite biased—it might have been saucer-shaped—so that on the average it turned up tails about nine times out of ten, then it is very likely that my selection experiment would have singled out this coin as the apparent best. In this case the estimate of 1/10 would not regress. In general, if the selected variable (or variables, when more than one is being selected) is outstanding, it will not regress.

Notice that my prior feelings about the probability of a head's turning up are very strong especially when compared with results from only 10 trials. Consequently I would probably use as my estimate—my posterior estimate combining prior with sample information—a number quite close to ½, say 11/20. But if the experiment had been to toss each coin 10,000 times and I selected one that turned up only 1,000 heads, I would have definite doubts regarding the fairness of my coin and my posterior estimate would be closer to 1/10. This is an example of the likelihood ratio, or the sample estimate, swamping the prior estimate.

Whenever variables are being selected from a pool on the basis of their good performance on a finite amount of data, we must be aware and take account of the selection and regression effect. An essential feature of the main study in this *Federalist* project is that allowance for this effect is made entirely through the prior distributions. In the previous section we saw an example of this. For the word *also* the estimates of μ_H and μ_M based on the (finite) sample were .28 and .71 (see Table 5). The effect of the prior was to modify the sample estimates to .31 and .67, which are closer together than the sample estimates. Of course, the closer together they are, the poorer the word is as a discriminator; so by taking the posterior estimates we are effectively discounting the sample evidence a little because we believe that the rates will regress towards each other when we look at independent data.

Actually we are planning to use the knowledge of the rates with which the two authors used *also* (and many other words besides) to help us make probability statements concerning the authorship of the disputed papers. If we did not deflate our sample estimates, our statements concerning the authorship would be too extreme. So it is mandatory to recognize and adjust for the regression effects.

The use of a prior distribution is not the only way to take account of the regression effect. (This paragraph is a digression from the main study.) The more usual non-Bayesian classification techniques do not incorporate the notion of prior distributions for parameters. One method that these techniques can use to overcome the problem is simply to select the variables from one set of data, then test the performance of these selected variables on new independent data. This procedure was used in the weight-rate study discussed below. The known works of Hamilton and Madison were split into two sets of about equal size. With one set the words were selected and weighted, then the final discriminant function was tested on the other set which was quite uncontaminated by the selection effect. This procedure might be followed even in a Bayesian study when the prior information is very vague, or when the validity of the model is questionable.

12. The Selection of Final Words for the Main Study

The 165 words that entered the main study (see Section 6) were reduced to 30 words, classed into 5 groups, before the disputed papers were analyzed. The 30 were selected because they were apparently good at discriminating between the known works of Hamilton and Madison. Since the prior distributions on the parameters had already taken care of the regression effect, the words could be selected for retention by whatever methods were available so long as they were independent of the disputed papers.

The words were grouped according to categories of use and source that were felt to bear on contextuality, so that the performance of different types of words (function words, adjectives and adverbs, etc.) could be evaluated.

Only 45 of the 165 words showed any appreciable discriminating ability as measured by the disparity between the estimated rates for the two authors. A few more of the 45 words were discarded because Madison's rates in *The Federalist* for these words were different from his rates in some of his papers exterior to *The Federalist*. Finally, personal pronouns and auxiliary verbs were eliminated since they were probably contextual. This left 30 words in five groups called B3A, B3B, B3G, B3E and B3Z. Table 6 displays these words, together with their estimated rates for the negative binomial analysis based on set 31 of the underlying constants.

13. Results from the Main Study

It is more convenient to report the results not in odds (for example 150 to 1 in favor of Madison) but in *log odds*, which are simply the natural logarithms of the odds: odds of 150 to 1 for Hamilton become log odds of 5, while odds of 150 to 1 for Madison (or 1 to 150 for Hamilton) become log odds of − 5. Table 7 converts odds to log odds.

Most of the following account of the results is taken from Section 6 of Mosteller and Wallace (1963). The account presents only a

TABLE 6. Final Words and Word Groups: Estimated Negative Binomial Parameters Based on Underlying Constants Set 31

Code No.	Word	μ_H	μ_M
B3A			
60	upon	3.24	.23
B3B			
3	also	.32	.67
4	an	5.95	4.58
13	by	7.32	11.43
39	of	64.51	57.89
40	on	3.38	7.75
55	there	3.20	1.33
57	this	7.77	6.00
58	to	40.79	35.21
B3G			
73	although	.06	.17
78	both	.52	1.04
90	enough	.25	.10
116	while	.21	.07
117	whilst	.08	.42
123	always	.58	.20
160	though	.91	.51
B3E			
80	commonly	.17	.05
81	consequently	.10	.42
82	considerable(ly)	.37	.17
119	according	.17	.54
124	apt	.27	.08
B3Z			
87	direction	.17	.08
94	innovation(s)	.06	.15
96	language	.08	.18
110	vigor(ous)	.18	.08
143	kind	.69	.17
146	matter(s)	.36	.09
151	particularly	.15	.37
153	probability	.27	.09
165	work(s)	.13	.27

sprinkling of the results from the 113 papers and the numerous prior distributions. Recall that each prior is characterized by a set of underlying constants.

TABLE 7. Conversion from Log Odds to Odds

Log Odds	Odds
0	1 to 1
2	7 to 1
5	150 to 1
10	22,000 to 1
15	3,300,000 to 1
20	480,000,000 to 1

A. *Checking the method.*

In Table 8 we present the total log odds for 11 papers by each author for three sets of underlying constants. For each author, we give his first 8 papers from *The Federalist,* and 3 papers exterior to *The Federalist.* Papers exterior to *The Federalist* are displayed to give a notion of what happens when the method is applied to a larger variety of writings, and these particular papers are chosen because they contain the one paper most poorly identified by the log odds for each author. Looking first at the negative binomial distribution for set 22 of underlying constants, we see that every Hamilton paper has positive, and every Madison paper negative, log odds. Since these papers contain the worst outcomes, the entire 48 Hamilton and 50 Madison papers have been assigned log odds in the proper direction by this distribution and set of underlying constants.

Looking now at the Poisson model we see that paper No. 134 has log odds pointing mildly in the wrong direction. As a whole, though, the log odds for the three sets of underlying constants point consistently and forcibly in the right direction. Just how strong these odds are can be better appreciated by consulting the brief conversion table, Table 7.

Since we know who wrote each of these papers, the log odds in Table 8 offer a check on the method. Essentially, each paper has been treated as if it were a disputed paper, and the log odds computed. And the evidence is that the method works well.

B. *Effects of prior distributions and of data distributions*

Beyond this, we can examine the effect of varying the underlying constants. Visual inspection will assure the reader that the variation in log odds from one set to another is modest compared to the variation from one paper to another. But the change in log odds from the negative binomial distribution to the Poisson is huge.

Table 8. Total Natural Log Odds for Papers of Known Authorship, 11 by Hamilton and 11 by Madison; Total for 30 Final Words; 3 Sets of Underlying Constants, 2 Distributions

Paper number	Paper length (thousands)	Hamilton					
		Negative binomial			Poisson		
		Set of underlying constants			Set of underlying constants		
		22	33	21	22	33	21
1	1.6	13.9	11.9	15.7	22.9	20.5	25.7
6	1.9	16.8	15.7	17.7	27.4	25.5	29.2
7	2.2	16.6	14.3	17.5	36.6	33.7	39.0
8	2.0	14.0	13.0	16.5	20.7	18.3	23.8
9	1.6	11.6	10.2	12.6	16.7	15.3	18.0
11	2.5	16.3	15.4	17.2	30.7	28.7	32.2
12	2.1	13.0	11.3	14.1	25.2	23.0	27.3
13	1.0	7.8	7.3	8.0	12.0	11.4	12.4
111	2.9	11.9	12.0	10.9	27.0	26.6	26.5
112	2.5	9.3	7.5	10.0	23.4	21.1	25.3
113*	1.2	3.0	2.2	4.0	2.8	2.0	3.8
Madison							
10	3.0	−17.5	−17.2	−18.2	−30.5	−29.5	−31.0
14	2.1	−20.0	−18.5	−22.6	−28.7	−26.5	−31.5
37	2.7	−20.2	−18.9	−23.4	−32.7	−30.4	−35.8
38	3.3	−16.5	−15.3	−19.6	−25.4	−22.9	−29.2
39	2.6	−24.6	−23.6	−26.6	−45.1	−42.5	−47.7
40	2.7	−19.2	−18.5	−20.9	−30.1	−28.6	−31.7
41	3.5	−15.6	−15.1	−17.5	−27.6	−26.5	−28.7
42	2.7	−11.9	−11.1	−13.4	−21.1	−20.0	−22.6
132	2.7	−20.3	−19.3	−22.9	−31.9	−29.3	−35.1
133	2.5	−13.3	−11.7	−15.6	−20.4	−18.7	−22.7
134*	1.7	−0.8	−0.1	−1.9	0.9	1.4	0.1

*The paper by each author that is most poorly identified.

C. Who wrote the disputed papers?

Next, the *piéce de resistance*, Table 9, presents total log odds for the joint and disputed papers. Attending to the 12 disputed papers, we see that every set of underlying constants gives odds for all papers strongly in favor of Madison. The weakest of these are papers 55 and 56, and the lowest odds for No. 55 are 240 to 1 (log odds of −5.5) in favor of Madison, not absolutely overwhelming, if one had strong initial odds in favor of Hamilton. Essentially, No. 55 does not have its share of marker words, no matter who wrote the paper, and the high-frequency words produced no information.

TABLE 9. Total Natural Log Odds for the Papers of Joint and Disputed Authorship. Total for the 30 Final Words. 3 Sets of Underlying Constants, 2 Distributions

Paper number	Paper length (thousands)	Negative binomial			Poisson		
		Set of underlying constants			Set of underlying constants		
		22	33	21	22	33	21
Joint							
18	2.1	−11.0	−10.8	−11.4	−20.1	−19.5	−20.5
19	2.0	−12.1	−12.0	−12.2	−18.6	−18.4	−18.3
20	1.4	−4.6	−5.0	−3.6	−7.0	−7.6	−6.0
Disputed							
49	1.6	−13.2	−12.2	−14.6	−18.1	−17.1	−19.3
50	1.1	−14.3	−13.7	−15.1	−18.2	−17.5	−18.9
51	1.9	−21.9	−20.9	−24.0	−33.4	−31.3	−35.9
52	1.8	−16.0	−15.7	−16.5	−23.1	−22.5	−23.4
53	2.2	−15.8	−15.0	−17.4	−22.0	−20.7	−23.6
54	2.0	−14.3	−13.6	−15.7	−22.9	−21.7	−24.3
55	2.0	−5.8	−5.5	−6.2	−7.1	−6.6	−7.6
56	1.6	−8.7	−8.2	−9.6	−10.6	−10.0	−11.4
57	2.2	−16.7	−15.7	−18.4	−26.1	−24.2	−28.6
58	2.1	−18.0	−17.1	−19.4	−26.3	−25.1	−27.4
62	2.4	−16.5	−16.0	−17.3	−26.9	−25.6	−28.0
63	3.0	−18.5	−17.7	−19.6	−32.2	−31.2	−32.9

D. *The behavior of word groups.*

To show how consistently the different word groups behave and to what extent each contributes to the total, we present the log odds by word groups for set 22 in Table 10.

All groups look quite consistent, considering their differing strengths—a weak set must have negative log odds occasionally. This general consistency is a further sign of good discrimination.

The set B3B is stronger than B3A (*upon*), which in turn looks nearly as strong as the other three groups put together. Recall that B3B contains the high-frequency function words: *to, this, there,*

TABLE 10. Log Odds by Words Group for Set
22 of Underlying Constants

Paper num- ber	Negative binomial					Poisson				
	Word group									
	B3A	B3B	B3G	B3E	B3Z	B3A	B3B	B3G	B3E	B3Z
Hamilton										
1	4.7	2.0	1.9	3.1	2.3	11.6	2.8	2.2	4.0	2.3
6	2.5	9.2	1.7	.3	3.2	5.2	14.3	2.1	.7	5.2
7	6.4	4.6	−.2	2.6	3.3	23.3	6.9	−.3	3.0	3.8
8	1.2	3.0	4.9	2.2	2.8	2.1	5.1	7.4	2.4	3.6
9	2.9	3.5	2.6	1.0	1.6	6.0	5.4	3.0	1.2	1.2
Madison										
10	−6.5	−6.8	−.9	−2.1	−1.2	−9.1	−14.1	−1.9	−3.5	−1.8
14	−5.0	−7.9	−1.4	−1.9	−3.8	−6.6	−12.3	−1.5	−2.5	−5.8
37	−3.2	−9.2	−3.1	−1.3	−3.4	−5.5	−16.1	−3.4	−1.2	−6.5
38	.3	−4.6	−6.4	−3.0	−2.9	.8	−8.4	−10.1	−3.4	−4.4
39	−5.8	−11.7	−.8	−2.7	−3.6	−7.9	−21.1	−1.4	−10.0	−4.7
Joint										
18	−2.1	−8.1	1.3	−1.0	−1.1	−3.6	−14.4	1.9	−2.7	−1.3
19	−4.8	−7.6	−.9	1.4	−.2	−6.2	−13.0	−.9	1.7	−.2
20	−.9	−7.6	.8	1.0	2.0	−1.6	−9.9	.7	1.1	2.6
Disputed										
49	−4.0	−5.5	−.8	−1.3	−1.6	−4.9	−9.4	−.9	−1.1	−1.9
50	−2.9	−9.0	−1.1	.2	−1.5	−3.4	−12.2	−1.2	.3	−1.8
51	−4.6	−9.3	−3.8	−1.9	−2.4	−5.8	−16.4	−5.4	−2.6	−3.3
52	−4.4	−10.2	.2	.2	−1.8	−5.6	−15.9	.1	.4	−2.2
53	−5.1	−6.4	−4.6	1.4	−1.2	−6.6	−10.1	−5.4	1.7	−1.7
54	−.2	−8.6	−1.3	−2.3	−1.9	−.6	−15.2	−1.7	−3.1	−2.3
55	−4.8	−.1	.8	−.7	−1.0	−6.2	1.1	.6	−1.4	−1.3
56	−3.9	−2.4	−3.1	1.0	−.4	−4.8	−3.1	−3.5	1.2	−.4
57	−5.1	−5.9	−2.6	−.9	−2.1	−6.7	−10.9	−5.4	−.8	−2.4
58	−4.9	−8.6	−1.3	−1.3	−2.0	−6.4	−15.1	−1.5	−1.0	−2.4
62	−5.5	−8.1	−.2	−1.5	−1.2	−7.3	−14.1	−.9	−3.2	−1.5
63	−6.6	− 8.4	−1.5	.2	−2.3	−9.2	−19.1	−1.6	.6	−2.9

on, of, by, an, also. So in the end the high-frequency words out-shone all marker words. While this does not prove that cleverness in selecting variables fails to pay, it does show that routine can pay.

E. *Summing up.*

In summary the following points are clear:

1. Madison is the principal author. These data make it possible to say with better foundation than ever before that Madison is the author of the twelve disputed papers. Weakest support is given for No. 55. Support for Nos. 62 and 63, most in doubt by current historians, is tremendous.

2. While the choice of prior distributions matters, it does not matter very much so long as they represent reasonably well the prior information which has come from a fair body of data.

3. The choice of data distribution is important. We notice that in the change from the negative binomial to the Poisson model the log odds are roughly doubled.

4. Routine pays off. We were surprised that in the end, it was the utterly mundane high-frequency function words that did the best job. Though we love them for their lack of contextuality, their final strength was as unexpected as it was welcome. The result is reminiscent of a hard fact perennially being discovered in the social sciences. For the forecasting of a great many facets of a man's behavior, it is hard to beat the usual tired old socio-economic variables and the standard personal background data.

5. The method performed satisfactorily on both *Federalist* material and on essays exterior to *The Federalist*. Such consistency of the method is encouraging in considering the method for other studies and in assessing the generality of the present inference. The disputed papers could be as contextually disparate as the Pacificus or Helvidius papers for all we know.

6. Two of the joint papers are mainly the work of Madison, the third presents a puzzle. The joint papers Nos. 18 and 19 seem mainly to be the work of Madison. No. 20 presents an interesting new problem: can we sort out the contribution of a possible, unwitting, third party, Sir William Temple, so as to assess properly Hamilton's share?

F. *Adjustments to the log odds.*

The log odds presented depend on many assumptions and approximations. When these are taken into consideration the log odds are decreased by about 25 per cent. Even after this deflation the odds cannot be taken entirely at face value. The possibility of what we call outrageous events, which we regard as outside the framework of the model, must be allowed for. For instance, the possibilitv of blunders or errors in calculation is always present.

To the statistician who asks how we can get odds of even thousands to one when we have only about 100 papers altogether, the answer is that the distribution theory, which is rather well founded on data, supplies some of this strength, but the major part comes from the independent, fairly modest contributions from many variables.

14. The Weight-Rate Study

The weight-rate study is based on the method of discrimination devised by R. A. Fisher (1936). The Bayesian analysis described in the preceding sections takes its name from the theorem published by the Reverend Thomas Bayes in 1763, but it is only within the last decade that statisticians have begun to think seriously of using Bayesian analysis directly in practical problems. So it is the Fisherian method, and not the Bayesian method, that has been given the title "traditional," or "classical."

One essential difference between a Bayesian analysis and the more traditional method is that the former attempts to assess prior information and then incorporate it into the model, while the latter does not. Critics of the traditional method feel that prior information should be used; "critics of the Bayesian plan usually agree that the inclusion of the information would be an asset, but they regard the proper assessment of this information as a hopeless task" (Mosteller and Wallace, 1964, p. 2). The researchers in this study found it to be, if not a hopeless task, at least a most formidable one. An idea of the relative sizes of a Bayesian and a classical analysis is gained from the fact that in their book describing these studies, Mosteller and Wallace devoted 154 pages to the main Bayesian study but only 15 pages to the classical weight-rate study. This comparison exaggerates the difference a little since much of the mathematics of the latter was omitted while the former was given a full mathematical treatment. The reason for this is twofold: the mathematics of the classical analysis is, for the most part, fairly straightforward while the Bayesian analysis is mathematically complex; secondly, unlike the classical methods, which have been well studied in the literature, Bayesian methods have been applied to actual life-sized problems on very few occasions. This *Federalist* project is one of the first published large-scale statistical studies that involve substantial analyses of data by Bayesian methods.

Nevertheless, a great deal more effort did go into the main study than into the weight-rate study. The Bayesian analysis also included some prior information that was neglected in the classical analysis; so it should not be surprising that the main study produced the more definitive conclusions concerning the authorship of the disputed *Federalist* papers. The researchers might have profitably done a larger job on the weight-rate analysis, but instead they put their extra effort into the Bayesian study.

In the main study the prior distributions on the word rates took account of the selection and regression effect. In the weight-rate study this effect is taken care of by the use of a calibrating set of papers, a procedure which is simple but which is expensive in terms of the amount of data available.

The plan is to construct a linear discriminant function, which is simply a weighted sum of the rates for words. The weights are chosen so that a paper which has typical Madisonian word rates gets a low (actually negative) score, while a Hamiltonian paper produces a high score. Building such a function is just like devising a psycological test to separate high-school students into two groups: one that would make better lawyers and another that would produce better doctors. The first group would probably do better on verbal questions and the second might excel on scientific questions. So if we gave verbal questions a negative weight (negative score) and scientific questions a positive weight, then added the scores on all the questions, prospective doctors would tend to have a positive total score while budding lawyers would tend to have a negative total score. In this way the test separates the students into lawyers (negative) and doctors (positive). Notice that to get a negative total score is not to do poorly in the test. We could just as easily have given the verbal questions a positive weight and scientific questions a negative weight, and then the doctors would score negatively.

The discriminant function to separate Hamilton from Madison is constructed using data from about half of the known papers for each author. These papers are called the *screening set,* and on the basis of the information contained in this set about word rates of the two authors, certain words are selected and weighted for use as discriminators. Once the words are chosen and weighted, the function is tried out on the other half of the material of known authorships, the *calibrating set.* This provides a test of the chosen function and also calibrates the weighted sum on material uncontaminated by the effect of selection, thereby taking account of the regression effect. The calibration gives us an idea how (known) Madison papers and (known) Hamilton papers score on this test function. Now when we apply the function to a disputed paper we can compare the new score with Madison's scores and Hamilton's scores, and decide who wrote the disputed paper.

The conclusions that may be drawn from this study are very similar to those of the main study: paper No. 55 is again the least Madisonian of the twelve. Its score is so close to the midpoint of the average score for the known Hamilton papers and the average score for the known Madison papers that we cannot make a definite classification one way or the other, although it is slightly on the Hamilton side. The rest of the disputed papers, except possibly No. 56, are undoubtedly Madison's.

For a more detailed description of the weight-rate study and of the two small-scale studies the reader is referred to Mosteller and Wallace (1964).

Perhaps it should be pointed out that these results are certainly not independent of the results of the main study; so the fact that this study has agreed with the main study, particularly insofar as it has judged No. 55 to be the least Madisonian of the twelve disputed papers, should not be construed as additional evidence for or against any of the papers. Fifteen of the twenty words used in the weight-rate study were also included in the thirty final words of the main study; so we would have been surprised had the conclusions reached from the two studies been very different.

15. Other Possible Discriminating Variables

The major effort in this attempt to solve the authorship problem went into the study of the differential use of individual words by Hamilton and Madison. The authors realize that the choice of words as the variables of interest can be easily ridiculed as linguistically and stylistically naive and uninteresting, but their defense against this criticism is strong: the use of words was feasible and highly effective for this discrimination problem, whereas other variables that came to mind appeared to have little or no discriminating value. But this is not to say that these other variables might not prove effective discriminators in other studies.

One of the variables that were tried and found to be useless for the *Federalist* study was sentence length. Another was word length. These two were discussed in an earlier section. Other variables that Mosteller and Wallace studied briefly were: (1) pairs of words, e.g., *effect* and *affect;* (2) use of comparative and superlative forms; (3) words with an emotional tone; (4) methods of enumeration; (5) conditional clauses and phrases; (6) the fraction of new material in the paper; (7) the uses of a word; and (8) the length of papers.

The reader can no doubt think of many other aspects of language and style that might be good discriminators. Large areas in the field of literary statistics remain to be explored in an effort to discover new measures of an author's style, measures that are stable within an author's writing but which differ from author to author. Plath (1961) gives a survey of the field of mathematical linguistics up to 1960. As he points out, "Investigations on the syntactive level, including the statistical study of patterns of coordination and subordination and of the types and depths of 'nesting' in sentences, may possible provide interesting new insights into certain aspects of literary style which have yet to be handled quantitatively." The "depth" of a sentence, a concept due to Yngve (1961), can be measured from the phrase structure tree of the sentence. Consider, for example, the sentence "The dog chased the cat." In the phrase-structure tree (Figure V) this sentence breaks into two parts, the noun phrase (NP) and the verb phrase (VP). The verb phrase splits

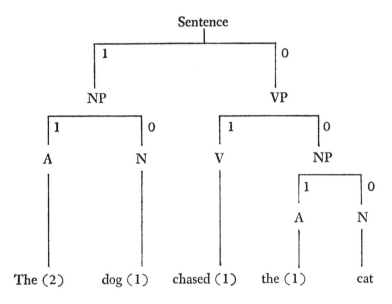

FIGURE V. Phrase-structure tree (depths in parentheses).

into verb (V) and another noun phrase. Then finally both noun phrases split into an article (A) and a noun (N). The depth of each word is calculated as follows: at each node (junction), number the branches 0, 1, etc. from right to left. To compute the depth of a word, add together the numbers written along all branches leading to that word. The depth of the sentence is defined to be the depth of the deepest word. Thus the depth of our sample sentence is 2, since the deepest word is the initial *the* (see Figure V).

Depth is one measure of how complex a sentence is, and could well be a variable that has a stable distribution within the writings of one author. In Yngve's model of sentence construction, the depth of the sentence is related to the amount of temporary memory storage that the listener needs in order to comprehend the whole sentence.

In the quotation above, Plath stated that concepts such as depth had not been treated quantitatively, but recently he has indicated (by personal communication) that he now has some data concerning the depth of the writings of some Russian authors. This is a by-product of work that he and others at Harvard have been doing on the machine translation of Russian into English. In the procedure that they use for translation, the amount of temporary computer memory storage (the depth of the predictive pool) required for the translation of a sentence is directly related to Yngve's depth. This amount of temporary storage is recorded for each sentence. Plath has noticed that the late writings of one Russian author were deeper in this technical sense than his early works. So it seems quite possible that the notion of depth could discriminate between two different authors.

Yet we should not be too optimistic about this or any other new variable until we have tried it out. After all, the depth of a sentence will be related to, and perhaps, highly correlated with, the length of the sentence. So measuring depth may be just an expensive way of measuring length, and sentence length did not discriminate between Hamilton and Madison at all. Until we try it out we can only speculate whether sentence depth will do any better.

When it becomes possible to perform syntactic analyses of English sentences on a practical scale — high-speed computers still take several minutes to analyze a complex Russian sentence — linguists will be able to study variables such as depth and use of words much more closely than they can now. But even when these studies become practicable, such simple characteristics of style as the frequency with which certain words are used may turn out to be just as good for use in solving authorship problems as the more complicated characteristics. And a study which uses simpler variables will likely be more economical: the problems of identification and counting will be fewer, and the use of a high-speed computer may be unnecessary.

The mere fact that a study has been carried out on a high-speed computer makes it no better a study than one requiring only desk calculators or even only paper and pencil. The worth of a study depends entirely on the data and ideas that go into it. In the *Federalist* project a computer helped in counting words in some papers, and performed most of the calculations for the main study. About half of the *Federalist* papers were typed on to punched cards, and the machine tabulated the total frequency of every word separately for each paper. Others of the papers were typed on to roll paper and counted by hand. At that time, counting by hand was cheaper than counting by computer, even though time on the computer was paid for at educational rates. However, the output of the computer was much better looking, came in multiple copies, and was easier to read and work with. In addition, the texts and counts of the papers that had been prepared for the machine were stored on magnetic tape; so the data was available for further computations. (A detailed description of the problems experienced in the counting and reconciliation of the counts made by hand and by computer is given in Mosteller and Wallace (1962).) But while the counting could have all been done by hand, the computations for the main study could not have been done in years without the computer.

To the man with an authorship problem Mosteller and Wallace offer some advice on getting started, and give a few sugestions for a small-scale attack which they believe might be widely effective. This is in Section 8.2 of the book. They include a table which should prove useful in picking out good words: the table lists the 165 words used in the study, along with the rates with which they are used by a number of authors. If our man with the authorship problem computes the rates from the known works of his competing authors, and compares them with the rates in the table, he should find a number of words that distinguish between the several authors.

16. Summary

This section quotes or paraphrases some of the conclusions reached by Mosteller and Wallace as reported in their book (1964) and J.A.S.A. paper (1963). It is in two parts: concerning the authorship of the disputed *Federalist* papers, and concerning authorship studies in general.

A. *The authorship of the disputed Federalist papers*
1. Our data independently supplement those of the historian. On the basis of our data alone, Madison is extremely likely, in the sense of degree of belief, to have written the disputed *Federalists,* with the possible exception of No. 55, where our evidence is weak: suitable deflated odds are 80 to 1 for Madison. No. 56, next weakest, is a strong 800 to 1 for Madison. The data are strong for all the rest, including the two papers historians feel weakest about, Nos. 62 and 63.

2. Among the joint papers, Nos. 18 and 19 look as if Madison wrote the lion's share. No. 20 requires a more subtle analysis of its possible contamination by third parties before Hamilton's share can be assessed.

3. We give little credence to the possibility that Hamilton wrote but Madison thoroughly edited the disputed papers, so that they finally looked Madisonian, rather than like a mixture of styles or a parody. The reader must appreciate that such a performance is not so trivial as changing two or three words. Even among the 30 words of the main study, Madison would have to make between 50 and 100 changes in each paper, to say nothing of the further changes these would induce. Since Madison could not know that we planned to use these 30 words, the total revision required, so that an analysis would show clear Madison rates, would have had to be on a scale even more vast.

4. Choice of prior distribution mattered little compared to other sources of variation.

5. Changes in the data distribution had enormous effects on the output, but both Poisson and negative binomial performed better in the disputed papers than the theory of these models forecast.

6. The main study shows stable discrimination for essays on various subjects, the writing spread over a quarter of a century.

7. The weight-rate, the robust Bayes, and the three-category studies give good support for the main study from the point of view of reasonableness of results. (Only the weight-rate and the main studies have been described in this paper.) Paper No. 55 is on Hamilton's side in these studies, although within easy sampling error of the border, and No. 56 is similarly inconclusive, although it is on Madison's side. These studies cannot be taken utterly at face value because of certain technical weaknesses. For this reason, their results do not take precedence over Results 1, derived from the main study.

B. *Authorship problems*

1. The function words of the language are a fertile source of discriminators, and luckily those of high frequency are strong. Our table of rates (discussed in Section 15) should help an investigator form a pattern of rates for a new author and speed him in solving easy authorship problems.

2. Context is a source of risk. We need variables that depend on authors and nothing else. Some function words come close to this ideal, but most other words do not. So many words and other variables depend on topics that their exploration for differences between authors would be a needless waste of funds, and worse, even screening them invites trouble, because some may accidentally survive. Grouping words or other variables in ways that relate not only to objective properties but also to the investigator's intuitive assessment of their trustworthiness offers a start on screening for context. Those groups which are not discarded out of hand can be studied

for their sensitivity to sources of writing. If the investigator has a variety of kinds of writing for each author, he can study variability in rates and have a basis for eliminating or lightly weighting variables or groups that show substantial heterogeneity among the kinds. If the bulk of the members of a group have excessive variability, he should consider guilt by association for the rest. No variable is entirely safe. He should investigate.

3. Hamilton's and Madison's styles are unusually similar; new problems, with two authors as candidates, should be easier than distinguishing between Hamilton and Madison. On the other hand, investigators with problems of selecting one author from many authors or of grouping a collection of essays into clumps by similar authors need all the help they can get.

References

Adair, Douglass (1944a, 1944b). "The Authorship of the Disputed *Federalist* papers," *The William and Mary Quarterly*, Vol. I, No. 2, pp. 97–122; *ibid.*, Vol. I, No. 3, pp. 235–264.

Brinegar, Claude (1963). "Mark Twain and the Quintus Curtius Snodgrass Letters: A Statistical Test of Authorship," *Journal of The American Statistical Association*, 58:85–96.

Cooke, Jacob E., ed. (1961). *The Federalist*. Cleveland: The World Publishing Company.

Fisher, R. A. (1936). "The Use of Multiple Measurments in Taxonomic Problems," *Annals of Eugenics*, Vol. 7, Pt. 2, pp. 179–188.

Mendenhall, T. C. (1887). "The Characteristic Curves of Composition," *Science*, Vol. 9, No. 214, supplement, pp. 237–249.

———— (1901). "A Mechanical Solution of a Literary Problem," *Popular Science Monthly*, Vol. 60, No. 2, pp. 97–105.

Miller, G. A., E. B. Newman, and E. A. Friedman (1958). "Length Frequency Statistics of Written English," *Information and Control*, 1:370–389.

Mosteller, F., and D. L. Wallace (1962). "Notes on an Authorship Problem," in *Proceedings of a Harvard Symposium on Digital Computers and Their Applications*, pp. 163–197, Cambridge Mass.: Harvard University Press.

———— (1963). "Inference in an Authorship Problem," *Journal of the American Statistical Association*, 58: 275–309.

———— (1964). *Inference and Disputed Authorship: The Federalist*. Reading, Mass.: Addison-Wesley Publishing Company.

Phillips, Patricia (1964). "A Statistical Approach to Some Literary Problems." Unpublished dissertation submitted to the University of Wales towards a Master of Science degree.

Plath, Warren (1961). "Mathematical Linguistics," in Christine Mohrmann, Alf Sommerfelt, and Joshua Whatmough, eds., *Trends in European and American Linguistics, 1930–1960*. Utrecht: Spectrum Publishers.

Whatmough, Joshua (1957) "Mathematical Linguistics," in *Proceedings of the VIIIth International Congress of Linguists*. Oslo University Press.

Williams, C. B. (1939). "A Note on the Statistical Analysis of Sentence-Length as a Criterion of Literary Style," *Biometrika*, 31:356–361.

Yngve, V. (1961). "A Model and an Hypothesis for Language Structure," *Proceedings of the American Philosophical Society*, 104:444–466.

Yule, G. Udny (1938). "On Sentence-Length as a Statistical Characteristic of Style in Prose: With Application to Two Cases of Disputed Authorship," *Biometrika*, 30:363–390.

_____ (1944). *The Statistical Study of Literary Vocabulary*. Cambridge University Press.

UNCONSCIOUS ORDERING IN THE PROSE OF SWIFT

Louis T. Milic

WHAT DOES it mean, to say we like a writer? Or a writer's style? Because I have always liked Swift above other prose writers, it occurs to me to wonder what this preference may signify. It is surely nothing as uncomplicated as a fondness for certain modes of narrative or certain themes or sujects. Some readers, it is true, regularly go into bookstores and ask for books about fishing or for something new in the way of satire; but the substance of a book (in that sense) hardly ever exerts so magical a pull after we have left our childhood reading.

Perhaps preference is derived from reputation. We know that there is an influence, but its role is not decisive. Readers may praise Milton, but they will not read him, as Dr. Johnson observed, unless they like him. We may read Hemingway or Salinger because others do so, because these writers are fashionable, which is a way of saying that they have responded to reality on behalf of the whole society in a fashion it is willing to accept as characteristic of itself. Such reputation is especially powerful when the writing is done in a prose which reflects current ideals of style: plainness, colloquiality, lack of affectation. But a response to reputation is temporary, not enduring enough to be a preference.

My preference for Swift is independent, I like to believe, of his high literary reputation of the moment and even of the generally high esteem in which his style has been held for two centuries — the word *perfect* has sometimes been used to describe it.[1] From a certain point of view Swift's style can even be made congruent with today's unambitious ideals of style. But it is not the style itself, I am convinced, that first leads to appreciation of any writer. That is usually the product of longer acquaintance. What really attracts the reader is something else, of which the style is inevitably a part, and that is the writer's personality.

The personality of a writer is an inferential structure built upon what we know or can guess about his subjects of interest, his reasoning, his feelings, his linguistic decisions, his attitudes. Since we do

---

[1] "Swift's style is, in its line, perfect . . .," Samuel Taylor Coleridge, *Select Poetry and Prose*, ed. S. Potter (London, 1933), p. 319; "The prose of Swift enchanted me. I made up my mind that this was the perfect way to write . . .," W. Somerset Maugham, *The Summing-Up* (New York, 1957), p. 20; there are many other examples.

not know him personally, cannot know him really, we must concentrate our attention on the symbolic properties of his work which distinguish him from other writers, his contemporaries, and even his siblings, if he has any. The greater the writer, usually the more numerous and impressive these differences, and the stronger the sense of personality conveyed.[2] Personality may thus be thought of as the reverse of humanity: it is the identity of a human unit as an individual, not his identification with the race in general. Personality, therefore, and one of its literary reflections, style, is the combination of drives to break away from the uniformity of the human mass and to establish, by expressing, one's particular indefinable uniqueness. Today, when all the forces of society, technology and industry combine to reduce human beings to equivalent easily-handled units, a strong interest has arisen in asserting the claims of individual personality. It is perhaps ironic that the machines which have a causative share in human depersonalization should be called on to assist in the rescue of the individual literary style.

Modern problems notwithstanding, the issue of individuality in the writer has been alive from the time of the ancients, although the modern stress on it is perhaps traceable to the influence of the Renaissance and the Romantic movement. Though the study of particular authors may date from the seventeenth century, the study of style did not begin as late as this. It has been pursued for a long time, but its findings have been anything but impressive. Comments on style have been the asides and afterthoughts of literary criticism. Impressionistic and subjective comment has held the field: anyone who wished to sum up a writer's individual manner dismissed him with an adjective; "heavy," "crisp," "masculine," "involuted," "lucid." The definition of *style,* moreover, has been so loose and so variable that these words might be taken to refer to the rhetoric or the diction or the grammar or the syntax or even the spelling and punctuation. A responsible methodology of stylistics has simply not been available, although some individual efforts of great power have resulted from the application of traditional rhetorical and philological procedures.[3]

Two factors have combined to produce a better state of affairs in stylistics: the development of technical means of handling the necessarily large quantities of data and the increase of knowledge in all phases of the study of language. The definition of style has come to be made in terms rather scientific than mystical: "a selection of non-distinctive features of language,"[4] rather than "style is the ulti-

---

[2] Such illustrations as Milton, Carlyle and Hemingway spring at once to mind.

[3] The work of Morris Croll, Leo Spitzer, Erich Auerbach and W. K. Wimsatt can be mentioned as illustrative.

mate morality of mind."[5] The relationship of the personality of the writer to his work, long recognized as a factor of weight, has come to be spoken of with a respect due to the recognition of how subtle and complicated the matter is. It has come to seem better to deal with the concrete and visible first and to leave speculation about the writer's personality for later.

Style, then, may be taken to be the sum of the individual choices made by the writer from the "non-distinctive" lexical and syntactic features of the language. This definition implies that the language provides the user with a variety of alternatives for the expression of any given meaning. We are free to consider this variety either a defect or a virtue in our language. This quality, which has been called redundancy, is simply nothing more than the duplication (or triplication) of information in a message. In such a sentence as "He told them the truth," the information that *he* is the subject is conveyed morphologically (case-form) and syntactically (word-order). But the amount of redundancy in an English sentence is not constant, as is shown by "John told the people the truth," in which only the word-order conveys the syntactic message. Nothing in the word-forms prevents the interchange between subject and object. A language might easily be constructed in which the redundancy had been deliberately reduced to somewhere near zero. In such a language, style would be nearly impossible: there would be no alternative ways to make a given statement. I say *nearly* in recognition of the fact that even artificial codes rapidly come to reflect the individual manner, or *style,* of the user.

Though redundancy provides choice and choice leads to style, which is a reflection of the unique mind performing the speech act, need we consider this opportunity to be necessarily a gain? The consequence of having alternative choices is a lowering of efficiency in the process of communication, inasmuch as it complicates the process of decoding, or understanding. If literary language were only communication, the aesthetic or stylistic ingredients of the message might reasonably be considered distractions on a level with the static which interferes with the communication of radio messages or stuttering in a public speaker.

But we welcome the wide range of choices made available by our language because literary men have very subtle and ambiguous communications to make and only a resourceful instrument like the English language provides the range and variety needed for literary expression. The study of style is based on the perception, collection,

[4]Leonard Bloomfield, *Language* (New York, 1933), pp. 498-9.
[5]A. N. Whitehead, *The Organization of Thought* (London, 1917), p. 25.

and tabulation of the idiosyncratic choices made by a writer in the attempt to express and communicate a literary message.[6] This kind of study, often called stylistics, has two main purposes: it can be attributive or interpretive. That is, it can serve to identify a given work as the product of a given writer by means of the individual fingerprints of his style; or it can be used to obtain a deeper understanding of the writer, his mind, his work, his personality.

It is evident that some characteristics of style would be better suited to attributive stylistics and others to interpretive stylistics, but it is possible to proceed as if both purposes could be served by the same procedure. In my study of the prose style of Jonathan Swift,[7] I was primarily interested in finding matter for interpretation but I used an attributive test as a check on the objectivity of the characteristics that I found. My concern with an attributive problem is reflected in the set of assumptions I was compelled to adopt before proceeding. Together these assumptions amounted to the definition of style which guided me.

The fundamental assumption is that the style of a writer is an idiosyncratic selection of the resources of the language more or less forced on him by the combination of individual differences summarized under the term "personality." This selection might be called a set of preferences except that this term suggests that the process is mainly conscious and willed. Although it is doubtless true that some part of the process of composition is deliberate and conscious, especially at the level of meaning, much of it is not fully conscious and it is this part which is of greater interest to the student of style. The reason is obvious: the unconscious stylistic decisions are less likely to be affected by the occasional and temporary character of a given composition (its subject matter) and are more likely to reveal something that the writer might deliberately wish to conceal.[8] If we are interested in his personality, such information would naturally be of great interest; and if we wished to attribute a work to him, we would place greater reliance on invisible tendencies which could not be imitated.

Two further assumptions are necessary if we are to make the

---

[6]The form-content distinction implied by this statement is not made without awareness of its aesthetic implications. It is, however, the prerequisite to any examination of *style*.

[7]*The Style of Swift: A Quantitative Approach*, scheduled to be published in 1966 by Mouton and Co., The Hague. For fuller treatment of the matters outlined here, this work should be consulted.

[8]This reserve is implied by the comment of Irvin Ehrenpreis: "He was struggling against a tendency to write in just the way he disliked." See Jonathan Swift, *An Enquiry into the Behavior of the Queen's Last Ministry*, ed. Irvin Ehrenpreis (Bloomington, 1956), p. xxxi.

fundamental one effective. We must assume, that is, that the stylistic consequences of the uniqueness of the personality are consistent and context-free and that they are measurable. Unless the stylistic characteristics recur consistently, they are not really characteristic, and unless they appear regardless of the subject matter of the composition, they must be of very low usefulness. They must be measurable, and therefore quantifiable, if any predictive or conclusive statement is to be made about them. Thus many usual aspects of stylistic analysis would be found useless for our purposes. Rhetorical devices (inversion, chiasmus, parallelism) are conscious, infrequent, traditional and highly visible, therefore unsuitable. Lexical choices are conscious and context-bound, and therefore unsuitable.[9] Similar objections can be raised against the study of imagery, metrics and prose rhythm. By eliminating unsuitable possibilities, we are left with the grammatical or syntactical component of writing as the best source of information about a writer's style.

The syntax of a writer's language is an element he is only very distantly aware of, though there must be a range of familiarity for different writers. Even grammarians tell us that they become conscious of their syntax only after they have already committed themselves to expressing their meaning in a given construction such as a relative clause or a participial phrase.[10] Although the generation of sentences and the processes involved in it are among the most mysterious of the many mysteries of the brain's linguistic operation, we do not have to be able to diagram the process in order to describe the results, the sentences actually produced by the writer. It is in the abstract grammatical classification and ordering of units performed by some unconscious part of the writer's mind while his consciousness is struggling with meaning that the stylistic process really takes place, in my view. In my study of Swift's style, I have concerned myself mainly with this underlying grammatical and syntactic substratum.

[9]The emphasis on quantification is not made without a keen sense of the inability of figures to measure affect. That something may be present ninety percent of the time does not mean that it will have nine times the importance of something present one-tenth of the time. Every tenth word, more or less, is *the* but we hardly notice it.

[10]For example, Paul Roberts says: ". . . it is a plain mistake to assume that conscious knowledge of the grammatical system is necessary to good writing. Some of our best writers know very little about grammatical analysis. Not only that, but writers who do understand the system do not apply this knowledge when they write . . . as I write these lines, I have no awareness at all of the particular structures that fall — which are subjects, which adverbs, which relative clauses," *English Sentences: Teacher's Manual* (New York, 1962), p. 2.

One feature of the study of style which has remained constant, despite the advance in technology, is the role of the observer. Nearly all studies of an author's style begin with an observation made by a reader. The difference between impressionistic and objective stylistics comes in what follows after. The impressionist makes observations and goes no further in the accumulation of data. He is satisfied that the phenomenon he has observed is typical of the writer, either in the sense of being meaningful of some peculiarity on his part or of being present in his works in approximately the same density everywhere. Both these assumptions rest on the further belief that the observation of idiosyncrasy he has made is indeed idiosyncratic of the writer and not characteristic of the genre or the period or the writer's social group or profession. An objective student of style is made uncomfortable by the uncontrolled extrapolation of the impressionist's procedure. He may place excessive reliance on the quantitative data but he feels that his conclusions will be sounder if he controls the variables quite closely.

Having made his initial observation, therefore, he examines the text of his author systematically to discover what quantitative order of frequency characterizes the peculiarity he has found. Its distribution in all the works of his author interests him as well. Moreover, he wants to know whether his contemporaries were given to the same peculiarity, and possibly whether writers at other, earlier and later, periods used it. In effect, then, the consequence of making a stylistic observation is the necessity of verifying its presence in a substantial number of texts. At least one difference, then, between impressionistic and objective criticism of style is the considerably greater amount of labor involved in objective work. The usual yield is a set of figures in the form of comparative tables showing the relative frequency of peculiarity X in Works 1, 2, 3, 4, 5. . . . of Author A and some works of Authors B, C, D . . . . The differences which will undoubtedly be found must be assessed for significance against the inevitable fluctuation of random variation due to sample size. Significance is determined according to criteria established in advance. If the observed peculiarity is found present at a significant level in the works of A and not of the others, it may be claimed as characteristic and used for attribution or interpretation, subject always to the necessary reservation that the quantifiable is not always the most meaningful.

In reading the works of Swift, I observed two peculiarities which I had never seen commented on in critical writings. One is the tendency to use accumulations of terms in series, thus:

". . . vast Numbers of our People are compelled to seek their Livelihood by Begging, Robbing, Stealing, Cheating, Pimping, Forswearing, Flattering, Suborning, Forging, Gaming, Lying, Fawning, Hectoring, Voting, Scribling, Stargazing, Poysoning, Whoring, Canting, Libelling, Free-thinking, and the like Occupations."[11]

This tendency to seriation, it turned out, had been noticed by several critics who treat them as syntactical, rhetorical, satiric or substantive, depending on their approaches, and variously label them juxtapositions, lists, catalogues, parallels, and series. The other peculiarity is Swift's addiction to connectives, especially in initial position, at the beginning of sentences.

The phenomenon of seriation has been considered to be related to the rhetorical ideal of *copia,* richness of texture, as opposed to bareness. In the form of doublets or triplets it is a formal rhetorical device which has been widely used in eighteenth-century prose, e.g., "a wise and salutary neglect," "the crimes, follies and misfortunes of mankind."[12] This type of structure is not necessarily pleonastic but, as a rhetorical device for structural symmetry combined with the diffusion of meaning, it generally is. Like many eighteenth-century writers, Swift used a doublet in every hundred words or so and a triplet in every thousand.[13] A series of four items or more has no such theoretical antecedents in rhetorical practice, though it has had a good deal of use from Rabelais to Henry Miller.

Swift's use of series, in the sense of a group of four or more similar grammatical units arranged in an order which permits them to be recognized as linked, is quite extensive. In 10,000-word samples from Dryden, Defoe, Steele, Addison, Goldsmith, Johnson, and Swift, only Steele had as many as ten series and Defoe had only one, whereas Swift had twenty-nine or one on every page, more or less. Moreover, Swift's series show a great range of variation in type. There are orderly lists of four nouns: "Temperance, Industry, Exercise and Cleanliness, are the Lessons equally enjoyned . . . ."[14] And there is also such a catalogue of undesirable members of society as the following:

"Here were no Gibers, Censurers, Backbiters, Pick-pockets, Highwaymen, House-breakers, Attorneys, Bawds, Buffoons, Gamesters, Politicians, Wits, Spleneticks, tedious Talkers, Controvertists, Ravishers, Murderers, Robbers, Virtuoso's; no Leaders or Followers of Party and Faction; no Encouragers to

[11]*The Prose Writings of Jonathan Swift,* ed. Herbert Davis (Oxford, 1939-in progress), XI, 236. All references to *Works* are to this edition.

[12]The examples quoted are from Burke and Gibbon, respectively. Comparative quantitative data about the use of doublets in eighteenth-century English writers may be found in Jan Lannering, *Studies in the Prose Style of Addison* (Uppsala, 1951), pp. 54ff.

[13]In 10,0000-word samples for six eighteenth-century writers the percentage of doublets ran as follows: Defoe, 1.11; Goldsmith, 1.30; Swift, 1.51; Addison, 1.55; Johnson, 1.72; Gibbon, 2.98.

[14]*Works,* XI, 253.

Vice, by Seducement or Examples: No Dungeon, Axes, Gibbets, Whipping-posts, or Pillories; No cheating Shopkeepers or Mechanicks: No pride, Vanity or Affectation: No Fops, Bullies, Drunkards, strolling Whores, or Poxes: No ranting, lewd, expensive Wives: No stupid, proud Pedants: No importunate, over-bearing, quarrelsome, noisy, roaring, empty, conceited, swearing Companions: No Scoundrels raised from the Dust upon the Merit of their Vices; or Nobility thrown into it on account of their Virtues: No Lords, Fidlers, Judges or Dancing-masters."[15]

Between these extremes, there are all kinds of grammatical and logical arrangements.

Single words, phrases, and clauses constitute the three basic types of series. As the complexity of the grammatical structure increases, the orderliness and recognizability of the series diminish. Thus, there are regular series, irregular series and chaotic series, the latter being barely recognizable as a single pattern:

"Are those detestable Extravagancies of Flanders Lace, English Cloth of our own wooll, and other Goods, Italian or Indian Silks, Tea, Coffee, Chocolate, China-ware, and that profusion of Wines, by the knavery of Merchants growing dearer every Season, with a hundred unnecessary Fopperyes . . ."[16]

The regular series of single words are most often nouns, but they may consist of adjectives, finite verbs, and verbals of all types. Any regular series may occur in initial or medial position but it is most often found at the end of sentences, especially the longer sort.

Although there are many regular series — mostly of single words — the striking feature of Swift's use of seriation is his avoidance of regularity. Chaotic series are often so because they contain a "nested" series of another type, as may be seen in the list of adjectives beginning with "no importunate . . ." in the long catalogue cited above, which is basically a list of nouns, types of members of society. The essential satiric procedure of the catalogue consists of indiscriminately lumping the respectable professionals of a type Swift disliked (attorneys, politicians) with criminals, triflers, and general undesirables. If the list were systematically arranged, the satire against the professional classes would be lost. The effect is successful only if they are all treated as equivalent units.

The *taxis* (arrangement) of such a series is a formula, but the *lexis* (vocabulary) is not. The insertion of the appropriate vocabulary into Swift's standard arrangement produces the rhetorical effect. The lexical component, it may be conjectured, is the conscious and satiric part of the device, whereas the impulse to catalogue or arrange seriatim is much less so. A satiric intention may also be observed behind the paradoxical continuator that Swift uses with some frequency. Continuators (*etc.* or some variant form) are normally

[15]*Works*, XI, 260-1.
[16]*Works*, XII, 79.

used for either of two purposes: for economy, to avoid the necessity of listing more than a few instances of self-evident sequence; for deception, to suggest the existence of additional matter of the same sort. Neither purpose is served when a continuator occurs at the end of a long sequence, but Swift regularly uses it in that position.[17] Two types are present, the plain neutral continuator and the satiric type. This latter works by the expansion of the formula by means of an unexpected classifying word which throws a new light on all the previous members of the series:
"I had been long conversing with the Writings of your Lordship, Mr. Locke, Mr. Molineaux, Colonel Sidney, and other dangerous Authors."[18]
But even the neutral continuator performs a function, which is the conveyance of copiousness implied by the very notion of series and catalogues.

Any series of items requires connection, if only to signal that the last item has been reached. The normal way to do this in English is to place the conjunction *and* between the last two items. Swift often violates this convention by using asyndeton (omission of connectives) or polysyndeton (connectives between all items). Both deviations emphasize seriation and diminish predictability. In effect, they represent another avoidance of regularity.

Connectives between items in series, however, offer little scope for variation and therefore little opportunity for individual expression. The other uses of connectives are richer in implication, to a great extent because connectives have enormous logical significance in prose, expository or argumentative. In discussing the use of connectives, the distinction between *lexis* and *taxis* is useful to recall. Some connectives fulfill grammatical functions, signalling relations between words, inclusion and subordination of clauses, modification of words by phrases and the like. In this, they operate syntaxically. Lexically, however, these and other connectives reveal the notional relationships between propositions, parts of an argument and other aspects of discourse to each other. Whether two clauses are joined by a coordinating conjunction or not (hypotaxis or parataxis) is a syntactic fact, regardless of the notional content of the connective (*and, or, but* . . .). The nature of the notional join, however, is of considerable importance to the argument of any discourse.

Both the taxis and lexis of connective use in Swift's prose were investigated and the results found very idiosyncratic. Initial connectives of three types were counted in samples of 2000 sentences

[17]In 28 out of the 200 series collected, that is, in 14 per cent.
[18]*Works*, X, 86.

from Addison, Johnson, Macaulay, and Swift.[19] The results are expressed in Table 1.

TABLE 1. Percentage of Initial Connectives in 2000-Sentence Samples of Addison, Johnson, Macaulay, and Swift

Connective	Addison	Johnson	Macaulay	Swift
C . . .	5.5	5.8	7.4	20.2
S . . .	7.1	6.2	4.1	5.4
SC . . .	3.3	1.4	1.5	8.3
Total . .	15.9	13.4	13.0	33.9

Swift's pre-eminence in this habit, or his addiction to it, is easily noted. His use of initial connectives is far greater than the other authors', and probably the population at large. If the sample is representative,[20] it would appear that Swift begins one sentence in three with a connective, one in five with a coordinating conjunction, one in six with *and, but,* or *for,* the favorite being *but.*

The real significance of this practice is revealed when it is observed that the notional range of these three favored conjunctions is rather narrow (additive, adversative and causal), merely a fraction of the available possibilities. The truth is, however, that they are in the main not used notionally but syntaxically, as the following passage will reveal:

"Lord Peter was also held the Original Author of Puppets and Raree-Shows; the great Usefulness whereof being so generally known, I shall not enlarge farther upon this Particular.

* another Discovery for which he was much renowned, was his famous Universal Pickle. * * having remark'd how your Common Pickle in use among Huswives, was of no farther Benefit than to preserve dead Flesh, and certain kinds of Vegetables; Peter, with great Cost as well as Art, had contrived a Pickle proper for Houses, Gardens, Towns, Men, Women, Children, and Cattle; wherein he could preserve them as Sound as Insects in Amber. * * * this Pickle to the Taste, the Smell, and the Sight, appeared exactly the

[19] Type C is equivalent to coordinating conjunction (*and, or*); type S to subordinating conjunction (*when, if*); and type SC to conjunctive adverbs or, as they are called by Paul Roberts, sentence connectors (*however, moreover*). In the numerical system described below, these types agree respectively with 41, 42, and 91.

[20] Within certain limits, all the samples in this study were drawn with the assistance of a random number table, in order to exclude bias. Sample 25 of Swift was drawn by a stratified sampling method in which part of every page of the work was sampled until the quantity needed was achieved.

same, with what is in common Service for Beef, and Butter, and Herrings, (and has been often that way applied with great Success) *but* for its many Sovereign Virtues was a quite different Thing. * * Peter would put in a certain Quantity of his Powder Pimperlim pimp, after which it never failed of Success."[21]

It will be observed that the passage reads easily and that there is no difficulty in assigning the proper relationships to the various parts of the paragraph. The paragraph has been shorn of four introductory connectives. As Swift wrote it, there should be a *but* where the single asterisk is, *for*s where the double asterisks are, and a *now* for the triple asterisk. Yet the logical sense has not been impeded. Some vague rhetorical function, perhaps concerned with the guidance of the reader, is accomplished by this pleonastic use of connectives.

This tendency to use connectives where they are not really needed is also characteristic of Swift's writing in yet another way, the accumulation of connectives both in initial and medial position. This practice, which most of the rhetoricians of the eighteenth century castigated Swift for,[22] produced such common pleonasms as *but however, and indeed, or perhaps* and such combinations as *and therefore, but though, for indeed if, and likewise because, and therefore when* and such a curiosity as *and therefore if notwithstanding*. Although a conscious purpose may inhere in such accumulations of connectives, it seems more likely to be a tendency of which Swift was not aware or which he found irresistible. His manuscripts and textual variants do not reveal him trying to curb this trait but engaged in a constant juggling of *but*'s, *for*'s *and however*'s.[23]

Curiously enough, this tendency did not interfere with the integrity of the message as this out-of-context and unpunctuated passage containing the four initial connectives demonstrates:

". . . and therefore if notwithstanding all I have said it shall still be thought necessary to have a bill brought in for repealing Christianity I would humbly offer an amendment that instead of the word Christianity may be put religion in general which I conceive will much better answer all the good ends proposed by the projectors of it."[24]

Swift's way with connectives, by the tenets of his time, was radical and improper. That he should persist in such unorthodox practice

[21]*Works*, I, 67-8.

[22]See Sterling A. Leonard, *The Doctrine of Correctness in English Usage 1700-1800* (Madison, 1929), p. 280 and passim.

[23]See, for example, the textual notes to *Gulliver's Travels, Works,* XI, and the work referred to in footnote 8, above.

[24]The original version reads: "And therefore, if, notwithstanding all I have said, it shall still be thought necessary to have a Bill brought in for repealing Christianity; I would humbly offer an Amendment, that instead of the *Word Christianity,* may be put *Religion* in general; which I conceive, will much better answer all the good Ends proposed by the Projectors of it." *Works,* 11, 37).

argues a likelihood of unconsciousness and therefore an inability to change. Whatever the degree of consciousness involved in Swift's habits of connection and seriation, the fact remains that these have a high degree of visibility and therefore may possibly be subject to the deliberate will. The same is not true for the grammatical sub-structure of any writer's prose and it is therefore this aspect of Swift which will now be examined.

Hardly anyone will quarrel with the contention that it is a rare writer who knows what percentage of the words he uses consists of nouns, adjectives, and so on. Swift himself considered the idea so preposterous that he put it into the mouth of the linguistic projector of Lagado, the inventor of the language frame, who had "made the strictest Computation of the general Proportion there is in Books between the Numbers of Particles, Nouns and Verbs, and other Parts of Speech."[25] Granted then that the configuration is hidden from the writer, to be helpful in stylistic analysis it must also be consistent, from page to page and work to work in a given writer, and it must be different in different writers.

This investigation of the grammatical sub-structure of Swift's prose style consists essentially of frequency distributions of parts of speech singly and in various arrangements. The procedure followed was to select random pages from a number of the works of Swift, each of the seven samples being 3500 words long. A set of control authors was also chosen: one author whose work was contemporary with Swift and whose style has been said to resemble his, Addison; two authors later in the same century but with styles vastly different from Swift's, Gibbon and Johnson; and one author from the next century, Macaulay. All the authors, be it noted, are famed for the individuality and quality of their styles. Two samples from each control were taken, each differing from the other in some way.[26]

Each word in each sample was classified as a part of speech according to a system based on Fries's but not identical with it.[27] Each word being represented by a two-digit code, the text of each sample was then punched consecutively on IBM cards, 36 words to the card, 100 cards to the sample, with only end-of-sentence punctuation indicated, thus:

‡‡ 42   11   02   61   05   31   01   51   31   07   31   01

Before I proceed to give an account of my leaving this kingdom . . .

---

[25]*Works*, XI, 168.
[26]See Appendix I for the constitution of the samples.
[27]See Appendix II for a full schedule of word-class codes with illustrations. The system is based on the one set forth by Charles C. Fries in his *The Structure of English* (New York, 1952).

Each set of cards was then presented to an IBM 1620 Electronic Computer programmed to make a count of the items in each word-class. The results produced by the first program are set out in Tables 2 and 3 below, for Swift and the controls, respectively.

An examination of Table 2 indeed shows that Swift was remarkably consistent in his use of parts of speech. His nouns amount to about a fifth of all his words and his prepositions to about an eighth. That this regularity is not inevitable may be observed in Table 3 where it is seen that Gibbon's use of nouns and prepositions is much higher and Macaulay's somewhat higher than Swift's. The claim that Swift's distribution of word-class preferences is consistent can be demonstrated by comparing Table 2 with Table 3. The greater fluctuation of the latter is easily perceived.[28]

Despite the internal consistency of the Swift samples taken as a unit, Table 2 shows that not all word-classes are equally reliable. Some classes (01, 31, 41, 51) are very consistent but some smaller classes (04, 81) exhibit a good deal of fluctuation. Some word-class fluctuation may be due to subject matter, as for example the high values of pronouns (11) in *Gulliver's Travels*, a first-person narrative, and of numerals (81) in *A Modest Proposal*. One way to reduce fluctuation is by grouping related word classes, such as the verbals represented by word-classes 05, 06, and 07. Verbals may appropriately be grouped since they represent a measure of finite-verb suppression, supposed to be a modern development in English prose.[29] The results of this grouping may be examined in Table 4. It is evident that Swift is regularly more dependent on the use of verbals than the control group of authors. This peculiarity can be used as a stable discriminator of his style.

Considerably more information may be quarried from the word-class frequency distributions, by making further groupings and comparative ratios, but since these do not have the discriminative power sought for here, they will be omitted in the interest of pursuing a more significant characteristic, the patterning of word-classes in

[28]A simple test of the consistency of Table 2 can be made by considering both it and Table 3 as drawn from one or more authors and computing the standard deviation of the seven or eight columns from their mean. Such a computation shows that the standard deviation of each word-class in Table 2 is much lower than the corresponding figure for Table 3. In other words, the scatter of figures around the mean is much closer in Table 2, the works of one author, than in Table 3, the works of a number of authors. To illustrate, Class 01 (nouns) shows a standard deviation of .93 for Swift and 2.60 for the Controls, a substantial difference.

[29]George O. Curme, *Syntax* (Boston, 1931), speaking of infinite forms of the verb, "No other part of our grammar is at the present time developing as vigorously," p. 448).

TABLE 2.   Word-Class Frequency Distribution of All the Whole Samples of Swift, with Computed Arithmetic Mean

Class	10	12	13	20	25	26	29	x̄
01 . . .	21.6	19.3	19.2	20.2	21.1	19.8	20.9	20.3
02 . . .	6.7	7.2	7.4	6.9	7.8	8.4	6.0	7.2
03 . . .	6.8	6.3	5.2	5.6	6.4	5.1	6.9	6.0
04 . . .	.5	.9	.6	1.2	.6	.7	1.0	.8
05 . . .	2.4	2.6	2.7	2.7	1.9	1.9	1.8	2.3
06 . . .	1.0	.6	.8	.8	1.3	1.3	1.5	1.0
07 . . .	.5	1.0	.6	.9	.3	.6	1.0	.7
08 . . .	.3	.1	.1	.1	.0	.0	.0	.1
11 . . .	5.7	7.5	6.9	6.7	8.5	9.3	5.1	7.1
21 . . .	7.1	7.5	8.2	8.1	5.7	6.0	7.8	7.2
31 . . .	15.6	14.7	15.6	14.9	15.9	16.3	14.4	15.3
32 . . .	.5	.6	1.0	.5	.5	.7	.4	.6
33 . . .	2.3	2.3	2.6	2.5	2.2	2.0	3.0	2.4
34 . . .	1.8	2.6	2.1	1.7	1.7	2.2	2.1	2.0
41 . . .	5.3	5.0	4.6	4.6	4.9	4.8	4.9	4.9
42 . . .	2.7	2.8	2.6	2.6	3.1	2.9	2.5	2.7
43 . . .	2.1	2.0	2.7	2.1	2.0	1.9	1.9	2.1
44 . . .	.0	.1	.1	.3	.0	.0	.1	.1
45 . . .	.3	.3	.5	.3	.4	.2	.5	.4
51 . . .	12.5	12.7	12.4	12.5	12.4	12.6	13.3	12.6
61 . . .	2.7	3.0	3.0	3.4	2.3	2.1	2.3	2.7
71 . . .	.1	.0	.0	.0	.0	.0	.0	.0
81 . . .	.6	.5	.7	.7	1.0	.9	1.8	.9
91 . . .	.7	.5	.3	.7	.4	.3	.9	.5

sequence.[30] The arrangement of word-classes in sentences is ultimately what syntax consists of. It is such a primitive syntax which is now proposed as the object of study, merely, that is, the systematic examination of sequential patterns of three word-classes, taken in overlapping sequence. For I believed at the outset of this research that an individual writer would use preferred sequences of three

---

[30]Nominal-verbal comparisons, adjective-verb ratios, connective, modifier and finite-verb groupings and other parameters of style are fully treated in my study, *The Style of Swift: A. Quantitative Approach.*

TABLE 3. Word-Class Frequency Distribution of Whole Samples of
the Four Control Authors

Class	Macaulay 61	62	Addison 65	66	Gibbon 71	72	Johnson 75	76
01 . . .	22.4	24.6	21.3	20.9	25.1	28.6	21.4	23.1
02 . . .	7.4	7.2	7.7	8.2	7.2	7.0	10.5	8.2
03 . . .	7.9	7.8	6.9	7.0	8.8	7.3	4.5	6.2
04 . . .	1.2	.9	.3	.4	.8	.5	.3	.7
05 . . .	1.4	1.6	1.7	1.5	1.3	1.0	2.6	1.6
06 . . .	.7	.8	.4	.4	.4	.3	.8	.7
07 . . .	.6	.5	.6	.7	.2	.3	.3	.6
08 . . .	.1	.1	.0	.0	.0	.1	.0	.1
11 . . .	6.2	4.2	7.7	7.5	2.5	2.0	8.1	6.4
21 . . .	8.2	7.2	7.1	6.8	5.7	5.1	7.6	7.9
31 . . .	14.9	16.4	16.1	15.5	19.3	19.4	14.7	14.4
32 . . .	.2	.4	.9	.6	.1	.0	.4	.2
33 . . .	2.9	1.5	2.4	2.6	1.4	.7	1.4	2.2
34 . . .	1.5	2.0	1.4	1.6	.9	1.0	2.0	1.8
41 . . .	4.5	4.0	4.1	4.6	5.3	6.6	5.0	4.8
42 . . .	2.3	1.7	2.6	2.7	1.7	1.1	2.3	2.6
43 . . .	2.1	1.8	2.4	2.8	2.2	1.0	2.3	2.4
44 . . .	.0	.0	.0	.0	.0	.0	.1	.0
45 . . .	.4	.1	.2	.4	.3	.2	.5	.4
51 . . .	12.7	14.5	13.6	13.3	15.0	16.3	12.2	12.8
61 . . .	2.0	2.2	2.2	1.9	1.6	1.1	2.6	2.2
71 . . .	.0	.0	.0	.0	.0	.0	.1	.0
81 . . .	.3	.4	.3	.3	.5	.7	.2	.3
91 . . .	.3	.2	.2	.2	.1	.0	.1	.5

word-classes and that such preferences would help to identify him.[31]

The second program, operating on the same sample decks of cards, collected units of three adjacent word-classes. In the sentence

[31]The choice of sequences of three words is dictated by the fact that anything larger would increase the number of possibilities beyond the usefulness of the present size of sample. I have taken it as an axiom that the sample must comfortably exceed the number of categories it is to be sorted into. For three-word sequences, this number is 24^3, the number of word-classes to the third power, or 13,824. On account of the redundancy of the English language, a number of these are not practical possibilities, e.g., 31 31 31. The practical total is estimated to fall between five and ten percent of the theoretical, or 600 to 1200, which is one-sixth to one-third the sample size. Four-word sequences can theoretically occur 331,776 ways, of which even a fraction is beyond reasonable sample size.

TABLE 4. Verbals as Individual Word-Classes and
Grouped (Group VB), in Percentages, for All
Whole Samples, Including Mean

	Swift							
	10	12	13	20	25	26	29	$\bar{x}$
05 . . .	2.4	2.6	2.7	2.7	1.9	1.9	1.8	2.3
06 . . .	1.0	.6	.8	.8	1.3	1.3	1.5	1.0
07 . . .	.5	1.0	.6	.9	.3	.6	1.0	.7
VB* . .	3.9	4.3	4.2	4.4	3.5	3.8	4.3	4.1

	Controls							
	Macaulay		Addison		Gibbon		Johnson	
	61	62	65	66	71	72	75	76
05 . . .	1.4	1.6	1.7	1.5	1.3	1.0	2.6	1.6
06 . . .	.7	.8	.4	.4	.4	.3	.8	.7
07 . . .	.6	.5	.6	.7	.2	.3	.3	.6
VB . .	2.7	2.8	2.7	2.6	1.9	1.6	3.7	2.9

*The VB value is not a total of the rounded word-class values, but a re-computation from the original raw data and may therefore not be equal to the sum of the three word-classes.

‡‡ 31, 01, 02, 51, 31, 01 ‡‡ the three-word sequences would be 310102, 010251, 025131, 513101, two fewer than the number of words per sentence, for no sequence can begin with either of the last two words of a sentence. The number of total three-word sequences in a sample is equal to the number of words less twice the number of sentences.

The expectation from this program was that individual authors would reveal syntactic preferences in their collocations of word-classes three at a time. The disappointing result, however, was that this preference could not assert itself against the context of linguistic uniformity. The perhaps not-too-surprising find was that the same structures predominated in all five writers in nearly the same amounts. The sequence 51, 31, 01 (preposition, determiner, noun) and its various inversions were the most common for all the writers. Although Addison and Macaulay show high consistency, Gibbon, Johnson, and Swift betray the most erratic fluctuation. It is unlikely, in sum, that either the particular favorite three-word structure or the percentage of its predominance can be used as a characterizing peculiarity. In fact, the inference is probably correct that the range

TABLE 5. Frequency of Occurrence of the Most Common
Single Three-Word Pattern (513101) as a Percentage
of Total Patterns

Swift samples . . .	10	12	13	20	25	26	29	
	4.3	5.4	4.9	4.9	5.5	6.3	5.1	
Control samples . . .	61	62	65	66	71	72	75	76
	4.8	4.8	4.9	4.9	6.6	7.6	5.5	5.0

of quantities evidenced in Table 5 is typical of the language as a whole. The use of prepositional phrases among all users of the language may be in the 4–8 percent range, subject to fluctuation by factors quite unrelated to individual choice. Even Gibbon's predictably high use of prepositional phrases is nearly matched by Swift's value in one sample of *Gulliver's Travels,* a very unlikely pairing.

Despite this unpromising, though interesting, result, the second program was not barren of useful information, but the manner of its becoming available furnishes a kind of lesson to users of computers. Intent as I was on uncovering the favorite patterns of the individual writers, I did not think of the possibility that information might come from another direction. As a routine measure, I included in the program a provision for a total of all the different three-word sequences in each sample. To my surprise these totals were far more individual than I had supposed possible and served as a potential identifying criterion.

TABLE 6. Total Number of Different Patterns per Sample

Swift	10	12	13	20	25	26	29	$\bar{x}$
	868	864	844	857	789	768	844	833
Controls	61	62	65	66	71	72	75	76
	755	669	657	752	497	440	680	769

Table 6 gives the figures. The consistency and elevation of the Swift figures is very suggestive of the value of the criterion. The lowness of the Gibbon figures also accords with intuitive expectation or with our sense that Swift's and Gibbon's styles are vastly different. The agreement among the three other controls suggests that 650-750 may be a typical or average performance for a literary work of the time.

A curious feature of this D-value, as it may be called, is its relationship to the size of the sample. Any attempt to convert the
value to another sample size on a strictly linear basis is bound to
be inaccurate. The reason lies in the peculiar arithmetic of combinations. In a small sample, say a sentence, the number of different
combinations would perhaps be as great as the number of items. As
the sample size increased, the number of recurrent patterns would
increase until the number of possibilities (possible combinations)
had been exhausted. Since, therefore, the curve describing this relationship is not a straight line, no estimate can easily be made of
relative values for other sample sizes.

The same program offered the opportunity to test another aspect
of syntax: sentence-initial structures. As was noted above, Swift's
reliance on connectives was significantly evident at the beginning of
his sentences, where these tended to occur singly and in groups
without any necessary notional aspect. Inasmuch as the data cards
made the verification of this result convenient, a third program was
devised, the purpose of which was to procure the frequency distributions of initial structures in all the samples.

Tables 7 and 8, below, show the percentages of occurrence of
each type of initial structure. For Swift the points of distinction are
the pronouns (11), determiners (31), conjunctions (41, 42), and
conjunctive adverbs (91). Among the controls, there is a striking
disparity between Addison's considerable use of initial pronouns and
Gibbon's avoidance of them, a difference probably reflecting the
distance between Addison's middle style and Gibbon's formal style.
Nearly all the controls use more initial determiners than Swift does
and he uses more initial connectives than they do. These polar and
obviously related characteristics constitute another set of consistent
discriminators. Table 9 below shows the relevant data.

With these discriminators at hand, it should be possible to form
some notion of the outward, or syntaxic, features of Swift's prose.
The interpretive aspect may be postponed while the criteria are
tested for their attributive force. A suitable object for testing is a
pamphlet whose authenticity has recently been questioned. I refer
to *A Letter of Advice to a Young Poet.*

At the moment, *A Letter of Advice to a Young Poet* is the only
work of any consequence in the Swift canon to be in doubt. At its
publication, in 1721, it was like nearly all Swift's significant works,
anonymous. It was not included in Swift's collected works published
by the Irish printer George Faulkner in Dublin in 1735, but neither
was *A Tale of a Tub* which Swift had by then tacitly acknowledged
as his. The *Letter* was included in Hawkesworth's edition of Swift's
works in 1768, reprinted in all subsequent editions, and until recently had been an unquestioned part of the canon.

TABLE 7. First Sentence-Elements by Word-Class as a
Percentage of Total Sentences, for Swift

Class	10	12	13	20	25	26	29
01	2.3	2.5	1.1		1.2	2.4	3.2
02	1.1			1.2		1.2	
03		2.5				2.4	
04							
05							
06					1.2		1.6
07							
08			1.1				
11	12.5	25.9	19.5	20.4	37.3	27.3	32.2
21	3.4	1.2	4.6	3.6			
31	20.4	18.5	16.1	18.1	20.4	23.8	9.7
32							
33		1.2	1.1				
34	3.4		1.1	1.2	2.4	1.2	
41	12.5	14.8	26.4	19.2	16.8	13.1	19.3
42	2.3	9.7	10.3	7.2	3.6	7.1	1.6
43	2.3	2.5	1.1			4.8	1.6
44				3.6			
45			1.1				
51	11.3	7.4	6.8	4.8	8.2	7.1	3.2
61	8.0	4.9	4.6	7.2	6.0	2.4	6.5
71	2.3						
81						1.2	
91	18.1	7.4	4.6	7.2	3.6	5.9	20.9
Total Sentences . .	88	81	87	83	83	84	62

Carl Van Doren in his 1930 life of Swift devotes some dozen
lines to the Letter, beginning, "Looking back over his career as a
wit he wrote an ironic Letter of Advice to a Young Poet, assuring
him that poetry did not demand religion or learning or even sense
of those who practiced it."[32] Ricardo Quintana, a few years leater,
delivers himself of the following encomium: "Yet the Letter to a
Young Poet is sui generis. Not only has it a peculiar importance by
virtue of the fact that Swift nowhere else discoursed of poetry at
such length, but it is also distinguished by the texture of its satire
and irony, for it is a grave discourse, evenly modulated, but with

[32]Swift in The Viking Portable Library Carl Van Doren (New York,
1945), p. 213.

TABLE 8. First Sentence-Elements by Word-Class, as a Percentage of Total Sentences, for the Controls

Class	Macaulay		Addison		Gibbon		Johnson	
	61	62	65	66	71	72	75	76
01 . . .	6.3	10.8	1.0	5.3	7.8	3.1	8.3	14.9
02 . . .							1.5	
03 . . .	1.3	2.5		1.1	1.1	1.0	1.5	.8
04 . . .	.6				1.1		.8	
05 . . .								
06 . . .	.6						1.5	
07 . . .								
08 . . .						1.0		
11 . . .	24.7	19.0	43.8	40.4	7.8	3.1	35.6	14.0
21 . . .		.6	3.1	3.2		1.0	1.5	.8
31 . . .	32.9	33.5	25.0	23.4	43.3	49.0	23.5	27.3
32 . . .								
33 . . .		1.9				1.0	.8	.8
34 . . .	.6	5.7	1.0		2.2	2.1	1.5	3.3
41 . . .	10.1	7.0	3.1	3.2	11.1	8.3	3.8	5.8
42 . . .	3.8	3.2	4.2	8.5	6.7	2.1		3.3
43 . . .							.8	1.7
44 . . .				1.1			3.0	
45 . . .	1.3		1.0		1.1			
51 . . .	11.4	9.5	5.1	7.4	14.4	25.0	7.6	18.2
61 . . .	5.1	4.4	8.3	6.4	3.3	2.1	2.3	9.9
71 . . .							3.0	
81 . . .	.6	1.3				1.0		
91 . . .	.6	.6	4.1					2.5
Total Sentences .	158	158	96	94	90	96	132	121

crushing irony lurking in every phrase."[33] This is not the language of men who doubt the authenticity of a work.

But after 1945, everything changes, for Herbert Davis has begun to question the authenticity of the *Letter*. As editor of Swift's prose works he has had occasion to examine it (and indeed all of Swift's work) rather carefully. Although its absence from Swift's collected works really creates his doubts about it, he finds also that it lacks "this very quality of directness and conciseness . . ."[34] which is Swift's

[33]*The Mind and Art of Jonathan Swift* (New York, 1936), p. 274.
[34]"The Conciseness of Swift," in *Essays on the Eighteenth Century Presented to David Nichol Smith* (Oxford, 1945), p. 27.

TABLE 9. Total Introductory Connectives (IC) and Total
Introductory Determiners (ID), as Percentages
of All Introductory Elements

	Swift							
	10	12	13	20	25	26	29	$\overline{x}$
IC	32.9	31.9	41.3	33.6	24.0	26.1	41.8	33.1
ID	20.4	18.5	16.1	18.1	20.4	23.8	9.7	19.6

	Controls							
	Macaulay		Addison		Gibbon		Johnson	
	61	62	65	66	71	72	75	76
IC . .	14.5	10.8	11.4	11.7	17.8	10.4	3.8	11.6
ID . .	32.9	33.5	25.0	23.4	43.3	49.0	23.5	27.3

hallmark. He does not in this attack specify further, but he returns
to the matter in the Introduction to the ninth volume of the *Prose
Works,* where he sets out a more detailed indictment.

There are three barriers to the credibility of the ascription of the
Letter to Swift, according to Davis: (1) no reference to it by Swift
or his friends, during his lifetime, has been found and neither
Swift nor Faulkner included it in the collected works; (2) the date
makes it unlikely because Swift was then at work on *The Bubble,*
a long poem, and was afflicted with a recurrence of his illness; and
(3) the same publisher (J. Hyde) had a year before brought out
another pamphlet which had been fathered on Swift and which
Swift in a letter to Charles Ford had specifically disowned *and* which
seemed to Davis to have stylistic affinities with the *Letter.*[35]

Despite the appearance of weight, the circumstantial part of this
bill of particulars is not very convincing. There are many reasons
why a work would escape notice, even if we had all of the author's
correspondence, which in Swift's case we do not. *The Story of an
Injured Lady* was not even published in Swift's lifetime, nor acknowledged by Swift, yet it is printed by Davis as genuine in the
same volume in which he dismisses the *Letter.* As for the timing,
that is surely speculation of the wildest sort: no one at two centuries' remove can profess to account for anyone's time, with that

[35]"Introduction," *Works,* IX, xxv-xxvi.

sort of accuracy. The third objection resolves itself to the un-Swiftian style that Davis believes to be characteristic of both the *Letter* and the disowned pamphlet. This consists of: (1) phrases like "but to proceed" to begin a new paragraph and other transitions; (2) parentheses like "I will take upon me to say," "as I was saying," and "and truly"; (3) "a heavy use of adjectives"; (4) a tendency to indulge in punning and word-play; (5) the unfinished condition of "the latter part" of the *Letter,* whose "last dozen pages" contain the phrases "another point," "once more," "to conclude," and five *lastly's.*[36]

After this, hardly any more unqualified statements about the value of the *Letter* were possible, of course. Murry, in his critical biography of Swift, calls it "an unsatisfactory piece,"[37] perhaps the first to do so. He had Davis's views on its authenticity available, but he does not reveal that he knows them. A scholar who was aware of Davis's doubts wrote on the persona of the *Letter* at about the same time as Murry, but he was not deterred by them from devoting some six pages to the strategy of its irony, saving himself at the end with: "All these conclusions about Swift's theory of poetry fall to the ground if he did not write the *Letter.*"[38] Another critic, wanting to discuss the work, but without contending the attribution, has recourse to the awkward stratagem of the skillful imitator.[39] Only Paul Fussell contests Davis's finding and he does so by evading the whole issue. The circumstantial evidence is ignored and the stylistic details nullified by maintaining that Swift here used a persona and therefore had not one but a stable of styles, could write like anyone.[40] None of this takes the question of attribution any further than where Davis left it.

To take the matter further, it is necessary to go back to the stylistic objections and to apply such objective quantitative criteria to the problem as have emerged from the examination of Swift's prose outlined above.

The procedure for comparing the *Letter* with both the Swift samples and those of the controls consisted of dividing it roughly into two halves, each of which approximated the right sample size. A third sample was constructed from what might be called the

---

[36]Ibid., pp. xxvi-xxvii.

[37]John Middleton Murry, *Jonathan Swift* (London, 1954), p. 323.

[38]William B. Ewald, Jr., *The Masks of Jonathan Swift* (Oxford, 1954), p. 98.

[39]J. Holloway, "The Well-Filled Dish: An Analysis of Swift's Satire," *Hudson Review,* Spring 1956, p. 22.

[40]Paul Fussell, "Speaker and Style in *A Letter of Advice to a Young Poet* (1721) and the Problem of Attribution," *Review of English Studies,* X (1959), 65.

"middle half," the second and third quarters.[41] These three samples were processed in the same way as the original sample decks, i.e., subjected to the three programs which were devised to reveal word-class frequency distribution, D-value and initial connective and determiner frequency. The results are displayed in Table 10 below.

Ocular comparison of the three samples shows good consistency among them and congruence with the Swift mean, though *Letter* I is most divergent and *Letter* II agrees best with the mean. A similar comparison of Table 10 with the figures for the Controls (Tables 3, 4, 6, and 9) shows a considerably greater kinship between the *Letter* figures and Swift than between the *Letter* and the Controls in any combination. The likelihood that the *Letter* is the work of Swift may properly be inferred.[42] But a question may be raised here about whether this procedure constitutes proof.

The answer is that proof is not within reach of any statistical technique which operates by means of quantitative probabilities. More important, the controls in this experiment are not by any stretch of the imagination proposed as likely candidates for the authorship of the *Letter*. They were selected as authors whose styles were distinctive in themselves and also had a certain relationship to that of Swift: thus, Addison is his contemporary; Johnson and Gibbon are later, with styles considered to be similar to each other but to contrast sharply with Swift's; and Macaulay is a century away. Since we cannot know who else may have written the *Letter*, we are reduced to showing that the evidence does not oppose the possibility that Swift may have written it. The comparative display which

---

[41]The first half (*Letter* I) runs from p. 327 of *Works*, IX, to the end of the sentence in line 12 on p. 336; the second half (*Letter* III) runs from the point just mentioned to the end of p. 345, excluding the last paragraph; the "middle half" (*Letter* II) runs from the second sentence of the third paragraph on p. 331 to the end of the third paragraph on p. 340, skipping two lines on p. 336 (from "Name" in line 10 to the end of the sentence.)

[42]If we estimate the statistical probability that the figures for *Letter* I, II, and III were drawn from the same population as the Swift figures, on the basis of the Student t-test, we find the chances to be as follows:

	VB	D	IC	ID
I	.001	.005	.01	.04
II	1.0	.05	.75	.20
III	.05	.20	.80	.05

The probability, therefore, that the VB value of *Letter* I is part of the Swift population is one in one-thousandth; on the other hand, the probability that the VB value for *Letter* II (which happens to be exactly the Swift mean) is part of the Swift population is precisely one. These probabilities cannot be taken wholly to the letter because of the probable divergence of the word-class distribution from a normal distribution.

TABLE 10 — Word-class frequency distributions and discriminator values for unknowns, with Swift means

	Letter I	II	III	Swift $\bar{x}$
01	19.8	19.9	21.4	20.3
02	5.7	5.9	6.1	7.2
03	7.1	7.4	7.4	6.0
04	1.0	.7	.5	.8
05	2.2	2.6	2.4	2.3
06	.5	.5	.6	1.0
07	.6	1.1	.8	.7
08	.2	.2	.1	.1
11	7.4	6.8	6.6	7.1
21	8.2	7.9	7.2	7.2
31	14.6	14.9	15.3	15.3
32	.5	.6	.7	.6
33	2.7	2.6	1.9	2.4
34	2.5	2.1	2.4	2.0
41	5.3	5.2	5.7	4.9
42	3.5	3.0	2.7	2.7
43	2.0	2.2	1.8	2.1
44	.0	.0	.2	.1
45	.4	.5	.4	.4
51	12.3	12.3	12.7	12.6
61	2.8	3.0	2.7	2.7
71	.1	.1	.0	.0
81	.1	.1	.2	.9
91	.5	.4	.5	.5
VB	3.3	4.1	3.8	4.1
D	901	869	855	833
IC	43.1	34.2	32.4	33.1
ID	8.3	17.1	14.1	19.6

follows (Table 11) reveals this relationship most clearly. All the figures have been normalized so as to facilitate comparisons of items of different numerical value.[43] The table shows that under each discriminator, there is a boundary between Swift-values and Control-

[43]The normalization operation consists of taking the Swift mean as equal to 100 and adjusting all other values to it. Thus a Swift sample value of 12 where the Swift mean is 10 would have a normalized value of 120. The procedure works to make different values commensurate.

TABLE 11. — Normalized values of four style discriminators, for Swift, Controls and Unknowns

VB		D		IC		ID	
	39 G		53 G		12 J	*I*	42
	46 G		60 G		31 G	29	49
	63 A		79 A		33 M	*III*	72
	66 A		80 M		34 A	13	82
	66 M		82 J		35 A	*II*	87
	68 M		90 A		35 J	20	92
	71 J		91 M		44 M	12	94
I	80		92 J		54 G	***100***	
25	85	26	92	25	73		
	90 J	25	95	26	79	10	104
III	93	***100***		12	96	25	104
26	93	13	101	*III*	98		119 A
10	95	29	101	10	99		119 J
II	100	20	103	***100***		26	121
100		*III*	103				128 A
13	102	10	104	20	102		139 J
12	105	12	104	*II*	103		162 M
29	105	*II*	104	13	125		171 M
20	107	*I*	108	29	126		221 G
				I	130		250 G

NB: Starred figures are Swift means; Roman numerals represent *Letter* samples; arabic numerals are Swift samples; and capital letters represent control samples.

values and that the samples representing the *Letter* are always well within the Swift boundary, and close to the Swift mean, especially *Letter* II. The quantitative data show, in other words, that the figures do not contradict the likelihood of Swift's having written it. This is not proof, of course, but the claim, it may be recalled, which threw the ascription to Swift into doubt was that the *Letter* was stylistically unlike Swift. It has been shown, I believe, that it is *not unlike* in the characteristics which lie below the surface.

In addition, it is not unlike Swift in the characteristics open to easy inspection. Four of the five stylistic criteria mentioned by Herbert Davis as invalidating the *Letter*'s claim to be genuine Swift are easily shown to be impressionistic and inaccurate. All the mechanisms he cites for rejecting the *Letter* are present in other works about whose authenticity there is no doubt and can be found even in the same volume as the *Letter*.[44] The density of adjectives is indeed greater in the *Letter* (all three samples) than in the Swift samples, the *Letter* samples being more than one percent higher than the Swift mean. Though not decisive, this is suggestive of a hand other than Swift's at work in the *Letter*.[45] The relationship of parts I, II, and III of the *Letter*, especially the relatively poor fit beween Letter I and the Swift averages, also suggests the possibility that an alien hand may have had a share in it. It is surely not an unwarranted conclusion to say that the *Letter of Advice to a Young Poet* looks very much like Swift's work, possibly tampered with by another hand, especially in the first quarter.

If this conclusion is accepted, the attributive uses of the word-class analysis here shown will have been demonstrated. But what interpretive inferences can be drawn from the same material? At the purely descriptive level, it is possible to say that Swift's high reliance on non-finite verbals makes his prose more modern (in that respect, at least) than even Macaulay's, who wrote a century later. His high D value implies a wider variety of syntactic patterns than some other authors. The low frequency of initial determiners, taken together with the high frequency of initial connectives, makes him a writer who likes transistions and who made much of connectives, both at the beginning of sentences and within sentences. His frequent use of series argues a fertile and well-stocked mind.

To proceed beyond this rather pedestrian account, to relate these devices of style to the personality itself, is not only more difficult, it is also riskier. The chance of error is great because no personality-syntax paradigm is available. Every speculation is as authoritative as any guess. Thus we can say that Swift's helter-skelter series show us the disorganization of his mind, and his non-notional connectives reveal the lack of logical structure in his thought. Saying thus, we should be making a case for the pathology of his mind, a matter

[44]Swift opens paragraphs as crudely elsewhere: "I must repeat . . . " (*Works*, IX, 50), "To return, then . . ." (74), "I will add one Thing . . ." (94), "But to return . . ." (XII, 99), "To return from digressing . . ." (124), "I now return . . ." (226). Parentheses abound: "Therefore, I say" (XII, 70), "if those (I say) openly profess . . ." (IX, 157), "I say, that in such a Nation . . ." (209). Concluding mechanisms are present also: in *The Publick Spirit of the Whigs*, in less than a half dozen pages, there are two Lastly's, "And to sum up all," and "His last demand" (*Works*, VIII, 62-8); elsewhere, in four pages, he uses "Further," "And whereas," "And again," "To conclude," and "Therefore, upon the whole" (VII, 292-5).

[45]On the basis of the Student t-test, the probability that the three *Letter* values for Class 03 come from the same population as the Swift figures is about .01 (1/100). If a hundred samples of Swift's work were drawn randomly, one sample would probably have 7.3 adjectives. But note in Table 2, that two of the Swift samples reach the values of 6.8 and 6.9 for adjectives.

that many have spoken about. But this is reaching beyond the known — neither syntactic stylistics nor personality theory is yet capable of making the leap.

APPENDIX 1.
DEFINITION OF WORD-CLASSES

01 Nouns: "The *captain* was very well satisfied."
02 Main finite verbs: "My master *alighted* at an inn . . . "
03 Descriptive adjectives: "No wise man ever wished to be *younger.*"
04 Descriptive adverbs: "I would *humbly* offer an amendment."
05 Infinitives: ". . . it will be a double charity to *admit* them."
06 Participles: ". . . *offering* to demonstrate . . ."
07 Gerunds: "Tools for *cutting* and opening . . ."
08 Quotations, foreign words: *"per annum"*
11 Pronouns (*I, them, himself, this, each, some, both, none*): "I have observed the wit . . ."
21 Auxiliaries (*may, does, be, have, must, can, will, let, ought*): "I *am* assured . . ."
31 Determiners (*a, an, the, some, every, his, many, all*): "Let me place *this* offer in a clear light."
32 Prepositional adverbs (*up, in, around, on, away, off*): "Jealousy like fire may shrivel *up* horns."
33 Intensifiers (*very, much, so, rather, too, more, quite, not*): "Young divines are *more* conversant."
34 Function adverbs (*almost, already, soon, perhaps, then, often*): "As I have *already* observed . . . "
41 Coordinating conjunctions (*and, but, for, nor, or, so, yet*): "But to return to madness."
42 Subordinating conjunctions (*because, when, if, as, although, since*): "*As* a war should be undertaken . . ."
43 Relatives (*who, that, which*): "The same spirits *which* would conquer a kingdom . . ."
44 Interrogatives (*who, when, where, how*): "*What* can be more defective or unsatisfactory . . ."
45 Correlative conjunctions (*either . . . or, not only . . . but also*): "They could *either* doubt it *or* forget it."
51 Prepositions (*with, of, on, by, in, up, behind, in relation to, as for*): "And *upon* this account it is . . ."
61 Pattern-markers (*there, it, to:*) ". . . *there* are more children born in Roman Catholick countries . . ." *It* is usual for clergymen . . ." ". . .Cartesius reckoned *to* see before he died."
71 Interjections (*Pray, No, Lord*): "O *faith*, I should be glad . . ."
81 Numerals (*one, eighth, eighteen, million*): "I again subtract *fifty thousand* . . ."

91 Sentence-connectors (*however, moreover, on the contrary, nevertheless*): *"Further,* they have liberty to garrison . . ."

APPENDIX 2.   Make Up of Samples and One-Tenth Sub-Samples

Sample	Author	Vol.	Page Number of Sub-Sample									
			1	2	3	4	5	6	7	8	9	10
10	Swift	I	20	7	154	30	48	26	57	104	88	100
12	"	III	110	93	29	30	99	159	64	36	145	79
13	"	III	49	60	165	124	115	39	24	151	149	139
20	"		II	IV	VI	VIII	II	IX	X	X	XII	III
			80	59	14	17	17	74	61	119	162	45
25	"	XI	(Stratified sample)									
26	"	XI	100	80	192	59	14	17	200	74	194	232
29	"	XII	(Continuous text)									
61	Macaulay[1]	I	562	72	231	411	64	36	536	593	303	631
62	"	II	176	450	737	583	49	456	666	775	671	564
65	Addison[2]	II	267	179	246	275	199	297	323	265	261	318
66	"	III	176	450	49	456	527	448	354	60	212	363
71	Gibbon[3]		II	II	III	I	III	III	III	II	II	II
			408	349	353	242	132	95	460	43	399	32
72	"		V	IV	VII	VI	IV	IV	VII	V	VI	VII
			272	487	136	420	256	200	216	369	316	142
75	Johnson		200	74	194	61	183	119	72	162	27	67
76	"		IV	III	I	I	II	III	IV	IV	I	IV
			118	39	366	59	121	418	256	200	150	152

[1]Thomas Babington Macaulay, *Literary and Historical Essays.* 2 vols. (London, 1923).

[2]Joseph Addison, *The Works of the Late Right Honorable Joseph Addison, Esq.,* 4 vols (Birmingham, 1761).

[3]Edward Gibbon, *The Decline and Fall of the Roman Empire,* ed. J. B. Bury. 7 vol. (London, 1896-1900).

[4]Samuel Johnson, *The History of Rasselas,* ed. R. W. Chapman (Oxford, 1927). *The Lives of the Poets.* 4 vols. (London, 1781).

STEPHEN CRANE'S THE O'RUDDY: A PROBLEM IN AUTHORSHIP DISCRIMINATION

BERNARD O'DONNELL

CASES OF doubtful or disputed authorship are not new to literary history. The Shakespeare controversy, for example, has been with us, with intermittant boiling points, for over two hundred years. The authorship of *The Imitation of Christ,* now generally attributed to Thomas à Kempis, was disputed for several hundred years. In the past, literary historians advanced tentative hypotheses based on stylistic and historical data; these hypotheses were often disputed by other literary historians. Conclusions were only rarely agreed upon. As a result, the determination of authorship often fell prey to calligraphers, cryptologists, even charlatans.

This is no longer the case. As electronic digital computers attract more and more attention in the humanities, scholars are renewing their interest in the problem of authorship determination. In the recent past a front-page story referring to the work of the Reverend Andrew Morton, a Scots minister and mathematician, has appeared in the *New York Times* headlined: "Cleric Asserts Computer Proves Paul Wrote Only 5 of 14 Epistles." Professor James McDonough of St. Joseph's College in Philadelphia has completed his study of the *Iliad,* analyzing authorship as peripheral to his main thesis. Professor Frederick Mosteller of Harvard has earned the praise of statisticians and historians alike for his analysis of the disputed Federalist Papers. Alvar Ellegard, a Swedish scholar, has published his findings on the authorship of the *Junius Letters.*

While there is some degree of excitement in all research, authorship determination has a certain dramatic flair. The *Times* hinted at the effect of Morton's findings were they to be substantiated. Shakespeare has not yet matched wits with the computer; you can imagine the rumblings in the scholarly world if the machine spells Shakespeare M-A-R-L-O-W-E.

The work I completed in 1963 is not quite so portentous. But it did involve an authorship dispute; and it did come closer to stylistic analysis than the previous studies, which had concerned themselves chiefly with vocabulary distribution and function-word frequencies; and it was quite exciting.

My study dealt with Stephen Crane's final work, a novel called *The O'Ruddy.* No serious literary study of this book had been made, though the possibility exists that the book was a new venture for Crane into the realm of the Comic Spirit. This is a novel of about 90,000 words. Crane had completed a manuscript of about 65,000 words when he died. Considerable mystery surrounds the completion of the book, but it was finished by Robert Barr, an English novelist, three years after Crane's death. Of the original Crane manuscript only Chapter 24 is known to exist. It would seem that Crane had written to this point. Barr, however, in a letter to Crane's widow demanding additional money, claimed that "only a fourth of the book is Stephen's." Since the evidence surrounding the completion of *The O'Ruddy* points to stylistic difficulty, my analysis was made on the basis of style.[1]

It was not the purpose of this study, fortunately, to define style. Nor was it designed to examine all the stylistic elements which could be found in a prose passage. It was an attempt to discover certain aspects of style, lexical and grammatical — objective entities in that they can be counted — which would differentiate one author's writing from that of another when these composite aspects, or profiles, were compared.

A pilot study to generate techniques for such work was designed and carried out.

Since the major study was an attempt to differentiate one author from another by using stylistic variables on a scale not previously attempted, the pilot study was conservative in its choice of variables. Basic aspects of style were intermingled with items which were unusual to the writings of one or the other authors, e.g., split infinitives, non-parallel structure. In studies of authorship determination, such a procedure is quite legitimate.[2] The results of the pilot study indicated, however, that many variables which are not idiosyncratic and which appear in practically all types of writing discriminate well when their pattern of interrelationships can be used.

This finding is highly pertinent to the variables chosen for the major experiment, since only those which are basic to the writing process — in that an incipient writer should be aware of their applicability and effectiveness — were used in the final list.

The purpose of this limitation was threefold. First, style is an amorphous, all-encompassing entity which cannot be meaningfully discussed except from a specific viewpoint. Second, since such a host of elements, in combination, represent style, only certain aspects can

[1]For further discussion of the problems surrounding the completion of *The O'Ruddy* and a more complete analysis of the issues touched on in these pages, see: O'Donnell, B., *An Analysis of Prose Style to Determine Authorship: The O'Ruddy, a Novel by Stephen Crane and Robert Barr*, doctoral dissertation, Harvard 1963 (to be published). The doctoral research was in part supported by National Science Foundation grant NSF-GP-683 in cooperation with the computation centers at Harvard and M. I. T.

[2]Frederick Mosteller and David L. Wallace, "Inference in an Authorship Problem," *Journal of the American Statistical Association* 1963, **58**: 275-309.

be used if they are to be handled within a statistically measurable framework. Third, this study, assuming success, took on the added significance of establishing the importance of these basic lexical and grammatical aspects of style in the study of the composing process.

The plan of using only those variables which are basic to writing style had to be further modified since an agreement among those involved in the study of composition of what is "basic" would be difficult to reach. Hence "basic" in this study meant that, in my opinion, these particular variables might be utilized in an introductory writing course. For this reason, a number of lexical and grammatical items which seemed either unique to the style of one of the authors (e.g., the unusual use of the prefix *mis-*) or too advanced stylistically to be considered basic (e.g., Crane's refined use of irony and certain other rhetorical devices) were not used, even though employing them might have enhanced prediction.

It is perhaps difficult, at first, to imagine the possible use of frequency counts of even the most meaningful variables, except for statistical purposes. A brief consideration of these counts would probably suggest their importance in the discovery of linguistic trends. Their relevance to the study of style, or more particularly to the development of style, is not so immediately evident. This relevance may become clearer if we discuss the variables from the viewpoint of their utilization.

The eighteen variables in the final listings were analyzed on the basis of their interrelationship within a paragraph. The first two, *words* and *sentences,* make up what may be called the superstructure of the paragraph. Both of course relate to length and are used by themselves as discriminators and as control factors when speaking of the frequencies of other variables. A paragraph of fifty words with five adjectives may show no difference, adjectively, from a paragraph of one hundred words with ten adjectives.

The next four variables, *clauses, dependent clauses, simple sentences,* and *past participial phrases,* might be referred to as the framework of the paragraph. In themselves they are sensitive to stylistic change. Aside from their importance from the standpoint of "what is said," involving choice for reasons of clarity, emphasis, and subordination of ideas, these variables directly relate to "how it is said," the essence of style. Ideas expressed in a series of independent clauses rather than in a series of simple sentences, or subordinated by a participial phrase rather than by a dependent clause, have a different impact on the reader even though the content is identical.

Frequency counts serve to focus attention on specific aspects of style which often, unfortunately, are taught in isolation from an actual piece of writing. Three of the major parts of speech were included among the variables: *verbs, adjectives,* and *adverbs.* The ease with which these parts of speech can be manipulated within a given context is a mark of the good writer. "But . . . but George . . . you can't . . . you can't mean that," (a) she said haltingly, (b) she stammered, (c) she said in a shocked voice — all say the same thing, but with a different nuance in meaning. The verbals, *participles* and *infinitives,* were also included for much the same reason. A consciousness of the possibility of interchange among these variables, gained by frequency counts, could then be sharpened by close inspection of the preference of one variable to another by a specific author.

Punctuation marks, necessary for clarity in any piece of writing, could be considered as part of the framework of the paragraph. Certainly periods and commas fall into this category. Other marks, such as *semi-colons* and *dashes,* have a certain flavor of their own not limited to clarity of expression. The *semi-colon* lies somewhere between the comma and the period in the degree of pause indicated. The *dash* is similar to the comma in that it requires a mental pause, but a longer one than the comma. The use of either of these variables indicates a conscious effort on the part of the writer to specifically equate or definitely separate the ideas he has expressed.

Metaphor, derived from the Greek word meaning "to transfer," may be defined: "A word that applies literally to one kind of object or idea is applied by analogy to another." It was selected, first, because the style of Stephen Crane is noted for its use; second, because of the forcefulness it adds to language; third, because it is an everyday occurrence in speech (*it's hot as hell; that comment threw him for a loss; he's a good egg*). *Color reference* was chosen for much the same reasons as metaphor (*he's yellow; he's true-blue; a scarlet woman*). It has the additional potential of introducing the young writer to basic symbols, which have no doubt been discussed with respect to his reading.

The two variables *impersonal constructions* (there is . . ., it seems . . ., etc.) and *initial conjunctions* (i.e., conjunctions appearing as the first word of a sentence) are not usually considered aspects of style that should be imitated. They were considered appropriate for this study, however, because of their value in discussing the style of writing in which they are used. *Initial conjunctions* are closely related to the variables *simple sentences* and *semi-colons.* They are usually used at the beginning of a simple sentence which may well have been attached to the preceding sentence. The sentence in which an *initial conjunction* is used often appears to be an afterthought of the writer. This pattern often is reworked in a final draft; it may be retained, however, if the after-thought effect is desired. *Impersonal constructions,* not usually found in good narrative prose, have a certain qualitative effect that usually can be better expressed by manipulation of the *verb* or *adverb* variables in a sentence. Improvement, however, does not always result from such change. It is difficult to see how the sentence "A tavern is in the town" is any improvement on "There is a tavern in the town."

Dialogue is used in this study to mean quoted expressions of one or more characters in the story which appear within a prose paragraph. That is, unquoted material precedes and follows the dialogue, all within a particular paragraph. Though not usual, this is a stylistic device in narrative writing that may be used with considerable effect: "But the new regiment was breathless with horror. 'Gawd! Saunders got crushed!' whispered the man at the youth's elbow. They shrank back and crouched as if compelled to await a flood." (S. Crane, *The Red Badge of Courage*). Since narrative writing is one of the basic forms of composition, and since this particular stylistic device is so forceful, *dialogue,* buried as it is, was included in our list of variables.

Certain of these eighteen variables were, at times, combined to form ratios, since the combination often contained meaning not attributable to a variable considered alone. In the case of *mean sentence length,* for example, not only is another meaning added to the variables *words* and *sentences* but it is a characteristic of style which has been established, in certain instances, to be a good discriminator.[3] The *verb-adjective ratio,*[4] was also included to see whether its effectiveness in differentiating between different types of writing was also applicable to discriminating authors within a specific type of writing. Certain other ratios, clause-dependent clause, sentence-verb, and clause-verbal ratios, which were used by George Hillocks in a brief study on student writing,[5] were included to see whether or not they also reflected nuances of more polished style.

This brief exposition only suggests the possibilities that these variables offer to the teaching of composition. It is an attempt, however, to establish the meaningfulness of these variables to research in this area. Further, these variables are unique in that no previous study of authorship determination has attempted to use variables which are so closely related to writing style.

Frequency counts of the chosen variables were based on sample paragraphs drawn from six novels, three written by Stephen Crane, three by Robert Barr. The novel was used since the book to be examined, *The O'Ruddy,* is a novel. Also, to insure that the fre-

[3]G. Udny Yule, "On Sentence Length as a Statistical Characteristic of Style in Prose," *Biometrika* 1939, 30: 363-390.

[4]D. P. Boder, "The Adjective-Verb Quotient," *The Psychological Record* 1940, 3: 310-343.

[5]George Hillocks, Jr., "An Analysis of Some Syntactic Patterns in Ninth Grade Themes," Euclid, Ohio, Central Junior High School (to be published).

quencies would be as representative as possible, these novels were selected on the basis that the writing covered a relatively short time span, approximately six years. Though no experimental data exist as proof, it is generally accepted that a writer's style may change over a long period of time. In a short period, however, a writer's style tends to remain stable, and any changes which do occur are not radical.

Each book was treated as a sub-population and the stratified sampling procedure recommended by Mosteller and Rulon[6] was used to obtain frequencies of the eighteen selected variables. One hundred paragraphs from each author were selected so that the sub-samples were proportional to the stratum sizes. This pool of two hundred paragraphs (approximately 10,000 words) constituted the set of known samples to be used to generate and to validate the predicting system needed to determine which parts of *The O'Ruddy* were written by Crane and which parts by Barr.

The paragraph was chosen as the sampling unit for several reasons: It is a basic unit of composition and, as such, clearly pertains to the chosen variables. Also, since the number of variables is relatively high, a large number of samples must be counted to avoid a possible positive bias in the multiple correlation coefficient. Counting 18 variables in each sample unit is time-consuming; therefore, choosing paragraphs rather than pages or chapters was both expedient and procedurally correct. A final reason was that an attempt was to be made both to separate *The O'Ruddy* into *chapters* of Crane and Barr and to explore the possibility of identifying unknown writing units as small as *paragraphs* within chapters. It was felt that the weighted variables would be more sensitive for predicting purposes if they were generated from a unit of this size. The generation of these weights was accomplished by multivariate statistical procedure.

Discriminant analysis is a multivariate statistical procedure designed to answer the question of which group an individual is most like. Philip J. Rulon labels this procedure "the statistics of taxonomy" and states: "Taxonomically, doctors, lawyers, engineers, administrators, and computer technicians are looked upon as representing six species, and the distinctions between and among species are studied by multiple discriminant analysis."[7] Essentially this statistic maximizes differences among discrete classes of things such that it is possible, data permitting, to decide which group an individual most resembles. Stated another way, discriminant analysis can be used

[6]Frederick Mosteller and Phillip J. Rulon, *Principles of Statistical Inference,* chapter 8, (unpublished).

to determine the probability that a person is a member of group A or B or C, given that he is an x, and a y, and a z.

In terms of this study the question asked was whether a paragraph (or a chapter) was most probably written by Crane or Barr given that it contains so many verbs, adjectives, dependent clauses, etc. Considering each author's writing to be one of two species, say species C and species B, this study will attempt to use the frequencies of the selected variables to accurately determine which of these two groups a given paragraph or chapter of *The O'Ruddy* is most likely a member. For example, a section of *The O'Ruddy* which has probability greater than .5 of being a member of Group C is assumed to have been written by Crane.

A *two-group* discriminant analysis, which is the appropriate model for this research, produces results equal to multiple regression procedures using a binary criterion vector. Operationally it is irrelevant which of the two statistics is used in this research.

An advantage of using the multiple correlation form for analysis of the variables is that stepwise regression techniques can preface the attempts to establish relationships and to generate regression coefficients. The twenty-three initially selected variables are a bit unwieldy. Stepwise regression procedures were used to obtain that minimum set of variables needed for maximum predictability.

The hypothesis that at least one subset of the twenty-three selected variables was significantly related to the criterion of authorship formed the base upon which this study rested. Little reason could be found to continue this research if no relationship were found to exist between the use of the selected variables and the identity of the author. On the other hand, demonstrating that only a moderate relationship exists would make pursuit of authorship determination worthwhile.

A multiple correlation was performed on 100 sample paragraphs, 50 from each author, with 18 selected variables as predictors. The magnitude of the relationship between these predictors and the authorship criterion would indicate the force with which the initial hypothesis could be advanced. The obtained multiple correlationship coefficient was .820. Analysis of variance of R yielded an F of 9.27 which (for 18 and 81 degrees of freedom) is significant well beyond the .01 level. The multiple R^2 (.67) indicated that 67 per cent of the differences between these two authors is being accounted for by the selected variables.

To determine the amount of faith which could be placed in these

[7]Phillip J. Rulon, "Distinctions Between Discriminant and Regression Analyses and a Geometric Interpretation of the Discriminant Function," *Harvard Educational Review* 1951, 21: 80-90.

results, the standard formula for shrinkage was applied. The corrected R is .775 which remains significant. These results clearly imply not only that it is tenable to advance an hypothesis of relationship but that it is justifiable to explore the possibilities of prediction.

The task at this point, then, is to see if these generated weights are transferable to new data. The b weights (derived from the above reported multiple correlation) were applied to the raw frequencies of 100 *uncontaminated* sample paragraphs, fifty for each author.[8] Forty-four paragraphs (of fifty) of Crane and forty-three (of fifty) of Barr were correctly assigned.

These results encouraged us to continue the experiment without further refinement, at least at this point. An attempt was then made to predict on known material that was considerably larger than the paragraph. This was deemed advisable since the initial predictions in *The O'Ruddy,* to orient sections of the book, would be done on chapters. The 100 uncontaminated sample paragraphs were grouped into chunks of about 1000 words. These groups resemble chapters of the novel in that chapters are made up of several paragraphs, though in most cases the chunks are considerably smaller. The smallness of size would be a further test of the sensitivity of the variables. It is logical to assume that it is easier to predict on a larger text than on a small one because of the increase opportunity for the variables to come into play. (Mosteller,[9] Yule, and Ellegard[10] all consciously attempt to avoid predicting small texts. Ellegard goes further in saying that 1000 words is the minimum text size on which accurate prediction can be made.)

The weights of the 18 variables were applied to raw frequencies of the variables in the 1000-word chunks. The results establish the transferability of these weights. The fact that all groups were assigned accurately — and substantially so — demonstrates the applicability of the generated system to relatively large units of several paragraphs. Attempts to predict chapters of *The O'Ruddy* could proceed with a certain confidence that assignments would be accurate.

The results of the application of the weighted variables to the chapters of *The O'Ruddy* were both dramatic and forceful. Chapters 1 through 24 were assigned to Crane; Chapter 25 emerged as a transitional chapter; Chapters 26 to 33 were strongly Barr's work.

---

[8]The term "uncontaminated" is applied to data which has not been used to generate the predicting weights; hence, an uncontaminated *known* sample may be treated as an unknown as a test of the procedures.

[9]Mosteller and Wallace, *loc. cit.*

[10]Alvar A. Ellegard, *A Statistical Method for Determining Authorship,* Stockholm, 1962.

The results of prediction of the individual paragraphs within the chapters were just as dramatic; they lend themselves, however, to further evaluation, possibly of a more literary nature. In Chapter 1, for example, two of the twenty-four paragraphs were assigned to Barr. Two possibilities exist here: Crane wrote them and they were mis-assigned (we do admit the possibility of some error); or Barr inserted them in this chapter for a specific reason. A literary analysis of the mis-assigned paragraphs would shed light on this. The results for our purposes, however, were quite satisfactory.

The point has been often made in this discussion that the stylistic variables used in this experiment are in themselves meaningful to those interested in developing student writing. The variables were chosen particularly with this relevance in mind. Hence, this study might offer to those researchers in composition an adaptable method for discovering lexical and grammatical patterns in student writing. If the pattern of a student's writing can be concretized, the task of spotting weaknesses and suggesting changes to correct them will be considerably lightened for both the teacher and the student. This analytic method could well be applied to examining "good" writing — the writing of accepted authors. The specific stylistic devices that these writers use would be identified and underscored by counts and correlations. Thus, for the first time perhaps, a student would understand what is meant by the Hemingway style or the Faulkner style.

Research in the field of composition is only beginning to develop. These grammatical and lexical variables, which were chosen for this study, could easily be overlooked because of their familiarity. It was the way in which these variables were used by Crane and Barr, however, that differentiated between their styles; therefore, the results of this study serve to highlight the importance of the variables in the study of the composing process.

A FACTOR ANALYSIS
OF THE VOCABULARY OF POETRY
IN THE SEVENTEENTH CENTURY

JOSEPHINE MILES AND HANAN C. SELVIN

BECAUSE, AS Kenneth Burke and many other critics have suggested, the clustering of terms is important for verbal and literary style, the use of the mathematics of factor analysis seems a possible way of getting at clusters not evident to the reading eye, yet underlying whole modes of expression. Professor Hanan C. Selvin, now of the University of Rochester, has worked out procedures for testing this belief, using a program written by Professor Alan B. Wilson of the Department of Education at Berkeley; and our results, however tentative and exploratory, may be of interest to those concerned with the study of literary style.

The question we asked is whether the main words of reference used by the poets of the seventeenth century tend to be grouped into clusters of use, so that one is more, or less, predictable in terms of another. And the further question is whether in the use of these words the poets also cluster in groups in ways familiar or unfamiliar to literary generalization. These are, in other words, two parts of a question about poetic style in the seventeenth century.

To put it more technically: will a factor analysis of the sixty nouns, adjectives, and verbs used at least ten times in a consecutive thousand lines by each of at least three of thirty poets in the seventeenth century reveal a number of factors useful for characterizing certain groups of poets and poetic habits of style? The representativeness of the thousand lines rests on the judgement that they provide a text long enough to show the poet's characteristic recurrences of word-use. For many poets, a thousand lines constitute their complete work. The stipulation of at least three poets aims to emphasize common uses rather than individual ones.

Factor analysis is a statistical procedure for measuring the extent to which groups of words have similar patterns of high and low use by various poets. In this paper, we shall speak of the words that make high contributions to a factor as forming a cluster. The reader should note that what Robert C. Tryon calls "cluster analysis" is a different, though related, procedure.

Our basic data are frequencies of word-use. These frequencies can conveniently be shown in a "score-matrix," Table 1:

TABLE 1.

30 17th Century Poets in chronological order.	60 Major Words: Adjectives, Nouns, and Verbs in alphabetical order. Here, the 11 Adjectives:										
	bright	fair	good	great	happy	high	new	old	poor	sweet	true . . . etc.
Jonson b. 1573	3	3	16	12		3	3	3	8	8	10
Donne 1576		5	20	6		15	6	7	5		20
Sandys 1578	2	14	2	12	7		5		8		
Fletcher 1582		19	15	25	10	8	11	7		6	
Wither 1588			10	10							10
Herrick 1591		6	14	4					6	17	7
Quarles 1592		13	25	10		5	13	5	18	8	8
Herbert 1593			10	20		6	4	3	6	6	5
Carew 1595	5	20	6	4						8	5
Shirley 1596	2	15	12	15			9	5	5		6
Waller 1606	12	30	15	20	5	10	10	7		12	5
Milton 1608	5	8	7	8	3	13	5	7		12	2
Suckling 1609		7	20	16			8				
Cleveland 1613			4	8	4			8		9	
Crashaw 1613	15	33	7	20		7	15	10	14	16	7

THE COMPUTER AND LITERARY STYLE

TABLE 1. (Con't)

30 17th Century Poets in chronological order.	60 Major Words: Adjectives, Nouns, and Verbs in alphabetical order. Here, the 11 Adjectives:									
	bright	fair	good	great	happy	high	new	old	poor	sweet	true ... etc.
More 1614	7	10	30	25	8	6	6	9		7	6
Denham 1615		3	12	22	6	5	5	20		1	5
Cowley 1618	5	20	4	15	7					2	5
Lovelace 1618	15	14	7	4	7		7		7	6	7
Marvell 1621	5	10		10			5	2		17	15
Vaughan 1622	5	10									
Dryden 1631		5	16	5		7	4	11		1	8
Roscommon 1633			13	12	4		8	6			
Oldham 1653			10	21			9	12	7		7
Blackmore 1655	8		7	16	7	10					
Creech 1659			13	19	5	7	10	9			6
Garth 1661				20			9	7			
Walsh 1663	9	7	7	12	12		7				9
Prior 1664	9	9	5	26							
Pomfret 1667	8	7		12	8						9

The figure "3" in the upper left-hand corner means that Jonson used the word *bright* three times in the thousand lines of *Underwoods*, his chief collection of poems. The blanks represent minimal or no uses. *Good* is the adjective Jonson uses most, sixteen times in a thousand lines. We take about ten times in a thousand lines, or a range from seven to twelve, as strong use; so Jonson can be seen to use five adjectives this strongly. Donne is quite similar in use of adjectives in general. Wither shares not at all in the use of these common adjectives, while Waller on the other hand is strongest in number and frequency of adjectives used, agreeing especially with Quarles, Shirley, and Milton. If we read the excerpt in columns down rather than across, that is, consider the vertical rather than the horizontal lines as pairs, we may note that some words, like *good* and *great,* are used strongly by almost every poet, especially in Waller's time. Others, like *poor* and *bright,* seem almost mutually exclusive, or like *poor* and *true,* selectively related.

So much one can see at a glance. But when the full matrix of thirty poets and sixty main adjectives, nouns, verbs is set up, the complexity is too great to be grasped in this way. It is difficult to look at 60 pairs of numbers and to estimate how closely one set resembles the other. The "coefficient of correlation" is a much better tool for this purpose than is simple inspection. And it is even more difficult to grasp the complexity of 435 possible pairs of poets, when each poet is paired with every other poet. The statistical procedure known as factor analysis is an efficient tool for reducing such complexity to a simple form, and, thanks to the computer, it is also economical. The calculations reported here took between one and two minutes on a large computer; they would have taken months on a desk calculator, years with pencil and paper. Factor analysis asks whether thirty poets really represent thirty distinct forms of behavior or whether they might be more fruitfully considered as representing a smaller number of more general patterns of word-use.

Table 1 therefore leads to two distinct but related lines of analysis: a study of the major patters of word-use (the "word-factors"), and a study of major patterns of poetic practice (poet-factors). The starting point for the study of poet-practice is the extent to which each pair of poets agree on use of terms — that is the extent to which each pair of horizontal lines is the same. Likewise, the starting point for the study of word-use is the extent to which each pair of words tends to be used together — that is, the extent to which each pair of columns is the same. The similarity is measured by the "coefficient of correlation," which approaches 1.0 as the two columns become more nearly alike and −1.0 as they become more different. A zero correlation means that the two columns show no systematic relation; in this case, knowing that one member of the pair is used frequently by some poet tells nothing whatever about the frequency with which he uses the other member of the pair.

Tables 2 and 3 represent the results of these two basic procedures; technically, they are the outcomes of "varimax rotation of principal-axis factor extractions." Note that, like Table 1, Table 3 is merely illustrative, not complete, showing just eleven adjectives of the sixty main words; that is, because of limits of space, just the top left-hand

TABLE 2.   Poet-Factors

Poets in chronological order	Factors: Correlation of poets with poet clusters				
	1	2	3	4	5
1 Jonson	.53	.48	.32	.11	−.35
2 Donne	.91	−.01	.13	−.05	−.10
3 Sandys	.53	.25	.20	.33	.44
4 Fletcher	.47	.27	.11	.38	−.05
5 Wither	−.07	−.08	.02	−.02	.25
6 Herrick	.63	.13	.36	.05	−.35
7 Quarles	.30	.34	.41	.35	−.08
8 Herbert	.35	.43	−.02	.17	.25
9 Carew	.86	.01	.18	.05	.11
10 Shirley	.70	.23	.31	.30	−.04
11 Waller	.59	.27	.19	.48	.10
12 Milton	.00	.02	.15	.71	−.03
13 Suckling	.75	.21	.26	−.08	−.34
14 Cleveland	.55	.03	.34	.00	−.14
15 Crashaw	.23	.19	.48	.65	.03
16 More	.30	.57	.15	.23	−.11
17 Denham	.49	.60	.12	.19	−.16
18 Cowley	.38	.38	.56	.05	−.18
19 Lovelace	.15	−.01	.66	.26	.14
20 Marvell	.09	.14	.54	.09	−.21
21 Vaughan	.04	−.27	−.24	.37	−.05
22 Dryden	.31	.60	.03	.03	.15
23 Roscommon	.06	.77	.17	−.12	.02
24 Oldham	.06	.76	.18	.14	−.29
25 Blackmore	.02	.70	.06	.05	−.07
26 Creech	−.00	.73	.07	.07	−.36
27 Garth	.80	.08	−.13	.09	.05
28 Walsh	.07	.24	.65	−.00	.21
29 Prior	.60	.21	−.27	.32	.04
30 Pomfret	.02	.56	.38	−.15	.16

corner of a table which presents in its entirety thirty poets and sixty terms. The partial tables show how the factor-matrix can be used; complete tables are of course the basis for the fuller generalizations made here.

In Table 2, which is complete, note that Jonson, as we might have concluded by reading the matrix Table I, is fairly moderate in his participation, looming large in no factor. Then note the very high number .91 for Donne in Factor 1. This means that Donne's word-usage has a great deal in common with that of every poet who has a high correlation with this factor — especially with Carew and Shirley for example, and least with Herbert, Wither, Milton. Factor I could well be called the Donne factor then, inasmuch as his practice defines it so fully, and as his choices are so little a part of any of the other four factors. Factors 2 and 3 are less identifiable with one poet's emphases, but seem relative to certain groups: Factor 2: Jonson, Quarles, Herbert; Factor 3: Jonson, Quarles, Herrick, Shirley. Factor 4 is clearly Milton's, shared especially by Sandys, Fletcher, Quarles, Waller. Factor 5 is Sandys's with Jonson, Herrick, and others in negative correlation, least apt to agree with Sandys. Participation in further Factors 6, 7, and so on, not shown, is so meager as to be marginal. In sum, the numbers in the table, the factor "loadings", show the degree to which each poet, in terms of his frequencies in choice of certain words, resembles the group which makes similar choices.

The numbers in excerpted Table 3, on the other hand, show the degree to which each word, in terms of its use by all the poets, appears in a text in company with the other words. The first column, Factor I, is closest to being identifiable by the word *good;* however, it is not vividly definable by any one adjective, but rather by its many strongly correlated verbs. Factor II, on the other hand, appears to represent that *poor* which we were able to discern in the matrix; now its relation comes clearer to other terms, not only to *true,* but also to *good, new, sweet.* In Factor III, the high correlation of *bright* and *fair* is most apparent. For Factor IV *true* is strongest; V and VI are mixed; and VII stresses *great* and *happy,* in contrast to *poor* and *sweet.*

Reading across the rows, note that for some words their appearance in certain contexts strongly defines them: *fair* in II and III, like *poor* and *sweet,* for example; *good* in I and II; *great* in VI and VII; *new* in II and VII; *true* in II and IV. Strong use thus seems to be limited to one or two chief clusters of use. The relation of *new* to *old* is particularly interesting: quite close in three factors, but with *new* dominating in II and III, subordinate in IV and V. By such clues we may gain insights into wider poetic views.

With these sections of the larger tables in mind, we may now

TABLE 3. Excerpt from Word-Factor Matrix

Words: 11 adjs. in alphabetical order:	Factors: Correlations of Individual Words with Word-clusters						
	I	II	III	IV	V	VI	VII etc.
bright	−.15	−.20	.79	.07	−.09	−.05	.03
fair	.08	.17	.84	.04	−.04	−.03	.04
good	.33	.41	−.05	.03	.07	−.05	.29
great	.12	.13	.19	−.31	.15	.26	.71
happy	−.12	−.27	.18	.33	−.10	−.12	.67
high	−.16	.08	.24	−.20	.27	.19	.13
new	.16	.60	.18	−.07	−.10	−.16	.34
old	−.15	.30	−.30	−.36	.31	−.26	.26
poor	.01	.83	.22	.04	−.09	.10	−.20
sweet	−.05	.40	.49	−.08	−.19	−.02	−.39
true	−.07	.56	.08	.52	−.00	−.27	.07

summarize the data for the two factor-analyses, for poets and for words, and then we may look at the relation between them; that is, try to render the matrix, by way of the factoring, into some generalization about seventeenth-century language in poetry

When we look at the groupings of poets in terms of the groupings of the sixty words they most use, the factors help us recognize more about these relations. The poets' Factor 1 associates almost half of the poets in a group in which Donne's uses are clearly dominant: Donne .91, Carew .86, Suckling .75, Shirley .70, Herrick .63, Prior .60, Waller .59, Cleveland .55, Jonson .53, Sandys .53, Denham .49, Fletcher .47. The so-called "sons of Ben" turn out to be even more strongly sons of Donne. Factor 2 shows other sons of Ben, in a different light: increasing classicism and its chronological source in him: Roscommon .77, Oldham .76, Creech .73, Blackmore .70, Denham .60, Dryden .60, More .57, Pomfret .56, Jonson .48, Herbert .43.

The other, smaller groups of mid-century: Factor 3, Lovelace .66, Walsh .65, Cowley .56, Marvell .54, Crashaw .48, Quarles .41; Factor 4, Milton .71, Crashaw .65, Waller .48; and Factor 5, the Sandys factor, .44 — to which there is strong negative correlation for non-Sandysian Jonson, Herrick, Suckling, and Creech.

For the larger number of words, a larger number of factors, seven, seem statistically and substantially important. Note that when the adjectives we have seen in Table 3 are seen in relation with nouns and verbs, only three or four carry weight, and these for only two or three factors. Factor I for words shows the following high degrees to which each word participates in and accounts for the whole factor: *bring* .94, *lie* .94, *world* .90, *go* .89, *time* .86, *thing, find, give* .85, *love* .71, *death* .68, *make* .51.

While on the face of it this list may not seem to reveal a meaningful homogeneity, it is, in fact, remarkably packed with verbs of action, and with a world-time-love-death–reciprocal-action complex which we may recognize as part of what has often been called "metaphysical." These terms together bear a very high proportion of the whole burden of metaphysical vocabulary.

The key terms of Factor II are *poor* .83, *keep* .74, *come* .71, *make* .61, *new* .60, *true* .56, *day* .56, *know* .55; though also active these are yet more adjectival and normative than the metaphysical. The adjective relations are visible in excerpted Table 3, as for Factor III also.

The third factor: *fair* .84, *bright* .79, *eye* .74, *heaven* .70 — aesthetic, sensory, with sublime associations. The fourth, emotional: *soul* .75, *love* .72, *fear* .69, *die* .64 *true.* 52 — a different interrelating of concepts; like Factor I, closely related to the vocabulary of the metaphysicals.

Factor V: four nouns, *god* (*s*) .81, *king* .76, *friend* .61, *power* .61. These appear to resemble or supplement Factor III. Factor VI with its substantive *earth* .68, *sun* .63, *sin* .61, *life* .59, *light* .56, *sea* .58, may, like Factor II, resemble and supplement the *great* .71, *happy* .67, *muse* .64, *art* .51, and *hear* .52 of Factor VII.

We have seen how highly Donne's uses account for Poet-Factor 1, and may note that, inasmuch as the first factor accounts for most, in Word-Factor I at least half the terms are strong for Donne, especially *death, thing, world, find, give, love, make.* His *sun, thing, keep* are characteristic of earlier colleagues, as *world* is of later ones. Jonson leads and exceeds Donne in the use of *great, god, life, light, man, nature, sin, call, fly, grow hear, know, see;* and of these, many are used especially frequently by one or another of the later so-called "classical" poets like Waller, Denham, Dryden, Oldham, Creech, Garth, and Prior: while some, especially *great, sin, god, life,* are also peculiarly characteristic of Sandys and Herbert as distinguished from the other religious poets.

What the mid-group of Lovelace-Cowley-Marvell-Crashaw-Quarles-Walsh especially shares is the aesthetics of *bright, fair, poor, sweet, day, eye, fire, heaven, world* and the verbs *find, keep, know, make, see* — the adjectives, even the metaphors as in *fire,* of a more domesticated metaphysics. This was their carrying on and modifying of the Donne tradition.

What the Milton-Crashaw-Waller group shares especially is its use of *high, new, old, sweet, god, heaven, night, come, give, hear, make*

— plus the Sandys factor combining *fair, earth, joy, night, soul;* with *joy* as strong only in Lovelace and Pomfret, with traces in Milton and Herbert; with *earth* as strong only in Prior; and with *soul* as strong also in Milton and Pomfret — a clearly Biblical grouping in addition to the more specially Miltonic of which it seems a part.

We may discern then a sequence of both kind and degree. Most pervasive throughout the century is the Donnic temporal and emotional, neo-Platonic, world of love and death. Next is Jonson's Aristotelean life and nature of norms, less personal and active, more abstract and evaluative than Donne's and thus including *sin,* as do Herbert and Crashaw who work apart from the Donne tradition. Classical nouns of value increase during the century, until they appear most strong in the satiric and descriptive work of the neoclassicists from Dryden on.

Next are the two mid-groups, both sensory and aesthetic, the one more classical earthly, the other more biblical heavenly, with appreciative adjectives and receptive verbs, with either *seeing* and *bright day* or *hearing* and *high night,* and the beginnings, in Sandys, of the cosmology of *earth* as distinguished from *world.*

The main poetic lines therefore seem to comprise: pervasive, speculative, cognitive and active, Poet-Factor 1 and Word-Factors I and IV; an early and late normative and ethical, Poet-Factor 2 and Word-Factors II, VI, VII; a middle aesthetic both human and heavenly, Poet-Factors 3, 4, 5 and Word-Factors III, V. The interweaving is strong, but the three major sources in reading, in Scholastic Petrarch, the Classics, and the Bible, are vividly clear, as well as the main progressions of the century away from its central metaphysical line toward the two others, human and sublime, which carry it into the next century.

Such lines we may note in the second stanza of Donne's *Good-Morrow,* in the words *good, soul, fear, love, make, new, world, go,* and *show.*

> And now good morrow to our waking soules,
> Which watch not one another out of fear;
> For love, all love of other sights controules,
> And makes one little roome, an every where.
> Let sea-discoverers to new worlds have gone,
> Let Maps to other, worlds on worlds have showne,
> Let us possesse one world, each hath one, and is one.

More classical in its generalizing terms of *love, muse, worth, thought, fate, art, friend* is Jonson's *To Francis Beaumont:*

> How I do love thee, Beaumont, and thy Muse,
> That unto me dost such religion use!
> How I do fear myself, that am not worth

The least indulgent thought thy pen drops forth!
At once thou mak'st me happy, and unmak'st;
And giving largely to me, more thou tak'st.
What fate is mine, that so itself bereaves?
What art is thine, that so thy friend deceives?
When even there, where most thou praisest me,
For writing better, I must envy thee.

And in *Lycidas,* the sensory *hearing,* on the *high* lawns of morning, after the fresh dews of *night,* the *bright* and risen star of *heaven*:

Together both, ere the high Lawns appear'd,
Under the op'ning eyelids of the morn,
We drove afield, and both together heard
What time the Gray-fly winds her sultry horn,
Batt'ning our flocks with the fresh dews of night,
Oft till the Star that rose, at Ev'ning, bright,
Toward Heaven's descent had sloped his westering wheel.

Certain emphases become more clear than we may often see them in critical histories: the primacy of the Donne tradition; the ethical allegiance of Herbert to Jonson; the early innovative forces of Sandys and Quarles toward the Biblical aesthetic; and the isolation of Vaughan from his religious confrères, in contrast to the surprising general continuity in Prior and Pomfret.

Certain doubts may be raised. How representative of each poet is each studied work? How representative of poetic vocabulary are the sixty major words here studied? How useful are they to establish main strands of emphasis, when they are only matters of degree and each poet's choices are in total unique? All of these doubts are in a sense one; that is, they concern statements made about tendencies rather than about totals, and thus are not exhaustive. But within their accepted limits, I think that the statements not only make sense but show the possibilities for making sense beyond our normal capacity for perception. Given the specific texts listed for our thirty poets, given the sizable proportions of whole vocabulary which we know these major terms represent, and given certain traditions of agreement beyond the simple facts of literal quotation or borrowing, we may well be able to see to what degree poets share in a major terminology, and to what degree style rests in the content of re-current reference. The strong appearance of certain factors, of certain terms like *world, poor, fair,* and of certain names like Donne's and Milton's shows the force of both persons and concepts in the creation of an art.

There is also some question as to whether there are certain types of factors which persist from era to era. Factors which we may desig-nate cognitive-active, normative-substantive, and aesthetic-qualitative factors, stress certain parts of speech; if we make a similar analysis of twentieth-century terms, themselves so very different in content, so much more fully aesthetic than in the seventeenth century, we yet may note a similarity of contrasts. The *black* and *green* of one factor and the *leaf* and *tree* of another are highly sensory for Roethke, Eberhart, Lowell. They can be seen in contrast to the *wind* and *water*, the *blue, sea, sky* of two other factors close to Stevens, less concrete. Still abstracter are *bright, dark, move,* or *life, death, world, love, nothing,* or active *know, hear, die, go,* with *earth* and *day,* the Eliot factor.

Thus there seems to be a similarity of factorial structure in the work of poets in two centuries as different as the seventeenth and the twentieth, a similarity that appears even when the two sets of words used are apparently very different. This kind of underlying similarity may be seen in fields of study which appear to have even less in common. Charles Morris and others have suggested the stability of action, receptivity, and judgment as factors. These are much the same as those found by Hanan Selvin in his study of qualities of leadership. Like modern artists, scholars may be pleased to find the lines of structure which run beneath the varied surface of art as of experience.

Here is the complete list of seventeenth-century works studied, with the complete list of sixty words emphasized (i.e., used about 10 times in the first 1,000 lines) by at least three of them. Jonson, b. 1573: *Underwoods* (first 1000 lines). Donne, 1576: *Songs and Sonnets.* Sandys, 1578: *Song of Solomon, Jeremiah.* Fletcher, 1582: *Purple Island.* Wither, 1588: *Vox Pacifica.* Herrick, 1591: *Hesperides.* Quarles, 1592: *Shepherds Oracles.* Herbert, 1593: *The Church.* Carew, 1595: *Poems.* Shirley, 1596: *Poems.* Waller, 1606: *Poems.* Milton, 1608: *Nativity, L'Allegro, Il Penseroso, Lycidas, Comus.* Suckling, 1609: *Fragmenta Aurea.* Crashaw, 1613: *Steps to the Temple.* Cleveland, 1613: *Poems.* More, 1614: *Psychozoia Platonica.* Denham, 1615: *Cooper's Hill* (1668 edn.). Cowley, 1618: *Mistress.* Lovelace, 1618: *Lucasta.* Marvell, 1621: *Poems* (through *Coy Mistress*), *Appleton House.* Vaughan, 1622: *Silex Scintillans, Poems.* Dryden, 1631: *Absalom and Achitophel.* Earl of Roscommon, 1633: *Poems* (through *Prospect*), *Horace's Art of Poetry.* Oldham, 1653: *Horace, Juvenal.* Blackmore, 1655: *Wit* (350 lines), *Nature* (500 lines), *Vanity, Happiness, Morning Thought.* Creech, 1659: *Odes . . . of Horace.* Garth, 1661: *Dispensary.* Walsh, 1663: *Poems.* Prior, 1664: *Poems on Several Occasions* (200 lines), *Solomon.* Pomfret, 1667: *Poems on Several Occasions—Choice, Death, Love Triumphant.*

Main words: bright fair good great happy high new old poor sweet true art blood day death earth eye fear fire friend god heart heaven joy king life light love man muse name nature night part power sin soul sun tear thing time world bring call come die find fly give go grow hear keep know lie live love make see. There are a few other main words, too many for the matrix, such as: seem show sing stand take tell think.

STATISTICAL METHODS IN LITERARY ANALYSIS

H. H. SOMERS

SUMMARY: A method is outlined which can be applied to literary texts in discussions about authorship. Overall statistical tests — the discriminant function of Fisher, the T² test of Hotelling — are discussed and applied to works of Philo Alexandrinus and the Epistles of Paul. Investigations into the discriminative power of various criteria are mentioned. The relation between stylistic features and stable personality traits is determined by factorial analysis. Three literary factors are found that seem sufficient to explain the greatest part of the common variance of the criteria used. Some measures are proposed for the main factors.

The first step in order to determine a supposed authorship of a given text is the analysis of the differences between the works of known authors and the text under test. In this contribution we shall consider mainly the problem of the statistical analysis of differences between texts and the relation of these differences to stable personality traits and to idiosyncratic characteristics of literary expression. We shall outline a method that can be followed in sampling, in the application of statistical tests, and in their interpretation.

From a theoretical point of view the problem to be solved is not very complex. In a population of known size (authors, styles, texts) one delimitates the section one wants to consider; for example, if the authorship of some Epistles of Paul is to be checked, one considers the population: biblical texts, epistolary genre, comments on the Bible, or, more generally, Greek religious texts of the first century.

Once the population has been defined, one needs to determine whether intra-text–variance is smaller than inter-text–variance, or, more specifically, for the determination of authorship, whether intra-individual differences are smaller than inter-individual ones.

This task might be very easy if one had for a given population a great number of texts for each author. But very commonly this condition is not realized: some texts are short; some authors have not left numerous works. Nevertheless we can still consider two subpopulations and limit our investigations to a comparison of two groups if we have to decide that a given text is a member of one of them. In the results we shall present here as an example of the method, we have chosen the works of Philo Alexandrinus and the collection of the Epistles of Paul. The homogeneity of this last collection has been questioned; it is assumed by exegetes that Philo

exerted some influence upon the redaction of the Letter to the Hebrews, which is commonly considered an epistle not written by Paul
himself. We are interested in seeing whether differences between
the two subpopulations are greater than the differences within these
two collections and whether statistical methods make it possible to
discriminate between them.

The second problem to be solved is the choice of criteria that will
sufficiently discriminate among texts and authors. The first condition to be imposed is that the criteria be adequately independent
of the content of the texts. Otherwise our differences could indicate
only that different subjects have been treated. The second condition
is that the dependence of the criteria upon the style or the destination of the text should be known; otherwise the criteria cannot be
used as indicators of authorship. It is known, for example, that one
finds more adjectives in the letters of W. James addressed to women
than in those addressed to men. If criteria exist which fulfill these
conditions, they are to be preferred. Actually such criteria do not
exist at all. Only when some conditions are kept constant, such as
literary style, the destination of the work, the subject treated, and
the conditions of production, can one assume, and not always safely,
that some criteria are relatively content-free and may be used as
indicators of personality. More technically expressed: only a part
of the variance within texts of the same author is due to personality
factors (measurement of this part is the first aim of the application
of statistical methods in order to determine authorship). This variance needs to be split into a part which is due to transient and
specific attitudes and a part which is due to more stable habits of
expression. A more cultivated intellectual habit of thinking can
increase the number of substantives used, while a more dynamic
empathy and active attitude can be habitually expressed by means
of an increased number of verbs. It is also possible to detect a
number of idiosyncrasies in the use of prepositions, subordinations,
conjunctions, and particles. In our example, which was intended as
an explorative pilot-study, we considered only the use of grammatical
categories: substantives, verbs, prepositions, adjectives, pronouns,
subordinations, conjunctions, negations, articles, particles, and the
number of words in segments of 500 letters. We were interested
in seeing whether it would be possible to evaluate the discriminative
power of these criteria.

The third problem to be solved is the sampling problem. One has
to determine the number of samples to be taken, their length, and
the type, dependent or independent, that would be the most useful
for the purpose. If the texts are long enough and sufficiently numerous, optimum conditions may be realized in the following way. The

number of samples required for reasonably significant figures is 100 ($N=100$). The length of text to be considered for example must be decided by taking into account the probability of the event. Counting tentatively the mean frequency of the event in segments of arbitrary length, one determines the length of text for which the probability of the event is .50. Taking 12–20 times the length of this segment as the sampling-unit length of text, one obtains a regular binomial distribution. After division of the whole text into parts of equal length, one determines by means of random tables for each criterion the N samples to be taken into account. This is random independent sampling of a finite population. But usually some of the criteria will be based upon "rare events." The texts at our disposition will be too short. Good results have been obtained in practice with samples 1000 words long. When even this is too much, one has to define minimum conditions of valid sampling. In our pilot-study we took 10 samples of the length of 500 letters (about 80 words) for each of 10 works of Philo and 9 Epistles of Paul (the 10th series of samples was composed of texts about the εἰκών theme). To simplify sampling further, one can admit dependent sampling: while the criteria chosen are mutually dependent within samples of about 80 words (we counted the frequencies for all criteria in the same samples), the results will be related. This is a useful procedure if one wants also to consider the relations between criteria within the same texts. Because with samples of very limited size most of the criteria are not normally distributed, but are distributed according to the Poisson-distribution, most parametric statistical tests require a previous normalization. This can be done according to the following formulas:

$$1°) \quad Y = \sqrt{X + 0.5}$$
$$2°) \quad Y = \sqrt{X} + \sqrt{X + 1}$$

(Both transformations are nearly equivalent).

The last problem to be solved is the use of appropriate statistical tests. Because the data are frequencies and the aim is to compare two collection of data, the χ^2-test may be expected to be the most adapted. The χ^2-test requires the independence of successive samples. Here two pitfalls are to be avoided. If the χ^2-test is used to compare two series of samples for the same criterion, one cannot be sure that successive samples taken in the same text are really independent. This needs a previous test. (A runs-test has to be used to detect successive dependence.) If the χ^2-test is used to compare frequencies for the two series of criteria, one commits an error neglecting the interdependency of these criteria. So for this purpose the χ^2-test is not appropriate.

Good statistical technique requires the use of overall statistical tests, which take into account the mutual dependence of the data. The most powerful tools are clearly the multivariate techniques when applied to normal or normalized data. Our aim is now to demonstrate the heterogenous character of the two collections of texts *and* the homogeneous character of both collections taken indivdually. For the first purpose the discriminating function of Fisher, for the second the T^2-test of Hotelling are the most adapted tests. The discriminant function of Fisher permits a maximization by means of a multiple regression formula ($X = a_1x_1 + a_2x_2 + a_3x_3 + \ldots a_nx_n$) of the differences of the X-scores for two or more collections of texts. This is exactly the solution of our problem: classify 20 or more texts correctly into two categories by means of only one common regression-formula. The results demonstrate that notwithstanding the minimum conditions we have been obliged to accept, we can accomplish this task by means of this powerful method. In Tables 1 and 2 one finds the mean frequencies for each criterion and for each work of Philo and each Epistle of Paul.

From Philo the ten following works are taken into account:

A. *De opificio mundi*
B. *De legum allegoria*
C. *De cherubim*
D. *De sacrificiis Abeli et Caïni*
E. *Quod det. potiori insid. soleat*
F. *De posteritate Caïni*
G. *De gigantibus*
H. *Quod Deus sit immutabilis*
I. *De agricultura*
J. *De plantatione*

From Paul the following are the letters and texts used:

E. *Epistola ad Ephesios*
H. *Epistola ad Hebraeos*
I. *Selectio textuum de imagine Dei*
K. *Epistola ad Corinthios prima*
L. *Epistola ad Corinthios secunda*
N. *Epistola ad Galatas*
P. *Epistola ad Philippenses*
Q. *Epistola ad Colossenses*
R. *Epistola ad Romanos*
T. *Epistola ad Thessalonicenses prima*

TABLE 1.   Number of Occurrences in the Texts by Philo

	Words	Subst.	Verbs	Art.	Pron.	Prep.	Adj.	Conj.	Part.	Sub'd.	Neg.
A	84.3	19.6	11.8	12.9	3.8	5.9	13.8	7.2	6.0	2.4	0.9
B	85.7	18.7	13.5	11.8	4.5	5.3	11.2	6.4	9.8	3.3	1.2
C	79.8	18.5	15.5	10.6	3.9	4.9	9.2	3.7	8.9	3.4	1.2
D	74.0	17.1	14.7	9.3	3.8	4.1	10.1	3.7	6.6	3.2	1.4
E	78.8	17.1	14.3	11.0	3.8	6.3	10.1	3.2	9.0	2.9	1.6
F	76.5	17.7	14.1	11.4	2.1	6.2	11.0	3.8	6.8	2.1	1.1
G	80.0	15.6	13.0	9.7	3.4	5.3	14.6	5.6	8.3	3.2	1.3
H	78.9	16.5	15.5	10.5	4.7	7.2	8.4	4.5	7.0	2.6	1.3
I	76.0	16.2	14.0	9.9	2.9	5.3	9.9	4.2	10.0	2.2	1.3
J	79.6	16.9	12.7	11.9	3.8	6.4	12.3	5.4	7.7	1.8	0.7

TABLE 2.   Number of Occurrences in the Texts by Paul

	Words	Subst.	Verbs	Art.	Pron.	Prep.	Adj.	Conj.	Part.	Sub'd.	Neg.
E	82.5	22.1	10.9	16.0	7.4	11.1	5.9	3.9	2.2	3.3	0.4
H	77.7	15.9	15.2	11.3	5.2	7.5	7.0	4.0	5.6	3.1	2.7
I	81.8	20.7	13.2	13.3	4.6	7.9	6.1	3.9	6.2	3.2	2.4
K	84.2	16.6	17.8	9.4	3.8	4.6	8.2	4.2	7.9	3.9	4.3
L	81.3	15.4	14.1	9.9	10.6	9.9	6.0	2.7	7.0	3.5	2.1
N	84.9	22.5	14.8	12.4	7.0	7.4	4.5	1.9	8.1	4.2	2.1
P	85.5	19.7	12.4	11.1	10.0	9.6	6.8	5.3	5.2	4.4	1.0
Q	84.8	20.8	13.2	14.2	7.5	11.5	4.9	5.3	2.3	4.2	0.9
R	86.1	21.4	13.3	15.0	8.0	7.1	3.6	3.0	7.7	3.3	3.7
T	81.6	17.0	14.1	10.8	10.5	9.6	5.8	5.1	4.6	2.8	1.3

To obtain the X-score for each work these figures are to be used in the formula:

$$X = 0.0997\, x_1 + 0.1264\, x_2 - 0.5404\, x_3 - 0.0986\, x_4 - 0.8596\, x_5 - 0.0312\, x_6 - 1.5699\, x_7 + 1.3884\, x_8 - 1.2194\, x_9 + 1.3141\, x_{10} + 3.9063\, x_{11}$$

where x_1 is the number of words, x_2 the number of substantives, etc. In Table 3 one finds the results of these computations. The results are quite clear: there is no overlapping between the X-scores. So the discriminant function is a valuable tool to assign a discussed text to one or another collection of texts.

For our second purpose we want to demonstrate *for the same data* that they are homogeneous within both collections taken individually, or that in the given collections the deviations of the means from the estimated population mean are not greater than those which could be expected by chance alone. The T^2-test indicates whether a vector of sample-means differs significantly from the vector of estimated population-means. If there is a work of Philo

TABLE 3.   A comparison of the works of Philo and Paul by
Means of the Discriminant Function of Fisher

Value of X			
Paul		Philo	
E	−4.1	A	−12.5
H	−2.2	B	−13.7
I	−0.3	C	−13.9
K	−1.8	D	−13.1
L	−9.6	E	−14.8
N	−4.9	F	−14.4
P	−6.1	G	−17.6
Q	1.2	H	−11.1
R	3.4	I	−15.8
T	−7.0	J	−18.0

or Paul that deviates from the population-means, the T^2-test would
be significative. The results shown in Table 4 do not attain any
degree of significance.

The application of two general overall tests indicates a very significant difference between the two collections of texts, but no significant differences greater than should be expected by chance alone
within each collection.

TABLE 4. Values of T^2 and x

	Philo			Paul	
	T^2	x		T^2	x
A	157	.389	E	423	.192
B	130	.124	H	139	.418
C	98	.505	I	172	.368
D	208	.324	K	45.7	.689
E	45.6	.689	L	185	.353
F	121	.440	N	138	.420
G	122	.101	P	52	.657
H	112	.471	Q	140	.417
I	79.2	.559	R	155	.392
J	89	.529	T	140	.417

For $P(T^2) < .10$, $x < 0.0016$.

The interpretation of this result indicates that it should be easy
to assign an unknown text to one of both collections, but much more
difficult to discriminate within each collection. This does not mean

that no true differences can be detected with refined methods, but that the interpretation should be very cautious, for it is known that when one calculates a number of tests, some of them should be expected to be significant only by chance!

For more refined analysis—each criterion can be submitted to test—there exist some well adapted non-parametric methods, such as the Kolmogorov-Smirnov-D-test for distributions. First we can test which are the criteria which truly discriminate between the two collections, then we can test the hypothesis that they are homogeneous within the two collections.

The application of the Kolmogorov-D-test to the distributions of each criterion of the two collections in order to detect the criteria which are truly discriminating gives the results shown in Table 5.

TABLE 5.   Probability of the D-Value of Kolmogorov

Number of words	.001
Substantives	.001
Verbs	-------
Articles	.001
Pronouns	.001
Prepositions	.001
Adjectives	.001
Conjunctions	-------
Particles	.001
Subordinations	.02

Almost all values are highly significant.

The same test can be applied within each collection. In order to maximize the chance to detect some significant difference we used the complete counts published by R. Morgenthaler, and we grouped the Letters of Paul into four groups:

    I. 1 Thess., 2 Thess., 1 Cor., Gal.
    II. 2 Cor., Rom.
    III. Eph., Col., Phil., Phem.
    IV. Hebr., 1 Tim., 2 Tim., Ti.

We subjected to the test two criteria: the use of the conjunction καί and the use of the article. There is no doubt that significant differences exist within the collection of Paul's Letters.

In order to estimate the magnitude of inter-individual differences versus intra-individual differences a sampling was made from several biblical texts: the book of Genesis, the Gospel of Mark, the Gospel

TABLE 6. Probability of the D-value

	Articles					Conjuctions			
	I	II	III	IV		I	II	III	IV
I.	____	____	____	.01	____		____	____	.01	____
II.	____	____	____	.01	____		____	____	.001	.01
III.	____	.01	____	____	.05		.01	.001	____	____
IV.	____	____	____	.05	____		____	.01	.01	____

of John, the Book of Wisdom, the Apocalypse, the Acts of the Apostles, etc. For this comparison classical two-way analysis of variance is recommended when applied on transformated scores, because of the possibility of a check upon random-sampling and the overall-character of the test. One can compare (see Table 7) the values of F for the collection of heterogeneous biblical texts with those obtained from Paul and Philo.

TABLE 7. Values of F for Biblical Texts (B), Paul (P), and Philo (Ph)

	B	P	Ph
Number of Words . . .	8.6	3.8	3.0
Substantives	4.0	2.9	0.7
Verbs	8.8	1.9	2.0
Articles	7.1	2.7	1.3
Pronouns	5.2	3.5	1.6
Prepositions	2.2	4.8	1.9
Adjectives	4.8	2.2	2.2
Conjunctions	4.8	4.1	2.4
Particles	8.2	7.3	2.4
Subordinations	1.6	1.0	1.5
Negations	4.3	5.2	0.7

The conclusion is that Paul's Letters are somewhat more heterogeneous than the works of Philo, but not so much so as the collection of biblical texts. The same analysis can be made in much more detail comparing each work of Philo with each other work of his and doing the same for Paul.

The three following tables present the results for one of the criteria: the number of verbs, for the biblical population, for Paul, and for Philo.

The biblical population is represented by the following works:

> A. Acts of the Apostles
> C. Apocalypse
> G. Book of Genesis
> J. Gospel of John
> M. Gospel of Mark
> S. Book of Wisdom

To these are added:

> E. Epistle to the Ephesians
> R. Epistle to the Romans
> H. Epistle to the Hebrews
> F. *De opificio mundi* (Philo)

In order to be statistically significant the value of F should exceed:

1° for the ten works together:

$$P (F) < .05 \qquad\qquad F > 1.96$$
$$P (F) < .01 \qquad\qquad F > 2.56$$
$$P (F) < .001 \qquad\qquad F > 3.38$$

2° for the comparison of two works only:

$$P (F) < .05 \qquad\qquad F > 4.41$$
$$P (F) < .01 \qquad\qquad F > 8.29$$
$$P (F) < .001 \qquad\qquad F > 15.38$$

Because of the fact that in a large number of F-values some will be significant by chance, careful statisticians exclude this possibility by increasing the critical value of F:

$$P (F) < .05 \qquad\qquad F > 10$$
$$P (F) < .05 \qquad\qquad F > 15$$

TABLE 8. The Values of F, for Number of Verbs, for the Biblical Population

	E	F	R	S	H	C	G	A	M	J
									$F_c = 8.6$	
									$F_r = 0.6$	
J	57.6	36	16	24.1	11.2	16	20	3.4	0.1	......
M	51.5	32	14	20.5	9.4	13.3	16.6	2.2	......	0.1
A	27	16.2	6.5	7.7	3.1	4.2	4.9	......	2.2	3.4
G	12	5.5	1.2	0.6	0	0	......	4.9	16.6	20
C	8.9	4.3	1	0.4	0	......	0	4.2	13.3	16
H	5.9	3.1	0.8	0.3	......	0	0	3.1	9.4	11.2
S	6.1	2.5	0.3	......	0.3	0.4	0.6	7.7	20.5	24.1
R	1.3	0.3	......	0.3	0.8	1	1.2	6.5	14	16
F	0.3	......	0.4	2.5	3.1	4.3	5.5	16.2	32	36
E	......	0.3	1.3	0.6	5.9	8.9	12	27	51.5	57.6

TABLE 9.   The Values of F, for Number of Verbs, for
the Works of Paul

								F = 1.915	
	E	H	I	K	L	N	P	Q	R	T
E	____	5.54	2.34	10.34	4.72	11.47	1.70	4.56	1.74	4.81
H	5.54	____	0.76	1.12	0.17	0.00	1.90	0.95	0.50	0.18
I	2.34	0.76	____	3.45	0.27	1.47	0.20	0.00	0.00	0.27
K	10.34	1.12	3.45	____	2.22	1.31	5.69	4.31	2.70	2.26
L	4.72	0.17	0.27	2.22	____	0.40	1.12	0.33	0.16	0.00
N	11.47	0.00	1.47	1.31	0.40	____	4.09	2.42	0.86	0.43
P	1.70	1.90	0.20	5.69	1.12	4.09	____	0.46	0.19	0.13
Q	4.56	0.95	0.00	4.31	0.33	2.42	0.46	____	0.00	0.33
R	1.74	0.50	0.00	2.70	0.15	0.86	0.19	0.00	____	0.14
T	4.81	0.18	0.27	2.26	0.00	0.43	1.13	0.33	0.14	____

The difference in results between the heterogeneous collection
of biblical texts and the homogeneous collections is striking. In the
very homogeneous works of Philo one finds a value of F as high as
11.02; nobody will wonder if slightly higher values are found in
the works of Paul.

Thus the results of the general tests have been verified by the
examination of the details.

Not only is it important to demonstrate whether differences are
statistically significant or not; their measurement is also important.
We want to know how much they differ.

For detailed comparisons the mean scores for each criterion can

TABLE 10.   The Values of F, for Number of Verbs,
for the Works of Philo

								F = 1.996	
	A	B	C	D	E	F	G	H	I	J
A	____	1.54	5.95	5.85	5.38	4.76	1.20	11.02	3.14	1.10
B	1.54	____	0.80	0.69	0.54	0.22	0.18	2.20	0.09	0.23
C	5.95	0.80	____	0.01	0.06	0.48	2.97	0.40	0.53	3.29
D	5.85	0.69	0.01	____	0.02	0.36	2.85	0.65	0.42	3.17
E	5.38	0.54	0.06	0.02	____	0.20	2.44	0.93	0.28	2.74
F	4.76	0.22	0.48	0.36	0.20	____	1.80	2.92	0.03	2.10
G	1.20	0.18	2.97	2.85	2.44	1.80	____	8.05	0.84	0.00
H	11.02	2.20	0.40	0.65	0.93	2.92	8.05	____	2.20	8.85
I	3.14	0.09	0.53	0.42	0.28	0.03	0.84	2.20'	____	0.99
J	1.10	0.23	3.29	3.17	2.74	2.10	0.00	8.85	0.99	____

be used, including their variances; however, an overall measure for the distribution of the means of all criteria together is provided by information theory.

Not only can one calculate the entropy of the distribution of probabilities for all criteria together, but more refinement is possible when one considers the sequential constraint in syntactic structure, taking into account the conditional probabilities of sequences.

According to the formula of Shannon the entropy of a distribution of probabilities is:

$$H = - \sum_i p_i \log_2 p_i$$

As example we consider: the first Epistle to the Thessalonians, the Epistle to the Hebrews, and the Gospel of John. One obtains respectively:

$$H = 3.06; \ H = 3.06; \ H = 2.95$$

If one calculates the conditional entropy from two-way tables where one enters for each criterion the number of times it is followed immediately by another (digram 1.2), or not immediately (digrams 1.3, 1.4, 1.5, . . . 1.n) according to the following formula:

$$H_1(n) = H(1.n) - H(1)$$

where $H_1(n)$ is the conditional entropy of the nth word when the first is known, $H(1.n)$ is the common entropy of the joint distribution calculated according to the following formula:

$$H(i,j) = \sum_{i,j} p(i,j) \log_2 p\ (i,j)$$

and $H(1)$ is the entropy of the first order, one obtains a conspectus of the evolution of sequential constraint within the grammatical structure of the text.*

The second part of the problem of authorship determination is the investigation of the exact relation between the variances of the criteria and stable personality traits. The human person has an amazing capacity for adaptation and imitation. So stable components of behavior appear amid great variability. In order to detect these components as expressing themselves in literary style, it is possible to examine the relations between criteria, their correlations, and the common factors underlying them. A factor analysis indicates three principal common factors. The first (A) is a general vocabulary-level factor which is expressed by the use of rare, abstract, long words; the second (B) is a bipolar qualificative-versus-

---

*Cf. H. H. Somers, "The Measurement of Grammatical Constraint," *Language and Speech* (London), 4:150–1`˙` (1961).

dynamic factor (verb-substantive opposition); the third (C) a factor of mental inhibition which opposes complex subordinative (use of particles, negations, subordinations) to simple narrative concrete style (articles, prepositions). Some specific factors indicate the idio-syncrasies of individual authors or works, such as the predilection of Philo for the use of adjectives.

Obviously the richness of vocabulary (factor A), indicating a level of general culture and of intellectual functioning, is a stable personality factor with slow evolution. In order to measure this factor, reliable and pure factor measures are to be found. A very simple measure is the Type-Token–Ratio of Chotlos, if taken always upon texts of 100 or 1,000 words. As is known the TTR is not stable if the length of the text is not constant. This is due to the properties of the distribution of word-types against the number of tokens (length of text). If one wants to compare texts where only the total length and the number of types are known, one can use the θ-measure, which Somers proposed.* This is computed according to the following formula:

$$\theta = \text{loglog } V \ / \ \text{loglog } N$$

where V is the total number of types; N, the total number of tokens.

This formula is based upon the empirical observation that θ is stable (N > 10,000) if the length of the text under consideration in-creases. For N < 10,000 the formula is:

$$\text{loglog } V = a + \theta \text{ loglog } N$$

(The constant a can easily be estimated from a TTR.) The applica-ion of the formula to Paul's Letters results in a chronological order-ing of them (see Table 11). The results confirm strikingly the

TABLE 11.   Values of θ and Evolution of Vocabulary

YEAR	θ
52: la Thess. and 2a Thess. . .	81
55: la Cor. and Gal.	81–82
57: 2a Cor. and Rom.	82
First Captivity	
60: Eph., Col., Phil., Phem. . . .	82–83
Second Captivity	
68: Hebr., la Tim., Ti., 2a Tim. . .	84–87

*H. H. Somers, *Analyse mathématique du langage*, Nauwelaerts, Louvain, 1959.

small heterogeneity we found in Paul's Letters, but suggests as an explanation a slow evolution of the vocabulary.

The second factor (B) has been discovered by Busemann and is usually measured by the Verb-Adjective–Ratio. Our factor analysis, however, isolates the adjectives as a specific factor, so we recommend the Verb-Substantive–Ratio as a relatively exact measurement of the B-factor. This factor is much more dependent upon genre, style, and personal attitude, upon pathological mental processes and habits.

The third factor (C) is one of the most important for authorship determination because of the presumed dependence upon stylistic habitudes, learning, preferences. In the Epistles of Paul, for example, the prepositions vary significantly from text to text; this is due to the content and the literary theme in Ephesians and Colossians, where the repetition of "in Christo" dominates. Some different attitudes or ideas of the author could very well explain these differences between texts.

Stable personality factors, acquired or inborn, exert an influence upon the fashioning of personal style. Detection of these personal features will be more easy if we possess exact descriptions of all elements of style in quantitative terms: then exact measurement of literary characteristics of speech can reveal individual differences useful in the determination of authorship. The formulation of laws and the investigation of causative factors will help to exclude casual errors.

References

Anderson, T. W. *An Introduction to Multivariate Statistical Analysis.* New York, 1958.

Busemann, A. "Ueber typische und phasische Unterschiede der Kategorialen Sprachform," Z. *Pädag. Psychol.,* 27:415–419 (1926).

Chotlos, J. W. "Studies in Language Behavior. IV. A Statistical and Comparative Analysis of Individual Written Language Samples," *Psychol. Monogr.,* 56:75–111 (1944).

Kendall, M. G. *The Advanced Theory of Statistics.* London, 1946.

Morgenthaler, R. *Statistik des Neutestamentischen Wortschatzes.* Zürich, 1958.

Pearson, E. S., and H. O. Hartley, *Biometrika Tables for Statisticians,* I. Cambridge, 1954.

Shannon, C. E. *The Mathematical Theory of Communication.* Urbana, 1949.

Siegel, S. *Non-parametric Statistics for the Behavioral Sciences.* New York, 1956.

Somers, H. H. *Analyse mathématique du langage: Lois générales et mesures statistiques.* Nauwelaerts, Louvain, 1959.

————. *Analyse statistique du style: Différences individuelles et facteurs psychologiques.* Ms., Louvain, 1960.

————. "The Measurement of Grammatical Constraints," *Language and Speech* (London), 4:150–156 (1961).

SOME INDICATORS OF AUTHORSHIP IN GREEK PROSE

Andrew Q. Morton and Michael Levison

In the study of ancient Greek literature a constant limitation upon scholarship is the uncertainty about the authorship of any work. When books were written and reproduced by hand, the rights and conventions of authorship were very different from what they are now, and what we would consider forgery and imposition were commonly practiced. Booksellers would put an author's name on any text which the name might sell. An unknown author would borrow the name of some illustrious colleague to give his views publicity which they would not receive under his own name. The head of a school, such as the medical school of Hippocrates, would issue under his name all the works which emanated from that school, a practice not yet extinct. Yet another motive for substitution of names is the eternal optimism of the human race. The old picture in the potting shed is a Rembrandt, the old letter in the church cupboard is Pauline. All these are reasons for not accepting the attribution of authorship on any piece of Greek prose without a critical examination.

In an examination of a piece of Greek prose designed to establish its authorship, stylistic evidence plays a large part, for independent evidence from contemporary history is rarely found and often difficult to interpret. Making a decision on the basis of an author's style is hazardous, for an author's style is affected by many things, by the subject on which he writes, by the relationship between his readers and himself, by his mood, by the literary form in which he expresses himself, and by many other influences.

Classical scholars have developed the subjective study of style to a high degree; but their work is carried out under two acute limitations. The first is that their examination is subjective, and subjectivity involves circularity. Suppose that two scholars are asked to examine two pieces of prose and decide whether or not they are by the same author. They will study the texts, make lists of stylistic evidence which may actually be identical, and yet come to quite contrary conclusions about the authorship. The differences which one scholar considers can only be explained by a difference of authorship, the other will explain by a change of mood or a development of mind. The root of this difficulty lies not in any caprice of the scholars but in the circular pattern of their argument. In essence each is saying that he recognizes the mind and style of this author in this work. If one asks how he recognizes the mind and style, he can only reply that he sees them in the genuine work.

The second limitation is best shown by an example. Plato wrote two prose works: one his first work, the *Apology,* and the other his last, the *Seventh Epistle.* These works differ in style, and the authorship of the *Seventh Epistle* has been much questioned. But the decision one reaches about the authorship of the *Seventh Epistle* depends entirely on what changes one thinks forty years might have brought in Plato's works, for there is no more Platonic prose to examine. Only when some general deduction has been made about Greek prose writers as a class can any conclusion be reached about the authorship of the *Seventh Epistle.*

The suggestion that objective criteria of style might be established was made in 1859 by Augustus de Morgan, then Professor of Mathematics at University College London. He argued that everyone knows writers who will use a long word wherever they possibly can, and that the average length of the words used by an author, to be measured by counting the number of letters in each word, might therefore be characteristic of the author. In statistical terms de Morgan was suggesting that all the individual works of an author might be samples drawn from the single population of all his works, and that the differences between works might be explained by the expected differences of random sampling.

It is interesting to note that de Morgan made his suggestion about one of the traditional problems of Greek prose, the authorship of the Epistle to the Hebrews. There is no evidence that his idea was tested on Greek prose, and the first development was the work of T. C. Mendenhall who, between 1896 and 1901, studied word length in English. It is now known that word length depends too much on subject matter to be a reliable indicator of authorship for individual works of Greek prose writers.

The first successful attempt to establish an indicator of authorship for Greek prose was made by W. C. Wake in 1946. Wake, studying the collection of more than 70 works coupled with the name of the great Hippocrates, decided to consider, among other things, their sentence length distributions. He examined the form of these distributions, and tabulated them for a number of writers directly comparable with Hippocrates. Since then, sentence length distributions have been recorded for nearly forty Greek prose writers who lived during the millennium which ended in 400 A.D. In every case the differences between works in the same literary form are only those expected in random sampling.

The interest of the present authors in this problem arose when they were asked by the late Professor G. H. C. Macgregor to determine the authorship of the Pauline Epistles of the New Testament. This is a collection of fourteen pieces of Greek prose which, if written by Paul, must have been written during a period of about fifteen years ending *c.* 65 A.D. Within the corpus there are certain recognized groupings. Romans, I and II Corinthians, and Galatians are all but universally accepted as the work of Paul. At the other end of the scale Hebrews was denied to Paul by the Revised Standard Version of the Bible in 1946, and this lead has been followed by the New English Bible in 1963. Another group, the Pastorals—I and II Timothy and Titus—are thought by many scholars to belong to a later era. I and II Thessalonians are subjects of much debate.

The problem of the authorship of the Pauline Epistles is made difficult by two factors. The first is their small size. Some, like Philemon with only 335 Greek words in its text, are so short that it is impossible to make any judgment at all about their authorship. The second difficulty is that there is no material with which the Epistles may be matched. If one has two pieces of prose A and B and a third piece C, and if one's task is to decide whether C goes with A or with B, then the problem is much simplified, for one can look at the purely personal habits of the authors involved. It is of no consequence that no other author might share these habits. If they are present in all the works of the author under examination, that is logically sufficient. But if one has two texts 'A and B, and the problem is to decide whether or not they were written by the same man, then one must establish rules about all writers of the class to which they belong before any conclusive decision can be made. It is therefore necessary to approach the problem of the authorship of the Pauline Epistles by making some generalizations about writers of the class to which they belong, that is to say writers of homogeneous continuous Greek prose. It is part of this investigation which forms the subject of the present paper.

Let us begin by considering the expression "homogeneous continuous Greek prose." It is hardly necessary to define Greek, or to say more of prose than that it is neither drama nor dialogue nor verse. "Continuous" implies that all the samples are one block of text, and not made up, for example, of the short pieces of prose which are often found between stretches of dialogue. Homogeneous prose is made up and set down by one man, and it is not copied from other sources or based on the text of another author. It is the free composition of one mind, consistent in all its parts.

The first step in the investigation was to approach some independent classical scholars, principally Professor K. J. Dover of St. Andrew's University and Professor E. G. Turner of University College, London, and to ask them to nominate a representative set of Greek prose samples. The samples chosen cover a range of authors; simple and complex stylists; long periods of time; wide ranges of subject matter; and a variety of literary forms. They were designed to be completely representative of writers of Greek prose, and to constitute a fair but searching test for any hypothesis supposed to apply to writers of continuous homogeneous Greek prose. They include works by Herodotus, Thucydides, Plato, Aristotle, Xenophon, Plutarch, Lysias, Isocrates, and Diodorus Siculus.

These samples can be supplemented by others chosen for their direct relevance to the particular problem under examination. For example Philo Judaeus, a Jew writing in Greek c. 40 A.D., makes a most relevant comparison with the Apostle Paul.

A list was next made of the various statistical features to be tested as potential indicators of authorship. By using a digital computer to help in the collection and tabulation of the data, a great deal of tedious counting was eliminated, so that many more features could be examined than in any previous investigation. Furthermore an accuracy of data unobtainable by manual counting was ensured. The samples were prepared for computer input by punching the text onto five-channel paper tape using a teleprinter with a Greek keyboard. The simultaneously produced typescript was proof-read and the tape then edited with the help of a tape reproducer in the usual manner.

Among the data selected for tabulation were details of sentence length, to extend the work previously undertaken by Wake, and details concerning the use of certain common Greek words, for example, the number of occurrences in the sample of the word καɩ, the number of times it occurs in a sentence once, twice, thrice, and so on. All the features listed could have been counted during a single pass of the text through the computer. Two passes were employed, however, and certain cross-checking figures output during each run affording a guard against possible malfunctioning of the computer. The computer nevertheless required only about two minutes per sample to complete its task.

When the standard samples had been investigated, it soon became clear that, in one sense, many of them were superfluous. Stylistic habits are much less affected by time and subject matter than by differences of literary form. Within the same literary form long periods of time and great contrasts in subject have little effect. This makes it possible to use as a reduced set of samples the Greek orators, especially Isocrates and Demosthenes. The Greek orators were not speech makers but professional speech writers. They would write a speech to suit the personality and circumstances of their clients, and used a wide range of literary forms to do this.

Isocrates has 21 works and 9 epistles in his Corpus, of which the work listed as the first one is regarded by the majority of scholars as spurious. He is remarkable for the length of his career. He began his last work, work 12, in his 94th year, laid it aside during a severe illness, and then completed it in his 97th year. His last production was an epistle dating from his 98th year, a year he did not live to complete. The extant works of Isocrates cover 63 years, an unparalleled period for writers of Greek prose. Though lacking the range of style found in Demosthenes, Isocrates goes in for elaboration. He claimed with pride that he had taken ten years to write one oration, and that another of his works contained no example of hiatus — the combination, supposed to be inelegant, of certain vowels at the end of one word and the beginning of the next.

Although the works of Demosthenes are spread over a shorter period, he is admitted to be the supreme stylist. Of him, the Oxford Classical Dictionary says: "His style varies infinitely according to the circumstances; sometimes as simple as Lysias, now polished like Isocrates, again almost as involved as Thucydides, he follows no scholastic rule."

It is not surprising that any hypothesis which applies to Isocrates and Demosthenes is found to apply to the other writers of Greek prose. All the influences which affect style are present in their works to the highest degree.

Sentence Length Distributions

The next stage of our investigation was a repetition and extension of the work undertaken by W. C. Wake on sentence length distributions, referred to previously. Sentence length distributions are positively skew and many of them can be fitted to log-normal distribtions. This does not mean that all writers do produce, or should produce, log-normal distributions, for there are many exceptions. Wake considered the distributions without making any assumptions about their form, and established the standard errors of the constants of the distributions in terms of quartiles and percentiles. He showed that the useful, and independent, constants of the distributions were the mean, the median, the first quartile, and the third quartile, and that the best measure of the proportion of long sentences was the ninth decile. The standard errors of these constants are given in Table 1.*

Where an author writes sentence length distributions which are log-normal, it is possible to calculate the standard errors of the constants of the distribution with more precision. On the other hand, no decision on authorship should be based on the evidence of sentence length in marginal cases where difference between the two methods changes a non-significant difference into a significant one.

*The tables referred to in this paper are assembled at the end of it.

Some examples of sentence length distributions are given in Tables 2–9.

The first (Table 2, i and ii) comes from the two second-century epistles of Clement and illustrates the fact that one should test the parts of works against each other before treating works as a whole. I Clement is large enough to provide four samples of 150 sentences and II Clement one sample of 150 sentences. The samples could all be drawn from a single population.

Tables 3 and 4 show distributions obtained from the famous historians Herodotus and Thucydides. Both wrote their books over a period of about thirty years and covered a wide range of subjects. In each case the sentence length distributions call for no comment; they are homogeneous.

Philo Judaeus was, as we have said, a Jew who wrote in Greek c. 40 A.D. Scholars are inclined to suspect that writing in what is in effect a foreign language must affect style; but the evidence of Table 5 is that it does not affect the consistency of sentence length distributions. Philo not only wrote in free composition, he also compiled commentaries on the Old Testament books. Table 6 shows that his commentaries are consistent with one another but differ from his free composition. This is only to be expected. His method is to copy a short sentence from Genesis and then write his comment upon it. It would appear that one can safely compare commentary with commentary, but not commentary with prose works.

The next example of sentence length distributions comes from the orator Lysias. He represents a puzzling problem in that the hallmark of his style is simplicity, and so any piece of prose which is written with elegant clarity is potentially by Lysias. Scholars have long argued that work 2 is not genuine, and Table 7 shows that this work has its mean, median, and third quartile more than three standard errors from the population constants.

We have already seen that the two authors whose works represent the most challenging and stringent test of a stylistic indicator are Demosthenes and Isocrates.

The Demosthenic Corpus comprises 61 works. Of these H. J. Rose, in his *Handbook of Greek Literature,* lists as definitely not by Demosthenes: works 7, 10, 11, 12, 13, 17, 25, 26, 33, 34, 35, 40, 42, 43, 44, 46, 47, 48, 49, 50, 52, 53, 56, 58, 59, 60, and 61.

Table 8 shows the sentence length distributions for the Demosthenic Corpus. If a range of three standard errors is accepted as the boundary of the population, then eleven of the eighteen works which are classified by Rose as spurious and are long enough to provide samples are rejected. The mean excludes 34, 40, 47, 48, 49, 50, 58, 59, 60; the median excludes 23, 40, 48, 49, 59, 61; the first quartile 23, 40, 49, 50, 59, 60; the third quartile 40, 49, 50, 58, 59; and the ninth decile excludes 40, 44, 49, 50, 59, 61.

One work usually considered genuine is also excluded; for work 23 has its median and first quartile outside the population limits. A look at the oration reveals why this is so. From sentence 75 in the text there is a remarkable run of short sentences—16 out of 25 have fewer than ten words. A reading of the text shows that Demosthenes is quoting from his opponent, and most of these 25 sentences have been put, in whole or in part, in quotation marks by the editor of the Oxford Text. If these 25 sentences are omitted from the sample, or replaced by the next 25 sentences, the sample is in order in all constants. It is such meaningful exceptions which give confidence in the use of sentence length distributions.

Table 9i shows the sentence length distributions of the works of Isocrates and Table 9ii the constants for the eighteen which have more than 90 sentences. Work 12 was Isocrates's last work, which was begun in his 94th year and eventually completed in his 97th. The majority of scholars are in agreement that work 1 is not by Isocrates. Though some believe it to be a compendium which he may have helped to edit, it is not Isocrates's own prose composition.

Not all of these sentence length distributions come from a single population. Taking three standard errors as the population limit, the means, for example, show that works 5 and 12 are not from the same population as works 2, 17, 18, and 19; the medians that works 2 and 17 are not consistent with work 4; while the third quartile differentiates work 4 and work 17.

There can be discerned among the works two distinct groups, one which includes works 4, 5, and 12, the other works 2, 17, 18, and 19. The difference between the groups might be explained in either of two ways. The first possible explanation would be the contrasts in literary form. Works 4, 5, and 12 are the elaborate orations, works 16–21 the informal forensic speeches which Isocrates later disowned as unworthy of his talents. Alternatively, the difference might be explained by the passage of time, for works 16–21 are his earliest productions and works 4, 5, and 12 belong to his later years.

The relative order of the works is known with greater precision than their actual year of publication, so that ranking might be an appropriate procedure. The rank correlation coefficient for mean sentence length and chronological order is 0.51, so that $t = 2.30$ for 15 degrees of freedom. As $t = 2.13$ for $p = 0.05$, this would be considered significant.

Scholars however unanimously prefer the contrast in literary form as the likelier cause. They expect epideictic works to show the elaboration which, in English prose, is found in Milton or Sir

Thomas Browne. It is therefore interesting to note that work 2, which resembles works 16–21, is referred to in work 15. Isocrates, defending his record, has sections read from works 4 and 8, and then asks for part to be read from work 2. He warns of its simplicity: "It is not however composed in the same style as the extracts which have been read. For in them each part is always in accord with that which goes before; but in this, on the contrary, I detach one part from another, and breaking up the discourse, as it were, into what we call general heads, I strive to express in a few words each bit of counsel which I have to offer" (*Antidosis*, 68).

Works 4, 5 and 12 are consistent and cover 41 years of Isocrates's career; works 2 and 18 are 28 years apart; works 15 and 18 are 48 years from one another. So within the same literary form, the sentence length distributions are consistent throughout Isocrates's long career. If we exclude in turn just the two extremes of genre (works 4, 5, 12, and works 2, 16–21), the distributions are consistent for 48 and 41 years respectively.

There are a few further remarks which should be made concerning sentence length distributions. Firstly, sentence length is periodic, groups of long and short sentences alternating, and a minimum sample of the order of 100 sentences is found to be necessary, although, Greek being an inflected language, sentence length is more sensitive than it is in English for the same size of sample. Secondly, there are situations in which sentence length distributions should not be used. They should not be used to compare dialogue with continuous prose. Commentaries written by one author on the works of another writer seem to be consistent with each other but not with the free composition of the same author. When dealing with fragmentary works, such as the later books of the historian Diodorus Siculus, great care should be exercised. Nonetheless all exceptions to homogeneity so far discovered have been meaningful exceptions, so that when used with respect for their limitations, sentence length distributions are an effective instrument of stylistic studies and make a firm foundation for further analysis.

Common Words

There is no subject more generally misunderstood or oversimplified than our use of words. We compose by selecting a word from a number of alternatives and placing it in a phrase, a clause or a sentence. But our choice of word is not a free choice; it is conditioned by many things. It is partly determined by the language we are using; for in English "the man shot the dog" is a very different statement from "the dog shot the man." It also depends on the subject matter, an influence which goes very deep and is consistently underestimated. When the Apostle Paul writes to the Romans about the relationship of his new religion to the Jewish law, this choice of subject not only implies frequent use of the word for "law"; it also means that certain illustrations and comparisons will be apt, and thus likely to be used, while others will be so remote and irrelevant that they will not occur.

Our choice of word is influenced by our cutural background. In his Pelican book *The Americans,* Gorer describes how a boy is sent supperless to bed for bad behavior but rewarded with a cookie or a candy for good behavior. This has so conditioned his vocabulary that all his compliments addressed to the female come straight from the larder; he calls her "sugar," "sweetie," "honey," and offers the ultimate compliment "You look good enough to eat."

Yet another influence on our choice of word is our character and the personal associations which we have with words. When one is trying to identify an author, it is this last influence, his purely personal choices, that one wishes to isolate.

The simplest way to look at the personal factors and exclude all the others is to examine the stylistic habits which embody the commonest words in the language, the words which are unavoidable and must be used in all subjects in every set of circumstances. These are the words which express general relations, whether relations of other words or relations of concepts; they are the conjunctions and particles, the filler words; they are the skeletal structure of our writing. These words are unduly neglected simply because the meaning and literary quality of a piece of prose lie in the rarer words, and the common words tend to slip past unnoticed.

In Greek the commonest word form is the definite article, occurring at rates of about 0.15. Then comes the conjunction καί, roughly the English *and,* with rates around 0.05; and the particle δε, very roughly the English *but,* which occurs at rates of about 0.03. The occurrence of the definite article is not suited to any simple test of authorship as it is tied to nouns, adjectives, and other words, all of which are part of the subject vocabulary. One promising line, now under investigation, is the proportion of nouns which have, or do not have, an accompanying definite article.

The Occurrence of καί

The conjunction καί is a word no writer of Greek prose can escape. Repetitions of καί constitute 5 per cent of all the words of Greek prose ever written, and of all Greek prose sentences in existence more than half contain at least one καί. The occurrence of καί is substantially independent of subject matter. Writing of gardening, of war and of cooking, you would expect to use different nouns and adjectives, but it is difficult to see why you should use *and* any more in one subject than another.

The simplest way to look at the occurrence of καɩ in a work is to divide the text into occurrences of καɩ and occurrences of all other words, and treat the rate of occurrence in terms of simple sampling. This is testing the hypothesis that an author writes all his works with a constant proportion of καɩ, and that the differences between works are only the expected differences of random sampling.

Table 10 shows the occurrence of καɩ in 36 samples from the *History* of Herodotus. For this table, χ^2 is 32.4 for 35 degrees of freedom, so that differences between the samples would arise by chance along just about one trial in two. Table 11 shows comparable samples from the *History* of Thucydides. In each case the sample is the first fifty sentences of the book, and for this table χ^2 is 14.0 for 31 degrees of freedom. Table 12 shows the occurrence of καɩ in a number of works of Plato, written over a period of more than thirty years. If the questioned Seventh Epistle is omitted from the table, χ^2 is 3.0 for 6 degrees of freedom; and if it is included χ^2 is 3.2 for 7 degrees of freedom.

These examples illustrate the fact that, for works in the same literary form at least, an author's habit of using καɩ remains unaffected by periods of time measured in decades and by wide ranges of subject matter.

Table 13 shows the occurrence of καɩ in the works and epistles of Isocrates. Taken as a whole the group is heterogeneous. If the works are split up into genres, following the editors of the Loeb text, then the groups of works in the same genre are homogeneous. For the epistles, χ^2 is 12.5 for 8 degrees of freedom; for the forensic speeches, works 16–21, 10.5 for 5 degrees of freedom; for the hortatory pair, works 2 and 3, 3.6 for 1 degree of freedom; for the epideictic works, works 9–12, 4.2 for 3 degrees of freedom; and for the two essays on education, works 13 and 15, χ^2 is less than 0.1 for 1 degree of freedom.

The suggestion is that comparisons between works in the same literary genre are straightforward. But it is sometimes desired to compare works in different genres. Such comparisons might be made in one of two ways. First, we might approach the statistical analysis in a different manner, treating the rate of occurrence of καɩ as constant withing each work but differing from one work to another. Now, for an event occurring at rate p, the mean number of occurrences in n trials is np, and the standard error of the proportion of events occurring is $\sqrt{(pq/n)}$, where q=1-p. For a rate of occurrences varying from one set of trials to another, however, this standard error increases, because it must include a term due to the changing rate in the population. The standard error of a variable rate of occurrence is

$$\left\{ \frac{p_0 q_0}{n} + \frac{n-1}{n} \left(\frac{pq}{n} \right) \right\}^{1/2}$$

where p_0, q_0 are the values for the whole population.

For the twenty-nine works of Isocrates, for example, the mean rate of occurrence of καί is 0.0469, if all the works are taken together. The mean of the twenty-nine sample means is 0.0468. The theoretical variance is 0.00053, and the value obtained from the samples 0.00057. For the first work, not by Isocrates, the proportion of καί is 0.0240, and the standard error of this proportion, including the term for the variable rate, is 0.005. Thus this work lies five standard errors from the mean for all the genuine works.

The disadvantage of this approach is that by increasing the standard errors one can tell nothing at all about small samples. The lowest rate of occurrence of καί which has been counted in any sample is 0.02, the highest 0.08. With small samples, such as the epistles and work 13, the standard errors would be so great that one would be unable to distinguish between the most extreme habits found in Greek prose writers.

The alternative procedure is to look at the occurrence of καί in sentences, a presentation which means much more to a classical scholar than any other way of displaying the information. Table 14 shows the occurrence of καί in sentences in the works of Isocrates and the fit of the data to a negative binomial of the same constants. If the distributions are assembled in a contingency table and compared with the negative binomial expectations, the values of χ^2 are as recorded in Table 15.

Only two values call for comment. Work 1, the rejected work, has $\chi^2 = 78.8$ for 2 degrees of freedom, a highly significant difference. Work 12 has $\chi^2 = 33.4$ for 4 degrees of freedom, which is also highly significant. This sample serves to illustrate the limitation of this method. Although work 12 shows a highly significant difference, the table does not reveal whether this difference is due to the occurrence of καί or to some feature of the sentence length distribution. A reference back to the rates of occurrence of καί in all the works indicates that the rate for work 12 is just about the mean rate for all the works, while an inspection of the sentence length distribution shows that this is anomalous. The sentence length anomaly is responsible for this highly significant difference. It would appear that the occurrence of καί in an author's works should be looked at by both methods; there are circumstances where one or the other alone could be misleading.

Other aspects of the occurrence of καὶ which have been examined are its occurrence in small samples, that is to say samples of twenty successive words (approximately the inverse of the rate of occurrence), also the spacing between successive καὶs, and the position of the first καὶ in the sentence. The occurrence in small samples gives a distribution similar to the distribution in sentences with a smaller variance. This might be expected, for the probability of finding 19 καὶs in a twenty-word sample must be near to zero, but Isocrates did write a sentence with 19 καὶs. The only advantage of using small samples is that it overcomes one of the rooted objections about which certain scholars argue, the punctuation of the texts. Ancient texts had rudimentary punctuation so that the markings are largely the work of the modern editors. It has been shown on a number of occasions that the differences between editors is negligible compared to sampling differences, but this is something scholars do not feel intuitively to be true. By avoiding sentence marking completely one can show that the results still stand.

The spacing between καὶs usually fits a negative exponential distribution, and the form of the distribution means that this cannot make a sensitive test. The same applies even more to the position of the first καὶ in the sentence. This habit differs from author to author, but only large samples and bold contrasts will give any positive result.

The Occurrence of δε

A special feature of the particle δε is that it has two distinct positions. It is commonly found as the second or third word of a sentence, and it also occurs in a number of constructions later in the sentence. This makes it possible to ignore the semantic context of the word and ask the simple question whether a sentence has δε as its second or third word.

Table 16 shows the occurrence of δε at the beginning of sentences in each book of the *History* of Herodotus, and Table 17 the comparable figures for the *History* of Thucydides. In each case the samples differ only by the expected differences of random sampling; for Herodotus χ^2 is 13.4 for 8 degrees of freedom, for Thucydides 5.5 for 7 degrees of freedom. Table 18 shows the occurrence of δε at the start of the sentences of the works of Lysias, and for the nine works χ^2 is 7.0 for 8 degrees of freedom. The widely disputed work 2 is not distinguishable from the other works in respect of this habit.

Table 19 shows the occurrence of δε at the beginning of the sentence for the works of Demosthenes. For the 27 accepted works with ninety or more sentences, χ^2 is 10.9 for 26 degrees of freedom. The proportion of sentences in these works with δε as word two or three is 0.225, while the proportion without is 0.775. Of the questioned works 14 are found to be more than two standard errors from the mean rate for the accepted ones. One of the accepted works, work 6, also lies more than two standard errors from this mean. An inspection of the work reveals the reason. The central section of the work, from sentence 25 to sentence 60, has a high proportion of sentences which begin with a few words taken from the opposing argument and placed, by the editor of the Oxford text, in quotation marks.

Table 20 shows the comparable data for the works of Isocrates, the only author to show heterogeneity in this habit. Examination of the data in order of relative chronology shows that the passage of time is unlikely to explain the variations satisfactorily. The alternative explanation, the difference in literary form, seems acceptable; for if the works are once again grouped into genres we find that the forensic speeches (works 16–21) have $\chi^2=4.2$ for 3 degrees of freedom, the hortatory pair (works 2, 3) has $\chi^2=3.0$ for 1 degree of freedom, the epideictic works (works 9–12) have $\chi^2=5.6$ for 3 degrees of freedom; the educational works (works 13, 15) have $\chi^2=0.5$ for 1 degree of freedom: the miscellaneous political speeches (works 4–8, 14) $\chi^2=10.0$ for 5 degrees of freedom. The only group with which the rejected work 1 would be compatible would be the hortatory pair, works 2 and 3.

This simple test is surprisingly effective. Though large samples, 200 sentences or more, are required to separate authors whose rates differ by a margin of five per cent, yet the habit is one in which authors differ widely, and large contrasts are found to be not uncommon.

The particle δε also occurs in a variety of constructions later in sentences. In this case the simplest procedure is to tabulate the number of such occurrences in each sentence of the sample, and examine the data in a contingency table. Application of this analysis confirms the results previously noted. Once again the sets of samples from the Histories of Herodotus and Thucydides are each found to display homogeneity. Those from the genuine works of Isocrates are heterogeneous, but reveal consistency when grouped according to genre; while work 1 does not conform to any of the groups.

Conclusion

What conclusions may be drawn from our investigations at this stage? First, it is clear that in order to test any hypothesis regarding authorship it is essential to look at a variety of authors and examine a wide range of works in different literary forms. It is apparent that stylistic habits vary little within the same literary genre compared to the variations found between genres. Undoubtedly authors have stylistic habits which persist for long periods and over a variety of subject matters, so that it is possible to establish statistical indicators of authorship, that is to say numerically expressible stylistic habits for which the differences between works of one author are just the expected differences of random sampling.

Situations can arise, however, in which great care must be exercised in making any judgment on authorship. If one has a group of works in one genre (or in similar genres) and an isolated work in a contrasting genre, it may not be possible to decide whether a statistically significant difference is due to the difference of genre or to a difference in habit. Yet another situation in which formidable difficulties are encountered may be illustrated from the works of Demosthenes. Some of the works in the Corpus are agreed not to be his—to have no connection with Demosthenes at all. Usually the statistically significant differences found in comparisons of habits are very large. But other works are speeches written by Demosthenes and given to clients who are thought to have amended them to suit their own ideas. The result is a mixed text and this type of work often gives rise to differences which are marginally significant. The decision about the Demosthenic authorship may depend as much on the interpretation of the adjective "Demosthenic" as on the statistical evidence.

This paper has briefly summarized part of a large-scale investigation into the unconscious habits of Greek prose writers. When such an investigation has shown that all authors of the class share certain habits but express the habits in their own way, then it is possible to separate the works attached to any author's name into those which there is no reason to deny him, those which there is good reason to deny him, and, possibly, a number upon which it is hazardous to judge. Attention can then be transferred to the personal habits of the individual writers—habits which are likely to be more sensitive indicators of authorship because they are personal—and the results can be checked against the primary indicators.

In the course of these investigations the authors have gathered statistical information about a number of Greek prose writers, Plato, Aristotle, Xenophon, Plutarch, Strabo, and Diodorus Siculus among them. The limitations of space preclude publishing these tables in full, but Dr. Levison will make them available to any scholar who would find them of special value in his research.

References

Demosthenes, *Orations,* ed. S. H. Butcher and W. Rennie. 4 vols. Oxford University Press; reprint 1958.

Herodotus, *Historiae,* ed C. Hude. 2 vols. 3rd ed. Oxford University Press; reprint 1962.

Isocrates, *Works* (Loeb Library). Vols. 1 and 2, ed. G. Norlin, 1928, 1929; Vol. 3, ed. Van Hook, 1945.

Lysias, *Orations,* ed. C. Hude. Oxford University Press, 1912; reprint 1960.

Plato, *Works,* ed. J. Burnet. 5 vols. Oxford University Press, 1900; reprint 1958.

Rose, H. J., *A Handbook of Greek Literature.* 4th ed. London: Methuen, 1951.

Thucydides, *Historiae,* ed. H. S. Jones. 2 vols. Oxford University Press, 1900, 1902; reprint, 1956, 1958.

Wake, W. C. "Sentence Length Distribution of Greek Authors," *J. R. Statist. Soc.,* 120:331–346 (1957).

TABLE 1. Standard Errors of the Constants of Sentence Length Distributions

Constant	Standard Error
Mean	Standard Deviation/ $N^{1/2}$
Median	$N^{1/2}/2Y$
First and Third Quartiles	$(3N)^{1/2}/4Y$
Ninth Decile	$3N^{1/2}/10Y$
Inter-quartile Distance	$(E_1 + E_2)^{1/2}$

where N is the number of sentences in the sample,

Y is the mean frequency for the cell in which the constant falls,

E_1, E_2 are the standard errors of the first and third quartiles.

TABLE 2 (i). Sentence Length Distributions — The Epistles of Clement

No. of words in sentence	1st Clement						2nd Clement			1st & 2nd Clement Total
	1	2	Sample 3	4	Remainder	Total	Sample 1	Remainder	Total	
1-5	26	26	32	27	11	122	21	9	30	152
6-10	42	45	42	43	20	192	41	16	57	249
11-15	34	42	41	33	22	172	43	15	58	230
16-20	13	13	19	22	12	79	18	11	29	108
21-25	16	9	8	8	14	55	14	8	22	77
26-30	6	5	4	8	4	27	7	4	11	38
31-35	5	5	1	5	4	20	6	3	9	29
36-40	3	3	--	1	4	11	--	--	--	11
41-45	--	2	1	1	3	7	--	--	--	7
46-50	2	--	--	--	--	2	--	--	--	2
51-55	--	--	--	1	--	1	--	2	2	3
56-60	1	--	1	1	2	5	--	--	--	5
61-65	2	--	1	--	1	4	--	--	--	4
66-70	--	--	--	--	--	--	--	--	--	--
71-75	--	--	--	--	1	1	--	--	--	1
76-80	--	--	--	--	--	--	--	--	--	--
81-85	--	--	--	--	1	1	--	--	--	1
No. of Sentences	150	150	150	150	99	699	150	68	218	917

TABLE 2 (ii).   Sentence Length Distributions —
The Epistles of Clement

Work	Mean	Stand'd Error	Median	Stand'd Error	First Quartile	Stand'd Error	Third Quartile	Stand'd Error	Ninth Decile	Stand'd Error
1st CLEMENT:										
sample										
1	14.6	0.9	11.0	0.9	6.4	0.6	19.0	2.0	28.3	3.1
2	12.9	0.8	10.5	0.7	6.4	0.6	14.9	0.6	25.0	3.7
3	12.9	0.7	10.1	0.7	5.6	0.6	14.7	0.6	20.6	4.6
4	13.3	0.8	10.8	0.9	6.2	0.6	17.2	1.2	26.3	2.3
Total	14.0	0.4	11.2	0.4	6.4	0.3	17.4	0.7	26.7	1.5
2nd CLEMENT:										
sample										
1	13.3	0.6	11.5	0.7	7.0	0.6	17.1	1.5	24.3	2.6
Total	13.9	0.6	11.9	0.6	7.1	0.6	18.2	1.1	23.8	1.0
Grand Total	14.1	0.07	11.3	0.33	6.6	0.26	17.6	0.6	26.5	1.2

TABLE 3 (i).   Sentence Length Distributions — Herodotus

No. of words in sentence	Book								
	1	2	3	4	5	6	7	8	9
1-5	16	6	7	8	13	8	10	9	13
6-10	35	33	48	38	47	30	36	42	45
11-15	47	34	37	49	43	35	46	43	54
16-20	39	39	34	38	32	41	38	33	28
21-25	24	26	21	24	26	29	23	27	23
26-30	16	22	23	15	14	30	19	18	14
31-35	11	19	6	15	9	10	10	10	6
36-40	5	5	11	8	2	3	4	9	9
41-45	4	4	6	2	5	6	4	4	4
46-50	1	6	2	----	4	5	5	3	----
51-55	1	1	3	1	2	1	3	1	2
56-60	1	----	2	----	----	1	2	----	1
61-65	----	----	----	1	2	----	----	----	----
66-70	----	----	----	----	----	----	----	1	----
71-75	----	1	----	----	----	1	----	----	----
76-80	----	2	----	----	1	----	----	----	1
81-85	----	1	----	----	----	----	----	----	----
86-90	----	1	----	----	----	----	----	----	----
101-105	----	----	----	1	----	----	----	----	----
No. of sentences	200	200	200	200	200	200	200	200	200

TABLE 3 (ii).   Sentence Length Distributions — Herodotus

Book	Mean	Stand'd Error	Median	Stand'd Error	First Quartile	Stand'd Error	Third Quartile	Stand'd Error	Ninth Decile	Stand'd Error
1	17.8	0.5	15.3	0.9	8.4	0.9	22.7	1.3	31.4	1.9
2	22.0	1.0	18.5	0.9	11.6	0.9	27.7	1.4	36.0	4.2
3	19.4	0.8	16.2	1.0	9.5	0.6	25.7	1.3	36.8	1.9
4	18.9	0.9	15.7	0.9	10.4	0.6	23.5	1.3	32.7	1.4
5	17.7	0.8	14.7	0.8	8.9	0.7	22.9	1.2	32.8	2.4
6	20.5	0.8	18.3	0.9	11.7	0.9	26.2	1.0	33.5	2.1
7	19.2	0.8	16.1	0.9	10.4	0.7	22.2	1.3	34.0	2.1
8	18.8	0.8	15.9	1.1	9.9	0.7	22.4	1.1	34.0	2.1
9	17.4	0.8	13.9	0.7	9.1	0.7	22.2	1.3	32.5	3.5

TABLE 4 (i).   Sentence Length Distributions — Thucydides

No. of words in sentence	Book							
	1	2	3	4	5	6	7	8
1-5	5	5	5	4	5	6	6	12
6-10	28	32	32	20	29	17	24	19
11-15	36	36	37	38	31	29	31	36
16-20	25	34	34	34	35	36	31	28
21-25	32	25	25	27	27	34	31	31
26-30	17	17	16	21	20	18	23	12
31-35	12	14	18	24	12	23	15	17
36-40	12	5	12	10	10	4	10	10
41-45	9	8	11	9	8	5	7	13
46-50	10	9	2	3	6	4	6	5
51-55	6	5	4	1	6	4	3	3
56-60	----	----	----	4	2	5	3	1
61-65	3	3	1	1	2	5	4	3
67-70	4	2	2	1	1	2	1	4
71-75	----	1	1	1	1	2	2	1
76-80	----	1	----	1	1	----	----	2
81-85	----	----	----	1	1	1	1	1
86-90	----	1	----	----	----	1	----	----
91-95	----	1	----	----	----	1	2	1
96-100	----	----	----	----	1	----	----	1
101-105	----	----	----	----	----	----	----	----
106-110	----	----	----	----	----	2	----	----
111-115	----	----	----	----	----	----	----	----
116-120	1	1	----	----	----	----	----	----
121-125	----	----	----	----	1	----	----	----
126-130	----	----	----	----	----	1	----	----
155-160	----	----	----	----	1	----	----	----
No. of sentences	200	200	200	200	200	200	200	200

TABLE 4 (ii). Sentence Length Distributions — Thucydides

Book	Mean	Stand'd Error	Median	Stand'd Error	First Quartile	Stand'd Error	Third Quartile	Stand'd Error	Ninth Decile	Stand'd Error
1	24.9	1.2	20.9	1.1	12.4	0.9	32.9	2.5	47.0	2.1
2	24.4	1.3	19.0	1.0	11.8	0.9	30.4	2.2	46.1	2.4
3	22.5	1.0	18.8	1.0	11.8	0.8	30.3	1.7	40.5	1.9
4	24.2	1.0	20.7	1.3	13.4	0.8	31.3	1.3	39.9	2.1
5	24.8	1.4	20.0	1.0	12.6	1.0	31.3	2.5	47.5	3.5
6	27.5	1.3	21.8	1.0	14.7	1.1	32.2	1.3	55.0	5.3
7	25.3	1.2	21.3	1.1	13.2	1.0	31.3	2.0	46.7	3.5
8	25.4	1.3	20.8	1.1	12.6	0.9	33.5	1.8	47.0	4.2

TABLE 5 (i). Sentence Length Distributions — Philo Judaeus

No. of Words in Sentence	1	2	3	4	5	6
1-5	7	9	12	9	16	12
6-10	27	34	29	34	30	25
11-15	42	46	27	45	39	28
16-20	33	27	32	27	40	29
21-25	21	19	26	19	25	14
26-30	21	20	14	20	20	18
31-35	12	9	14	10	13	8
36-40	14	13	11	13	6	3
41-45	13	4	7	4	8	5
46-50	2	7	9	7	--	3
51-55	4	1	6	1	--	5
56-60	1	4	2	4	--	--
61-65	2	--	3	--	1	2
66-70	--	4	2	4	--	--
71-75	--	--	2	--	--	--
76-80	--	--	1	--	--	--
81-85	--	1	--	1	1	--
86-90	--	--	--	--	--	--
91-95	--	1	--	1	1	--
96-100	--	1	--	1	--	2
101-105	--	--	1	--	--	--
116-120	1	--	--	--	--	--
121-125	--	--	1	--	--	--
146-150	--	--	1	--	--	--
No. of sentence	200	200	200	200	200	154

1. On the Creation
2. Sacrifice of Cain and Abel
3. Cherubim

4. Worse Attacks the Better
5. Posterity of Cain
6. Giants

TABLE 5 (ii).   Sentence Length Distributions — Philo Judaeus

Work	Mean	Stand'd Error	Median	Stand'd Error	First Quartile	Stand'd Error	Third Quartile	Stand'd Error	Ninth Decile	Stand'd Error
1	22.7	1.0	18.6	1.1	11.9	0.7	29.8	1.5	41.2	1.6
2	22.6	1.2	17.0	1.3	10.8	0.7	28.7	1.5	43.7	5.5
3	25.8	1.5	20.0	1.1	11.7	1.1	33.6	2.2	49.4	2.4
4	22.4	1.2	17.2	1.4	10.8	0.7	29.0	1.5	43.7	5.5
5	21.6	0.9	17.1	0.9	10.6	0.8	25.0	1.2	38.5	3.5
6	20.2	0.9	17.1	1.1	10.3	1.0	27.1	1.5	41.6	2.3

TABLE 6 (i).   Sentence Length Distributions — Philo

No. of Words in Sentence	Allegorical Interpretation of Genesis			
	Sample 1	Sample 2	Sample 3	Total
1-5	22	20	25	67
6-10	47	44	47	138
11-15	37	46	27	110
16-20	38	38	41	117
21-25	22	24	16	62
26-30	17	9	13	39
31-35	7	9	11	27
36-40	5	5	2	12
41-45	3	3	11	17
46-50	1	--	--	1
51-55	--	--	1	1
56-60	--	--	2	2
61-65	--	--	1	1
66-70	--	1	1	2
71-75	1	1	--	2
76-80	--	--	2	2
No. of Sentences	200	200	200	600

TABLE 6 (ii).   Sentence Length Distributions — Philo
Allegorical Interpretation of Genesis

Work	Mean	Stand'd Error	Median	Stand'd Error	First Quartile	Stand'd Error	Third Quartile	Stand'd Error	Ninth Decile	Stand'd Error
1	16.3	0.7	14.2	0.9	8.0	0.7	21.4	1.4	29.1	1.2
2	16.3	0.7	13.9	0.9	8.4	0.7	20.4	1.3	29.9	2.4
3	18.2	1.0	15.1	0.9	7.7	0.7	23.1	1.9	35.0	1.9
Total	16.9	0.5	14.3	0.6	8.0	0.4	22.5	0.9	31.3	1.4

TABLE 7 (i). Sentence Length Distributions — Lysias

No. of words in Sentence	Work									
	1	2	3	6	7	12	13	14	19	20
1-5	10	1	4	12	2	15	11	3	7	4
6-10	21	19	10	20	15	35	46	14	39	35
11-15	30	20	20	36	23	48	40	16	26	23
16-20	18	13	20	30	16	28	33	14	27	12
21-25	15	18	14	14	10	22	24	16	32	20
26-30	13	17	10	6	10	13	16	11	10	7
31-35	6	12	5	6	8	10	10	3	9	5
36-40	6	12	5	12	1	11	7	5	4	3
41-45	2	12	3	1	5	6	7	5	5	1
46-50	1	4	3	2	2	5	2	6	2	--
51-55	1	--	2	--	3	2	1	2	1	--
56-60	2	2	1	1	--	3	1	1	1	1
61-65	1	--	--	1	--	--	1	--	1	1
66-70	--	1	--	--	--	1	--	--	--	--
71-75	--	4	--	--	--	1	1	--	--	--
76-80	--	1	1	--	--	--	--	--	--	--
90-95	--	--	--	--	--	--	--	1	--	--
96-100	--	1	--	--	--	--	--	1	--	--
101-105	--	2	--	--	--	--	--	--	--	--
121-125	--	1	--	--	--	--	--	--	--	--
No. of Sentences	126	140	98	141	95	200	200	98	164	112

TABLE 7 (ii). Sentence Length Distributions — Lysias

Work	Mean	Stand'd Error	Median	Stand'd Error	First Quartile	Stand'd Error	Third Quartile	Stand'd Error	Ninth Decile	Stand'd Error
1	19.2	1.2	15.6	1.6	10.1	0.8	25.2	1.9	35.3	2.8
2	29.2	1.7	24.7	1.6	13.8	1.3	37.1	2.1	47.5	4.4
3	22.3	1.0	18.5	1.2	12.6	1.0	27.8	2.1	40.3	5.0
6	18.5	1.0	15.4	1.0	10.5	0.7	22.8	1.8	36.2	1.5
7	21.0	1.2	17.3	1.5	12.0	0.9	27.6	2.1	41.5	2.9
12	20.0	1.0	15.4	1.3	10.0	0.9	25.8	2.4	39.1	1.8
13	18.8	0.9	15.5	1.1	9.2	0.7	24.2	1.2	35.0	2.1
14	23.1	1.6	20.6	1.5	12.3	1.3	29.8	1.9	48.0	7.4
19	19.0	0.9	16.9	1.2	9.4	0.7	28.8	2.8	33.7	2.1
20	17.2	1.0	13.7	1.2	8.4	0.7	22.5	1.2	29.9	3.2

TABLE 8 (i). Sentence Length Distributions — Demosthenes

No. of words in sentence	Work											
	3	4	6	7	8	9	10	13	14	15	18	19
1-5	20	29	17	6	26	28	14	9	15	3	31	28
6-10	25	19	19	12	35	40	38	10	19	12	29	42
11-15	27	29	17	18	30	35	39	24	21	21	36	33
16-20	25	30	14	14	30	35	21	15	20	19	25	26
21-25	16	10	7	14	15	20	18	9	20	16	19	11
26-30	7	6	7	11	21	17	21	12	7	11	16	14
31-35	3	9	5	10	13	10	16	7	7	12	10	13
36-40	6	7	2	8	10	7	4	4	6	3	7	9
41-45	2	4	2	3	7	3	11	2	2	2	4	4
46-50	2	2	2	1	4	4	4	3	5	2	6	4
51-55	--	4	4	--	1	5	1	1	1	1	5	3
56-60	1	4	--	1	1	1	3	1	1	--	4	3
61-65	--	1	--	--	--	2	3	2	1	1	1	3
66-70	1	1	--	--	1	2	1	1	--	--	2	2
71-75	--	2	--	1	3	1	4	1	1	--	1	1
76-80	--	1	2	--	--	--	1	--	--	--	1	--
81-85	1	1	1	--	1	--	--	--	--	--	--	1
86-90	--	--	--	--	1	--	--	1	1	--	1	1
91-95	--	--	1	--	--	--	--	--	--	--	--	1
96-100	--	--	--	--	1	2	--	--	--	--	--	--
101-105	--	--	--	1	--	--	--	--	--	--	--	1
106-110	--	--	--	--	--	--	--	--	--	--	1	--
111-115	--	--	--	--	--	--	--	--	--	--	1	--
151-155	--	--	--	1	--	--	--	--	--	--	--	--
No. of sentences	136	159	100	101	200	212	199	102	127	103	200	200

TABLE 8 (i) (contd.) Sentence Length Distributions—Demosthenes

No. of words in sentence	Work												
	20	21	22	23	24	25	27	29	30	32	34	35	37
1-5	20	19	34	44	36	28	13	23	7	14	8	14	42
6-10	29	29	24	36	34	29	33	37	16	13	27	32	38
11-15	38	31	34	41	34	38	30	28	10	23	35	24	47
16-20	29	31	31	19	28	31	40	26	12	18	28	14	27
21-25	26	26	32	23	18	24	29	21	15	6	21	19	33
26-30	22	14	17	13	20	12	20	23	15	6	12	12	13
31-35	11	11	12	5	9	7	15	7	6	3	9	5	6
36-40	9	12	7	4	4	7	5	7	7	6	5	8	6
41-45	7	8	4	4	7	9	9	8	3	3	3	6	4
46-50	1	4	2	3	1	4	5	5	4	3	2	..	1
51-55	2	5	..	5	1	3	..	2	..	2	1	2	3
56-60	..	..	1	2	3	4	2	..	1	..	1	2	1
61-65	1	4	..	..	2	1	1	2	2	1	1	1	..
66-70	1	..	..	1	..	..	2	..	1	1	1	..	..
71-75	..	1	..	..	1	1	2	2	1	..	1	..	..
76-80	2	1	2	..	..	1	..	..	..	..	1	1	..
81-85	1	1	..	..	..	1	..	..	..	..	..	..	..
86-90	1	1	..	..	..	..	..	..	..	..	1	1	1
91-95	..	..	..	..	2	..	..	..	..	..	..	..	1
96-100	..	..	..	..	..	..	..	..	..	..	..	..	..
106-110	..	1	..	..	..	..	..	..	..	..	..	1	..
111-115	..	1	..	..	..	..	..	1	..	..	..	..	..
116-120	..	..	..	..	..	..	1	..	..	..	..	..	..
No. of sentences	200	200	200	200	200	170	207	192	100	99	157	142	223

TABLE 8(i)(contd.). Sentence Length Distributions—Demosthenes

No. of words in sentence	Work											
	38	39	40	41	43	44	45	47	48	49	50	55
1-5	11	25	5	9	27	12	23	6	8	7	5	5
6-10	21	30	13	15	29	25	28	31	25	15	24	19
11-15	15	36	13	23	31	47	39	41	15	24	29	26
16-20	18	24	19	10	26	44	41	24	28	18	20	17
21-25	13	12	14	10	21	22	21	18	21	25	16	17
26-30	5	17	15	15	12	21	13	27	14	11	18	6
31-35	5	7	17	3	16	10	12	15	11	10	15	9
36-40	5	4	9	5	7	10	11	11	9	12	6	1
41-45	2	3	3	3	10	3	5	2	6	10	8	3
46-50	2	2	8	1	4	3	_	4	4	8	7	1
51-55	1	1	4	2	6	_	_	4	3	2	3	1
56-60	_	1	3	1	2	_	3	3	1	1	2	1
61-65	_	1	1	1	1	7	1	2	_	4	1	2
66-70	_	_	2	_	5	_	1	1	1	5	1	_
71-75	_	_	2	_	1	_	_	3	1	_	1	_
76-80	_	_	_	_	2	1	1	3	1	3	2	_
81-85	_	_	2	_	_	_	_	1	_	_	2	_
86-90	_	_	1	_	_	_	_	1	_	1	_	_
91-95	_	_	_	_	_	_	_	2	_	_	_	_
96-100	_	_	_	_	_	_	_	_	_	_	_	_
101-105	_	_	_	_	_	_	_	_	_	_	1	_
106-110	_	_	_	_	1	_	_	_	1	_	_	_
116-120	1	_	_	_	1	_	_	_	_	_	1	_
130-135	_	_	1	_	_	_	_	_	_	_	1	_
156-160	_	_	_	_	_	_	_	1	_	_	_	_
No. of sentences	99	163	132	98	200	199	200	200	149	154	165	108

TABLE 8 (i) (contd.) Sentence Length Distributions—Demosthenes

No. of words in sentence	Work					
	56	57	58	59	60	61
1-5	8	25	23	7	3	5
6-10	28	31	26	23	11	18
11-15	21	37	30	24	27	23
16-20	25	32	22	27	16	23
21-25	16	26	21	22	18	26
26-30	12	20	11	16	15	20
31-35	12	9	17	21	9	11
36-40	1	8	13	11	6	6
41-45	2	5	5	12	1	3
46-50	3	2	4	5	4	5
51-55	4	3	2	6	4	2
56-60	--	--	3	4	--	2
61-65	2	--	3	7	--	--
66-70	1	2	--	3	--	--
71-75	1	--	4	2	--	2
76-80	2	--	4	--	--	--
81-85	2	--	--	2	--	--
86-90	--	--	--	1	--	2
91-95	--	--	2	--	--	--
96-100	--	--	--	1	--	--
101-105	--	--	--	2	--	--
106-110	--	--	--	1	--	--
126-130	1	--	--	--	--	--
131-135	--	--	--	1	--	1
141-145	--	--	--	1	--	--
156-160	--	--	--	1	--	--
No. of sentences	141	200	200	200	114	149

TABLE 8 (ii). Sentence Length Distributions — Demosthenes

Work	Mean	Stand'd Error	Median	Stand'd Error	First Quartile	Stand'd Error	Third Quartile	Stand'd Error	Ninth Decile	Stand'd Error
3	17.2	1.1	14.3	1.1	7.8	1.0	21.6	1.6	34.0	5.9
4	19.9	1.4	15.4	1.1	7.8	1.4	21.9	2.7	40.3	4.7
6	20.0	1.8	15.1	1.8	7.1	1.1	25.7	3.1	45.0	7.5
7	23.8	1.8	20.2	1.8	12.0	1.2	30.4	2.2	38.6	1.9
8	20.6	1.1	16.5	1.2	8.4	0.9	28.3	1.5	40.0	2.1
9	19.8	1.1	15.4	1.0	8.1	0.8	25.3	1.8	44.7	7.3
10	22.3	1.1	17.0	1.7	9.7	0.8	29.6	1.5	43.7	1.8
13	22.7	1.8	19.3	1.7	11.9	0.9	33.6	3.1	44.5	7.5
14	20.5	1.3	17.1	1.4	9.4	1.3	25.2	3.6	39.4	2.8
15	21.4	1.1	18.7	1.3	12.6	1.1	27.8	2.0	34.5	1.3
18	21.7	1.4	15.8	1.4	8.3	1.1	25.0	1.6	37.9	3.0
19	21.0	1.3	14.6	1.1	7.5	0.7	28.6	2.2	45.0	5.3
20	20.7	1.1	17.2	1.2	10.1	0.8	30.0	1.3	37.7	2.3
21	23.0	1.3	18.4	1.1	10.3	1.0	24.2	2.2	44.4	2.6
22	18.3	0.9	16.3	1.1	8.3	1.3	22.2	1.0	33.3	1.8
23	16.4	1.2	12.4	0.9	5.8	0.9	25.0	1.3	34.0	4.2
24	18.6	1.1	14.4	1.0	7.1	0.9	25.0	1.7	36.3	5.3
25	20.2	1.1	15.7	1.2	8.8	1.0	27.6	2.6	37.8	2.3
27	21.5	1.1	18.4	0.9	11.0	1.0	27.0	1.6	40.7	2.4
29	20.3	1.1	16.5	1.3	8.4	0.8	30.0	1.3	40.5	2.6
30	23.7	1.5	21.7	2.5	11.0	2.2	25.2	1.4	43.3	5.0
32	19.2	1.4	14.8	1.1	7.6	1.7	24.7	3.6	41.7	5.0
34	22.7	1.1	16.5	1.1	10.6	0.8	26.5	1.3	38.3	3.8
35	20.6	1.4	15.4	2.1	8.3	0.8	22.0	2.2	39.9	2.2
37	16.5	0.9	13.4	0.8	6.8	0.9	21.9	1.0	30.6	3.7
38	17.9	1.3	14.2	1.7	7.7	1.0	20.7	1.7	40.0	7.5
39	16.9	0.9	13.7	0.9	7.6	0.9	22.6	2.3	31.9	2.7
40	29.6	1.7	25.7	1.9	15.5	1.3	36.7	1.5	53.5	4.3
41	20.1	1.4	16.0	2.2	10.1	0.9	27.2	1.4	38.2	3.0
43	23.3	1.4	17.5	1.4	9.3	1.1	31.3	1.9	46.3	5.3
44	19.5	0.8	16.8	0.8	11.4	0.7	22.7	1.4	29.8	1.0
45	19.3	0.9	16.2	0.9	9.8	0.8	24.3	1.5	36.4	1.8
47	25.7	1.5	19.6	1.5	11.6	0.7	28.7	1.1	38.6	1.8
48	23.5	1.3	19.7	1.1	11.4	1.8	30.4	2.4	42.6	3.1
49	26.4	1.4	22.6	1.2	13.4	1.1	37.3	2.2	49.1	2.3
50	27.7	1.7	21.4	2.0	12.1	1.0	40.5	3.5	81.3	2.8
55	19.6	1.1	16.2	1.5	10.6	0.9	24.1	1.3	34.0	1.7
56	22.8	1.6	17.7	1.2	9.9	0.9	28.2	2.2	47.2	5.9
57	18.7	0.9	16.1	1.1	9.0	1.0	24.8	1.2	35.0	2.4
58	22.9	1.3	19.7	1.6	10.2	1.0	32.1	1.8	47.5	5.3
59	31.3	1.8	24.3	1.6	14.2	1.3	39.6	2.8	61.4	3.1

TABLE 8 (ii) (contd.). Sentence Length Distributions — Demosthenes

Work	Mean	Stand'd Error	Median	Stand'd Error	First Quartile	Stand'd Error	Third Quartile	Stand'd Error	Ninth Decile	Stand'd Error
60	22.9	1.1	20.0	1.6	14.5	0.9	33.1	2.6	38.0	2.7
61	24.6	1.6	21.0	1.2	13.1	1.2	31.7	2.1	48.5	3.7

TABLE 9 (i).   Sentence Length Distributions — Isocrates

No. of words in sentence	Work											
	1	2	3	4	5	6	7	8	9	10	11	12
1-5	6	--	3	7	8	2	5	7	6	3	4	11
6-10	58	15	17	13	26	14	18	17	13	13	7	19
11-16	60	36	34	30	32	25	35	24	25	17	11	23
16-20	38	28	29	27	33	42	38	30	40	17	16	16
21-25	12	22	23	17	30	40	16	31	25	18	22	27
26-30	6	16	17	29	18	19	16	24	17	22	16	19
31-35	7	3	12	13	12	15	13	15	6	9	3	18
36-40	3	4	8	8	9	11	10	10	6	9	6	14
41-45	2	3	3	13	1	7	12	16	8	6	3	10
46-50	--	4	5	9	7	3	4	4	7	6	7	6
51-55	--	2	2	7	4	3	5	6	5	1	3	7
56-60	--	1	--	4	4	8	1	5	5	--	3	7
61-65	1	2	1	5	1	--	3	4	4	3	--	1
66-70	--	--	--	4	3	2	4	1	1	--	1	2
71-75	--	--	--	--	1	2	1	2	--	1	--	1
76-80	--	--	2	2	3	1	1	1	1	2	1	4
81-85	--	--	--	1	2	2	--	--	1	--	--	1
86-90	--	--	1	1	2	--	--	1	--	1	--	2
91-95	--	--	--	2	--	1	--	--	--	--	--	3
96-100	--	1	--	1	--	1	--	--	1	--	--	3
101-105	--	--	--	2	2	--	--	--	--	--	--	--
106-110	--	--	--	--	--	--	--	--	--	--	--	2
111-115	--	--	--	2	2	1	--	--	--	--	--	--
116-120	--	--	--	--	--	--	--	--	--	--	--	1
121-125	--	--	--	--	--	1	--	1	--	--	--	1
126-130	--	--	1	1	--	--	--	1	--	--	--	--
131-135	--	--	--	--	--	--	--	--	1	--	--	--
136-140	--	--	--	1	--	--	--	--	--	--	--	--
146-150	--	--	--	--	--	--	--	--	--	1	--	1
156-160	--	--	--	--	--	--	--	--	--	1	--	--
186-190	--	--	--	--	--	--	--	--	--	--	--	1
No. of sentences	193	137	158	200	200	200	182	200	172	130	103	200

TABLE 9 (i) (contd.). Sentence Length Distributions — Isocrates

No. of words in sentence	Work								
	13	14	15	16	17	18	19	20	21
1-5	--	3	5	2	11	3	5	1	1
6-10	4	17	20	13	19	24	21	3	13
11-15	2	16	20	12	29	30	16	7	13
16-20	9	18	31	10	28	30	26	6	12
21-25	7	21	37	13	15	19	24	10	10
26-30	5	12	22	14	13	14	11	5	2
31-35	2	8	15	13	10	11	4	5	--
36-40	3	10	16	4	13	8	6	4	4
41-45	3	5	8	2	3	4	4	1	1
46-50	2	5	9	4	3	3	4	1	--
51-55	2	--	5	3	2	4	3	1	--
56-60	--	3	5	3	2	1	2	--	1
61-65	--	4	--	--	2	--	1	--	--
66-70	--	2	1	--	--	--	--	--	1
71-75	--	--	1	1	--	--	1	--	--
76-80	1	1	--	--	1	1	--	--	--
81-85	--	--	1	--	1	1	--	--	--
86-90	--	--	--	1	--	--	--	--	--
91-95	1	--	1	--	--	1	--	--	--
96-100	--	--	1	2	--	1	--	--	--
101-105	--	--	1	--	--	--	--	1	--
111-115	1	--	--	--	--	--	1	--	--
121-125	--	--	--	1	--	--	--	--	--
No. of Sentences	42	124	200	99	152	155	128	46	58

Table 9 (ii).   Sentence Length Distributions — Isocrates

Work	Mean	Stand'd Error	Median	Stand'd Error	First Quartile	Stand'd Error	Third Quartile	Stand'd Error	Ninth Decile	Stand'd Error
1	14.9	0.6	12.7	0.6	6.8	0.5	18.7	0.8	24.9	1.7
2	22.3	1.1	18.0	1.0	12.7	0.8	25.6	1.8	39.1	4.4
3	23.7	1.3	19.4	1.1	12.8	0.8	28.8	1.5	39.6	2.4
4	29.5	2.3	26.0	1.2	15.0	1.0	42.3	2.4	63.0	4.2
5	30.0	1.3	20.2	1.2	12.5	1.0	31.3	2.5	44.6	21.2
6	28.0	1.3	22.1	0.9	16.1	0.7	32.8	1.9	53.3	7.1
7	25.1	1.2	19.9	0.9	13.2	0.8	33.3	2.2	46.0	5.1
8	28.2	1.3	23.5	1.1	15.3	1.0	36.0	3.1	52.0	3.5
9	26.7	1.5	20.4	1.3	14.8	1.2	32.5	5.0	51.8	3.9
10	28.6	2.0	24.2	1.6	12.5	1.4	34.2	2.7	47.5	2.9
11	26.5	1.5	23.1	1.2	16.2	1.3	32.1	7.1	48.4	2.2
12	33.8	2.0	26.1	1.9	14.4	1.3	41.5	3.1	70.0	10.6
14	25.5	1.4	21.9	1.3	13.4	1.5	33.8	3.0	46.6	3.4
15	27.9	1.3	23.2	1.0	15.8	1.0	35.0	2.0	48.3	2.4
16	29.1	2.1	24.8	1.9	14.4	1.8	36.6	5.4	70.0	15.0
17	22.6	1.1	18.0	1.1	11.4	0.9	29.6	2.1	39.8	1.4
18	23.0	1.3	18.4	1.0	11.9	0.9	28.7	1.9	40.6	4.6
19	22.0	1.2	19.2	1.1	11.9	1.5	26.8	2.2	41.5	4.3

TABLE 10. The Occurrences of καὶ in the History of Herodotus

Sample	Occurrence of καὶ	Number of Words in Sample
1	31	946
2	27	772
3	37	935
4	38	903
5	46	1,111
6	54	1,355
7	40	1,130
8	43	910
9	33	973
10	38	1,045
11	37	916
12	29	953
13	34	834
14	37	1,035
15	43	990
16	34	962
17	32	719
18	40	944
19	41	887
20	42	1,065
21	28	964
22	46	1,109
23	39	1,023
24	42	982
25	47	1,074
26	39	844
27	26	820
28	42	1,102
29	36	1,037
30	38	972
31	25	871
32	44	870
33	32	1,042
34	21	795
35	26	755
36	45	907
Total	1,332	34,552

TABLE 11.   The Occurrence of καί in the History of Thucydides

Sample	Occurrence of καί	Number of Words in Sample
1.1	96	1,370
1.2	69	1,165
1.3	66	1,266
1.4	87	1,209
2.1	79	1,242
2.2	78	1,201
2.3	97	1,202
2.4	74	1,232
3.1	81	1,092
3.2	66	1,123
3.3	76	1,168
3.4	58	1,111
4.1	81	1,155
4.2	89	1,310
4.3	76	1,278
4.4	68	1,126
5.1	98	1,276
5.2	92	1,352
5.3	105	1,409
5.4	119	1,428
6.1	81	1,185
6.2	107	1,369
6.3	98	1,158
6.4	74	1,245
7.1	74	1,080
7.2	91	1,295
7.3	105	1,371
7.4	96	1,313
8.1	109	1,313
8.2	98	1,165
8.3	95	1,163
8.4	91	1,228
Total	2,774	39,851

TABLE 12. The Occurrence of καὶ in some Works of Plato

Work	Occurrences of καὶ	No. of Words in Sample
LAWS		
Sentences		
1-200	180	3,353
201-400	185	3,489
APOLOGY		
Sentences		
1-200	161	3,087
201-400	197	4,100
PHAEDO	156	2,944
CRITO		
Sentences		
1-200	143	2,673
THEAETETUS	119	2,071
EPISTLE SEVEN	473	8,798
	1,614	30,515

Mean rate of occurrence — .0525

TABLE 13.   The Occurrence of καὶ in the Works of Isocrates

Work	Occurrences of καὶ	No. of Words in Work
1	69	2,903
2	140	3,006
3	213	3,737
4	311	6,539
5	250	5,352
6	220	5,600
7	249	4,572
8	270	5,635
9	250	4,601
10	171	3,721
11	119	2,748
12	342	6,750
13	60	1,322
14	121	3,182
15	241	5,499
16	133	2,872
17	151	3,369
18	125	3,562
19	146	2,923
20	44	1,120
21	46	1,095
Total for Works 2-21	3,602	77,205

Epistle		
1	15	585
2	59	1,278
3	20	420
4	48	824
5	10	281
6	47	888
7	46	780
8	37	664
9	62	1,134
Total for Epistles 1-9	344	6,854

TABLE 14. The Occurrence of κα in Sentences — Isocrates.
The Data fitted to a Negative Binomial Distribution

Sentences having	Observed	Expected
No κα	1,034	1061.1
One	727	685.3
Two	373	382.5
Three	208	202.4
Four	102	104.1
Five	42	52.5
Six	28	26.4
Seven	15	13.2
Eight and over	11	12.2
Total	2,540	2539.7

TABLE 15. The Occurrence of κα in Sentences in the
Works of Isocrates

No. of κα sentence	1	2	3	4	5	6	7	8	9	10	11
No κα	140	59	51	72	81	92	76	77	55	57	36
One	41	39	53	48	63	47	42	51	57	30	38
Two	8	26	27	40	25	38	29	31	28	19	16
Three	4	8	14	18	11	11	18	23	11	11	7
Four	----	2	7	9	11	5	7	11	12	8	4
Five	----	1	2	5	3	3	5	3	5	3	----
Six	----	2	2	3	2	3	2	1	1	1	2
Seven	----	----	2	3	1	----	2	3	1	1	----
Eight	----	----	----	1	1	----	1	----	1	----	----
Nine	----	----	----	----	2	----	----	----	----	----	----
Ten	----	----	----	----	----	----	----	1	1	----	----
Eleven	----	----	----	----	----	1	----	----	----	----	----
Nineteen	----	----	----	1	----	----	----	----	----	----	----
No. of sentences	193	137	158	200	200	200	182	200	172	131	103
Chi squared	78.8	5.0	6.5	8.1	4.4	5.4	2.1	4.2	9.8	1.5	6.4
Degree of Freedom	2	3	4	4	4	4	4	4	4	4	3

TABLE 15 (cont'd.).   The Occurrences of καί in Sentences in the Works of Isocrates

No. of καί's in sentences	Works						
	12	14	15	16	17	18	19
No καί	76	54	82	41	71	76	53
One	43	45	57	24	43	51	40
Two	33	10	26	15	15	15	15
Three	11	8	21	10	16	8	11
Four	13	3	5	3	5	5	5
Five	12	4	5	----	2	----	1
Six	4	----	4	2	----	----	3
Seven	2	----	----	2	----	----	----
Eight	4	----	----	----	----	----	----
Nine	2	----	----	----	----	----	----
Eleven	----	----	----	1	----	----	----
No. of sentences	200	124	200	98	152	155	128
Chi squared	33.4	8.4	4.6	0.5	6.1	11.5	1.6
Degrees of Freedom	4	3	4	3	3	3	3

TABLE 16.   The Occurrence of δε at the Beginning of Sentences in the Works of Herodotus

Book	Sentences having δε as 2nd or 3rd word	No. of sentences in sample
1	91	200
2	89	200
3	100	200
4	97	200
5	98	200
6	98	200
7	70	200
8	92	200
9	92	200

Chi squared 13.4 for 8 Degrees of Freedom.

TABLE 17. The Occurrence of δε at the Beginning of
Sentences in the Works of Thucydides

Book	Sentences having δε as 2nd or 3rd word	No. of sentences in sample
1	95	200
2	95	200
3	90	200
4	90	200
5	97	200
6	81	200
7	85	200
8	82	200

Chi squared 5.5 for 7 Degrees of Freedom

TABLE 18. The Occurrence of δε at the Beginning of
Sentences in the Works of Lysias

Work	Sentences having δε as 2nd or 3rd word	No. of sentences in sample
1	43	126
2	49	140
3	38	98
6	44	141
12	73	200
13	81	200
14	34	98
19	51	164
25	24	83
30	30	90

Chi squared 7.0 for 8 Degrees of Freedom

TABLE 19. The Occurrences of δε at the Beginning of
Sentences in the Works of Demosthenes

Work	Sentences beginning with δε	Sentences in work	Work	Sentences beginning with δε	Sentences in work
1	18	91	32	28	100
2	23	90	33	40	118
3	26	136	34	48	158
4	37	159	35	41	142
5	13	54	36	36	202
6	9	100	37	59	223
7	33	101	38	23	99
8	39	200	39	35	163
9	51	212	40	46	132
10	34	199	41	24	98
11	11	47	42	23	110
12	17	65	43	63	200
13	36	102	44	59	200
14	29	127	45	67	200
16	25	84	47	80	205
17	20	76	48	49	153
18	43	200	49	50	155
19	40	200	50	64	168
20	35	200	51	13	68
21	40	200	52	27	87
22	45	200	53	32	74
23	42	200	54	41	143
24	39	200	55	24	109
25	46	200	56	37	143
26	18	73	57	47	200
27	66	207	58	39	203
28	18	83	59	73	200
29	44	192	60	23	114
30	22	100	61	35	149
31	4	51	Total	2193	8641

TABLE 20.   The Occurrence of δε at the Beginning of
Sentences in the Works of Isocrates

Work	Sentences beginning with δε	Sentences in Work
1	31	193
2	21	137
3	35	158
4	54	200
5	63	200
6	73	200
7	43	182
8	67	200
9	48	172
10	46	130
11	28	103
12	47	200
14	36	124
15	64	200
16	36	99
17	53	152
18	65	155
19	39	128
Total Work 1 excluded	818	2740